Praise for the B........ ....
MC5: Sonically Speaking

"Brett Callwood's new book spills the beans with firsthand interviews and an enthusiastic take on their incredible career, from revolution and imprisonment, to drugs, death, and glorious reformation."
—Jo Kendall, *Kerrang!*

"The only band who ever disturbed the smug equanimity of the Who back in the early Grande days. I will enjoy the inside story."
—Pete Townshend, the Who

"All MC5 aficionados and rock fans worldwide absolutely *must* read this book. Through interviews with the surviving members and a host of others, the past gets placed in excellent perspective to the present. Great job!"
—Dennis Thompson, MC5 drummer

"When I was talking with Brett Callwood about my time in the MC5, it reminded me that when we were in the middle of creating whatever it was that we created, we became a circle of five that was really one. Nobody could penetrate that circle, not even the people that we lived with. Callwood does a great job of letting the reader into the circle for a look around."
—Michael Davis, MC5 bassist

"Callwood has done a great job of providing an excellent rendition of an amazing story, and it's high time too."
—Paul Raggity, *Rock Sound*

"The book paints a picture of a hectic and somewhat controversial start to the MC5's career, with edgy stage stunts and crowd clashes. Essentially, it is another read that romanticizes the sixties, making you wish you were around when it all happened . . . [Brett Callwood's] passion instills a sense of enthusiasm and makes this a thoroughly enjoyable read."
—Jas Grieve, *Big Cheese*

"The MC5 were always much more than a band with great tunes, and Brett Callwood realizes that. This book documents the music, the politics, and the attitude of the greatest band ever to come out of the Motor City, and is a definite buy for anybody who wants to know where punk really started!"
—Diamond Dave, Total Rock Radio

"*Sonically Speaking* is essentially a story of a potentially great and innovative group that burned bright for a brief moment and then self-destructed, and gained that dubious legendary status many years later, after the tragic deaths of their two key members: lead vocalist Rob Tyner and guitarist Fred Smith."
—Pete Makowski, *Classic Rock*

"Their legacy and influence far outweighs their short career, and Brett's passion for the band shines through every page."
—Geoff Nicholls, *Rhythm*

"Brett Callwood has written—and written well—the long-awaited definitive biography of the MC5, nailing down the important information in the correct order, paying close attention to the actual facts, as opposed to accepted myths and legends, and telling the true story of the MC5 from beginning to end. If I enjoyed it this much, how you think you're gonna like it?"
—John Sinclair, former MC5 manager

"It's an eminently readable tome that, aside from anything else, may make you think twice before rolling a comforting doobie."
—*Guitarist*

"Callwood has picked up the challenge, producing an objective insight into the men who were the MC5 and their immediate entourage. It's to his credit that he's not only talked to the remaining members of the band but key figures like former manager John Sinclair."
—Malcolm Dome, *Metal Hammer*

"Sincere and straightforward."
—Iggy Pop

MC5

MC5

Sonically Speaking

A Tale of Revolution and Rock 'n' Roll

Brett Callwood

A Painted Turtle book
Detroit, Michigan

First published in the UK by Independent Music Press © Independent Music Press, 2007.

14 13 12 11 10   5 4 3 2 1

Library of Congress Cataloging-in-Publication Data

Callwood, Brett.
MC5 : sonically speaking : a tale of revolution and rock 'n' roll / Brett Callwood. — North American ed.
  p.   cm.
Includes bibliographical references and index.
ISBN 978-0-8143-3485-0 (pbk. : alk. paper)
1. MC5 (Musical group)   2. Rock musicians—United States—Biography.   I. Title.
ML421.M42C35 2010
782.42166092'2—dc22
[B]   2010008384

∞

Designed by Brad Norr Design
Typeset by Westchester Book Group
Composed in Minion, You Are Loved, and Trade Gothic

Contents

Acknowledgments

There are a lot of people who made this book possible. First, I need to thank Dennis Thompson, Michael Davis, Wayne Kramer, Fred "Sonic" Smith, and Rob Tyner. If you guys hadn't lived your lives in the manner that you did, I wouldn't have a story to write. And a big thank-you to Dennis, Michael, and Wayne for being so open during their interviews with me. You are three of the nicest men I have ever had the pleasure of meeting. Angela Davis—nothing seemed to be too much trouble over the course of writing this book, and your pasta and meatballs rock. Thanks also to the following people for help with my interviews in Detroit and Los Angeles: Margaret Kramer, Russ Gibb, Gary Grimshaw and Carl Lundgren (thanks for the cover), Jackson Smith, and Deborah Pietruska-Nathan. Thank you to John Sinclair, Pun Plamondon, Brian James, Gary Rasmussen, Leni Sinclair (thanks for the photos), Ginger, Mark Arm, and Lisa Kekaula for further interviews on the phone and at All Tomorrow's Parties. Sue Rynski for the photos. Ian Fortnam at *Classic Rock* magazine—cheers for the help with the Kramer interviews, fella. Nina Antonia, a big thank you for your help with the Gang War research. Phil Durr for lending me his sofa in Detroit for the week of the original research trip. Dave Allison, Scott Hamilton at Small Stone, Steve Zuccaro, Eric Hoegemeyer, Bronwyn Bunt, Sue from Slot, the Detroit Red Wings, and the Detroit Tigers. The people at the Banana Bungalow/Orbit hostel for giving me a cheap bed in L.A. Ben Myers, for his help and support.

Becky Tyner, Marshall Crenshaw, Sirius Trixon, Robert Gillespie, and Ralph Serafino for the U.S. edition additions.

Sian Llewellyn and Scott Rowley at *Classic Rock*; Louise King, Kim Willis, Chris Barnes and Phil Ascott at *Rhythm*; Kate Hodges at *Bizarre*; Steve Harvey, Russell Welton, and Ben Cooper at *Acoustic* and *Bass Guitar*; Michael Leonard and Mick Taylor at *Guitarist*; Stephen Lawson at *Total Guitar*; Paul Rees at *Q* (formerly of *Kerrang!*); Daniel Lane of *Kerrang!* (formerly of *Metal Hammer*); Bill Holdship and

Brian Smith at *Metro Times*; B.J. Hammerstein and Rachel May at *Metromix* and the *Detroit Free Press*; Jerry Vile at *Essential Detroit*; Gary Graff at the *Oakland Press*; Phil Freeman of the sadly deceased *Metal Edge*; Scott Heisel at *Alternative Press*; Tony Timpone at *Fangoria*; Andy Chapelle, Jennette Smith, and everyone at *Crain's Detroit Business;* Tom Sharrard at *GrokMusic.com*; and Adam Budofsky at *Modern Drummer*—thanks for the schooling, guys.

Martin Roach at Independent Music Press—thanks for taking a chance, sir.

Kathy Wildfong, Maya Rhodes, Kristin Harpster Lawrence, Margaret Erdman, Sarah Murphy, Emily Nowak, and M. L. Liebler at Wayne State. Thank you for your support and guidance. Lindsey Alexander—thanks for the impeccable copyediting.

Chris Mann, Glenn and Vanessa Morgan, George Dobell and family, Matt Wilson and family, Paul Cummings and family, Alex Kane, Clare Pproduct and Anti-Product, the Reverend Geza X.

Limey mom and dad, Yankee mom and dad, brothers Scott and Kris, Grandma Marga and Grandma Mimi.

My beautiful wife, Toni. None of this would have been possible without you. You're the most talented, creative person I have ever met and you'll forever be my muse. You're the princess in my Detroit rock 'n' roll fairy tale. You're everything to me and it's an honor to be bound to you for eternity. I love you with all of my heart forever, Toni Callwood.

Preface

The book that you hold in your hands is the second edition of a biography that was originally published in the UK in 2007. *Sonically Speaking* was the first book that I ever wrote, and I was delighted when the subsequent reviews in the British press were overwhelmingly positive (I believe the final score was 13–3 in my favor, with regard to good reviews over bad). Even more encouraging was the fact that the surviving members of the MC5 and people around them also liked the book. Of course, it wasn't perfect. There were some obligatory typos, and I had misspelled a couple of place-names around Detroit.

At the beginning of 2008, I relocated to Detroit from London. After numerous trips there, and having made many great friends, I realized that Detroit was the only place where I truly felt at home, where I felt a sense of belonging. The process of getting a work visa was relatively painless, thanks to Jerry Vile of the annual *Essential Detroit* magazine and the *Dirty Show* (the biggest erotic art show in the world, I believe) stepping up to the plate and sponsoring my application, plus a whole host of local and national publications giving me work, and a letter packed with kind words about my achievements from the National Writers Union.

Not only that, but on Valentine's Day 2008, at that very same *Dirty Show*, I met the woman who is now my wife. My Detroit fairy tale was complete; here I am, surrounded by the best bands in the world that make up the best music scene in the world, and I'm in love too. Toni and I got married at the Omni Hotel in Detroit, on the Detroit River, on May 24, 2009. Dennis Thompson of the MC5 was in attendance, as was Niagara of Destroy All Monsters. Geza X, the legendary producer of the Germs, the Avengers, and Black Flag, was our reverend.

Married and settled into our house in the Detroit suburb of Berkley (where Rob Tyner lived for a long period), I was able to find the time to set up a publishing deal for both *Sonically Speaking* and my second book, a biography of the Stooges, with Wayne State University Press, hence the book that you're holding.

While it is essentially the same book, I did take the opportunity to fine-tune it with regard to correcting every mistake I found or that was found for me (thanks to John Sinclair, Becky Tyner, and my wife in particular for being so vigilant). I also rejigged some of the narrative so that it flowed better, and I added a little bit more material.

I spoke to Dennis Thompson to find out what had happened in the MC5 camp since the first edition of my book went to press. I spoke with Becky Tyner to get a better feel for Rob Tyner and his personality, as I felt that the first edition was lacking in that area. On a similar note, I spoke to musicians Robert Gillespie and Ralph Serafino, who had played with Tyner in the controversial "New MC5." This was an area that I had only briefly mentioned in the first edition, but as I delved into the story, I realized that it warranted further attention.

Finally, I spoke with Marshall Crenshaw, the Detroit singer/songwriter (who's also from Berkley), who played second guitar with the DKT/MC5 on their first U.S. tour.

I tried to keep the additional material to a minimum, as I wanted to keep the spirit of the first edition—a book that I'm incredibly proud of—alive.

Ultimately, as I read over this edition, I'm happy that, while I haven't fixed something that was never broken, I've just given it a little bit of spit and polish.

Enjoy.

Introduction

My introduction to the MC5, like many other people's, came in the form of the song "Kick Out the Jams." It's the band's anthem, their most famous song, and also the track that has been most frequently covered. In 1990 a film came out called *Pump Up the Volume*, starring Christian Slater. It was a fairly typical teenage rebellion movie, but I loved it then and still do now. Slater played the part of a goofy schoolkid who at night became Happy Harry Hard-on, a pirate radio DJ. His filthy talk and excellent taste in punk rock had the entire school, and indeed the town, up in arms. Cue teachers ranting and kids getting up to all kinds of shenanigans. Like I say, it's pretty standard, albeit well played out, stuff, but the soundtrack is phenomenal. The likes of Soundgarden, Concrete Blonde, and the Pixies all make an appearance, but the highlight of the disc is easily a version of "Kick Out the Jams" performed by legendary hardcore troupe Bad Brains and former Black Flag vocalist Henry Rollins. Having Bad Brains and Rollins together on the same song is reason enough to celebrate, and their "Kick Out the Jams" is as violently forthright as would be expected. So began my mission to find out more about the band that had created this incredible song. Soon I had (well-worn) copies of all three MC5 albums in my collection, alongside various bootlegs and discs by spin-off bands like Sonic's Rendezvous Band, Destroy All Monsters, and Gang War. I became a pretty obsessive collector of all things Kramer, Tyner, Davis, Thompson, and "Sonic" Smith. The MC5 was, it seemed to me, everything that was good about music. In Wayne Kramer and Fred Smith, they had the finest guitar partners ever to swap riffs. Of course, that's a personal opinion. But as good as Sylvain and Thunders of the Dolls are, or Richards and Jones of the Stones, or Slash and Stradlin of Guns N' Roses, or Perry and Whitford of Aerosmith, the MC5 duo had *something else*. Their fearsome proto-punk delivery was matched by their sheer ability, and those two attributes together are not all that common in one guitarist, never mind two. As Kramer says later in this book, he never thought it was OK to not play well.

Rob Tyner's voice was pure Detroit; like his homeboys John Lee Hooker and the many Motown hit-makers, Tyner bled emotion through his raw larynx, but unlike many of the punk vocalists who followed his lead, Tyner could really sing, too. He was the archetypal rock 'n' roll front man—part James Brown, part Mick Jagger, and part Tina Turner. Not only that, but his Afro has become an iconic piece of rock imagery.

The rhythm section of Dennis "Machine Gun" Thompson and Michael Davis was as raw as anything that punk would later produce. So raw in fact, that both would employ the services of a teacher during the recording of their second album due to problems nailing their parts. But all of that stuff, while undoubtedly difficult to deal with at the time, has just become a part of the glorious legend.

When the news came through at the beginning of the new millennium that the band was going to reunite, I was over the moon. I don't buy any of the "destroying the legacy" crap that people infected with snobbery seem to enjoy throwing at bands on the reunion trail. I wanted to hear the surviving members of the MC5 play their songs on stage, because I didn't have a chance to see them the first time. The same thing goes for the Stooges and the New York Dolls. I didn't make it to the infamous 100 Club reunion show, but I saw them at London's Astoria soon afterward and they were fantastic. Granted, this wasn't the MC5 of legend—they were even billing themselves as DKT/MC5 to make the distinction clear. But for people of my generation who were unable to see the original band, this reunion/reinvention was a godsend.

In 2003, not long after I began writing for *Classic Rock* magazine, I was sent to Detroit to interview an up-and-coming blues-rock band called Gold Cash Gold. Despite lacking the conventionally perceived glamour of a trip to L.A. or New York, this was a dream assignment for me. The home of the MC5 and the Stooges, and I was going to be there on a record company's dime (God bless Times Beach Records). I fell in love with Detroit that week, and as well as continuing to adore the music that the place produced, I became a big fan of the Detroit teams in a number of U.S. sports (the Red Wings in hockey, the Tigers in baseball, the Pistons in basketball, and even the Lions in football). I'm told that Detroit is a city in despair, that it's all very "ghetto" (whatever that means). But on the occasions that I visited (and now, since I've moved there), I found the place to be warmer and more welcoming than anywhere else in the States. Is Detroit pretty? Conventional wisdom says no, although there is beauty in its industrial landscape and glorious, if oft-abandoned, architecture. But it does have the best bars in the world, and with a generally blue-collar population and a whole lot of garage bands, that goes a long way.

In 2005, DKT/MC5 were due to play the Download Festival at Donington Park, and I was commissioned by *Total Guitar* and *Bass Guitar* magazines to write a preview piece for their news sections. I interviewed Wayne Kramer and Michael Davis, and in doing so I became acquainted, if only over the phone and via e-mail, with their respective managers, who also, in both cases, happen to be their wives. I found Angela Davis and Margaret Kramer to be so incredibly helpful, so willing to do what they could to assist, that it was almost odd that they were both connected to the same band.

So when I began to think about which band I wanted my first book to be about, there was really very little to ponder. Other artists might generate more sales, but there are few bands that I could get as enthusiastic and passionate about as the MC5. When Martin Roach, the owner of Independent Music Press in my native United Kingdom, expressed an interest in publishing a history of the MC5, I contacted Angela Davis, and she was once again incredibly helpful. The very week that the project was confirmed, I began interviews over the phone with the band. Soon afterward, I organized a return trip to Detroit and another one to L.A. to meet with the three band members, as well as their former acquaintances and colleagues.

It was while I was in Detroit, however, that the only real complication I encountered throughout the entire process of writing this book manifested itself. While I was writing, legal discussions were taking place between the surviving members of the MC5 and Future/Now Films, which had made a documentary about the band. The city of Detroit listened intently as the filmmakers and the MC5 negotiated the details of the film's release. So when I came to conduct interviews in the Motor City, there was little else anybody wanted to talk about. Still, I managed to get some excellent material. I also got to see the Red Wings in the flesh (and treated myself to a big foam finger—well, you've got to).

While visiting Detroit, I was able to meet with MC5 drummer Dennis Thompson at his home. I'd already decided that I liked Dennis after numerous telephone conversations, but in the flesh he proved to be unlike anyone I'd ever met before. He has a habit of speaking incredibly fast, and someone who doesn't know him might misread him as combative, but in fact there are few kinder souls. Throughout the entire process, he was a generous and wonderful source of anecdotes, and as I was coming to the end of writing the book, he supplied me with this gem:

> We had a planned "assassination" of Rob Tyner. Our road manager Steve "The Hawk" Harnadek was the shooter. This was at the Grande Ballroom, in our heyday. We used to pull pranks like this quite often. We'd sit down and concoct these ordeals. They call it performance art now. Rob had a blood pack, and toward the end of the show, Harnadek shoots him with a starter pistol. Rob fires the blood off and falls down. We all put on a big act onstage and drag Rob into the dressing room, and the crowd goes crazy. They're trying to kill Steve. We barely got him into the dressing room, and people are pounding on the door. It's pandemonium and mayhem. Russ Gibb [the former manager of the Grande Ballroom] had to call the cops and empty the place. That backfired. It was fun, though.
>
> Early on, when the band was younger, Rob had pulled his back on stage. He was lying on stage, unable to get up, with his legs straight up, singing. He was in excruciating pain and could not move. We let him sing a couple of songs like that, saying, "Get me off the fucking stage." Wayne and Fred put their guitars down, grabbed a leg each, and dragged him off the stage while people were laughing.

In 2009, while collecting new material for the U.S. edition of this book, I met with Becky Derminer, wife of Rob Tyner. I was concerned that the original UK version was lacking in Tyner, so this was my first attempt to correct that. Becky and her family welcomed me into their home, before Becky and I went on a tour of the band's old stomping ground in Detroit. It was a wonderful experience, and I hope I've carried some of the passion for her husband's music that she instilled in me forward into the book. As an Englishman, I was amused to learn that Tyner had impersonated an English accent in order to woo Becky at their first meeting.

The MC5's story is a unique one. From their initial semi-revolutionary existence under the guidance of manager John Sinclair and the extracurricular role they played as spokesmen for the rock 'n' roll youth, through two record contracts, alcoholism, drug use, jail time, infighting, the breakup of the band, the tragic passing of two members, countless projects that came and went after the MC5, a shocking reunion, and court battles, the MC5 have taken the best and worst traits of just about every rock 'n' roll band in history. As Russ Gibb told me when I met with him in Detroit,

"The MC5's story is one that needs to be told, because it's the classic American success story, but maybe minus the dollar sign. But it's a success story nevertheless—to come from Lincoln Park and get recognition and respect, and they were doing what they wanted to do."

The members of the MC5 made three of the greatest albums ever recorded, but they didn't get rich; they did not make millions of dollars from the band despite the MC5's now iconic status. The fact that Wayne Kramer would work as a carpenter and Dennis Thompson as a toolmaker after the band's breakup is evidence of that. If success is judged purely on financial grounds, then the MC5 were a relatively high-profile failure. But if success is judged on artistic merit, respect from fellow musicians, and a legacy that future generations will discover and embrace as much as they will the Beatles, the Stones, and the Pistols, then the MC5 have triumphed in sparkling fashion. They've enraged authority on all levels over the years, from parents to the FBI, and in doing so, they have simply done their job as a rock 'n' roll band. James Dean made only a handful of movies, and his image wouldn't have been nearly as enduring if he'd been partial to wearing an argyle sweater rather than that biker jacket. This is why the MC5 will also live on—they're the very opposite of "disposable" or "pop" music, and despite what recent trends may suggest, it takes a lot more than a load of chunky guitar riffs to turn pop into rock.

Thanks to the help of many of the main players, especially the three surviving members of the band, this book covers the many highs and (possibly more) lows that this group of five "factory rats" from Detroit have gone through, right up to the present day. I've tried to keep it balanced, which wasn't always easy as my research coincided with the aforementioned court case. But above all, I've tried to write with the same level of passion that the MC5 have always performed with. It's the very least they deserve.

In the Beginning . . .

1

T he MC5 could not have been born in any city other than Detroit. Aside from the fact that the Motor City gifted the 5 with their name, the band's sound is as at home in Detroit as the Beach Boys' sound is in California. The blue-collar, hardworking tradition of Detroit's people has resulted in their tremendously dry sense of humor, and a desire for music that's as open and raw as their everyday life. Just listen to the pained, impassioned croak of local bluesman John Lee Hooker or, more recently, the primal retro-stomp of the White Stripes for evidence.

The Detroit of the late 1940s and 1950s that Robert Derminer, Fred Smith, Michael Davis, Wayne Kambes, and Dennis Tomich were brought up in was a relatively prosperous place to live. Dennis Thompson was born Dennis Tomich on September 7, 1948, in Highland Park, Michigan, and grew up in the downriver industrial suburb of Lincoln Park. "It was essentially built as a blue-collar town during the boom, the construction boom, after World War II," Thompson told me in late 2006. "When we were growing up, all of our dads had work at the factories, because there was a lot of work. It was the heyday for the USA."

At this point in Detroit's colorful history, it really was "the Motor City," due to the number of car manufacturing plants spread across the area. Thanks to the amount of work available, a young Detroiter (as people from the city refer to themselves) could get a job at a plant right out of high school, earning a decent living without having to go to college. There's an obvious and very visible contrast between the ghettos in the Metro Detroit area, and places like Grosse Pointe, where the upper crust lives. Thompson told me that he places Lincoln Park at number eight on a scale from one to ten in terms of nice, safe living in Metro Detroit. It was undoubtedly a safe place to live when he was growing up there. The drummer feels that Lincoln Park High School is very different today: "Times have changed, with hip-hop, sports clothes, and backward hats. Back in my day, it was just fights at the football game on a Friday night. The kids would drink beer and have fights with the kids from different high schools. Normal stuff, no real violence."

Thompson feels that he was lucky to have a happy upbringing, with his dad, John Tomich, working two jobs—he was a journeyman toolmaker and designer in the automotive field and was also an electrician with a two-year degree. Thompson has one brother and one sister, both of whom are approximately ten years older then him. His father was willing to put them through college but they both declined. Thompson's birth was a happy accident, and although he attended some college, he eventually left to go on tour with the MC5.

Thompson's mother's name was Leona, or Lee to her friends. She was a singer on the radio until she developed chronic bronchitis. She was the family matriarch and raised three children. Thompson remembers her as "a homemaker of the highest caliber. I miss her dearly."

In fact, Leona Tomich's mother and two brothers were all working musicians during the early days of big band. Back in the 1930s, during the Depression, the future Mrs. Tomich was very young and had a widely admired voice. Her meeting John Tomich was a direct result of her vocal prowess—she was singing at the local Detroit radio station, which was common for local singers of that era, and John heard her. Unfortunately, after an attack of bronchitis, which turned into chronic bronchitis, her range was never the same, so she was forced to change careers. John and Leona got married, had kids, and moved into a brand-new house in Lincoln Park.

At four years of age, Dennis discovered his love of percussion when he started experimenting with the bongos, playing along with his older brother's band. His brother was fourteen at the time and played with an instrumental rock band that practiced in the family basement. Thompson recalls that his "earliest favorite song was 'Twinkle, Twinkle, Little Star,' and 'Do You Love Me' by the Contours. I remember playing with my family in our basement at Christmastime. My sister played the piano and sang. My mom sang, and my brother played guitar with me on the drums. If the whole family was over, we would play and they'd all sing along. It was really cool. Great memories."

Born in Detroit on June 5, 1943, to parents Milton and Edna Mae Davis, Michael Davis is five years older than his MC5 bandmates, except for Rob Tyner, who was only a year younger than Davis. His father worked for the Ford Motor Company, starting out as a welder on the production line during the war, and later rising to the business office, where he became the production control supervisor. Davis's mother worked in a dry-cleaning business when the future bassist was an infant, and later worked from home as a typist. The family lived in Detroit on a street named Epworth. Their home was a two-story wood-frame house with a porch and a backyard. Epworth was a busy street with a trolley that ran down the middle of it. Davis's first word, besides "mama" and "dada," was "streetcar" (though he pronounced it "steee-cah"). The animal-loving Davises had cats and a dog named Brownie. Young Michael's grandmother lived with them, and she took him to the markets and other places where she felt she could spend quality time with her grandson. Davis remembers the neighborhood as being glum, with two huge oil refinery tanks standing across the street from his house. A favorite pastime was when his grandma would take him downtown to the Broadway Market for a ham sandwich. Over the years, the Davis family moved often, until finally, Michael's parents were able to buy a house. It was located on the far northwest side of Detroit, where, at the time, there were still cornfields and a farmhouse or two. "Occasionally," Davis recalls, "a pheasant would fly up in front of me when I was in the fields." Nowadays, this area is much like any other inner-city neighborhood.

Davis maintains that Detroit was a fine place for a child to grow up during the 1950s, and he remembers a promising beginning to a multicultural Detroit. The era gave no hint of the troubles that would hit the city in 1967:

> Things were a lot different at that point. Rock 'n' roll was a mainstream kind of thing—AM radio and all that. Detroit was all right—it was an industrial city. There was a good feeling around Detroit. It wasn't like it is nowadays. It was going through a transitional period where all of the inner cities throughout the country were basically in a process of erosion. All the white people were moving to the suburbs, and all the cities were starting to become abandoned by middle-class white culture. It started in the late 1950s, and moved from the inner cities outwards. That was named "the white flight."

Davis's point is valid, and the suburbs were being built to accommodate that "white flight." Davis was comfortable because he identified with the more bohemian culture, which was in its infancy, with jazz music, coffeehouses, and folk singers. Beatnik culture was leaking into mainstream culture, creating an exciting backdrop to Davis's formative years. Seemingly overnight, there were alternatives to straitlaced

American life. The American dream was becoming distorted, and the cultural changes were attractive to many because the new lifestyle was so experimental. As Davis remembers, "You didn't know where the thing was going, but it was a lot of fun. People would have beatnik parties, where they'd dress up in sunglasses, goatees, and berets. So it was crossing from something that was strictly underground into something that was more acceptable to middle-class kids. Everything was fine. Cultures were merging, in a sense of white culture and black culture. The things that black people were doing—their kind of music and the hipness of black people—were being discovered by middle-class white kids. The merging of those cultures was very attractive—it was people coming together."

Davis's first school of note was Dossin Elementary School, built in 1949–50 to accommodate the expanding Detroit metropolitan area. He later attended Cass Technical High School. His father insisted he attend Cass when his teachers at Dossin said that he had special aptitude in art and the performing arts. The family was delighted that Davis was willing to accept, as Cass was considered a prestigious school, with Diana Ross listed among its alumni. Still, Davis didn't want to go, as all of his friends were going to local high schools in the suburbs. Naturally, his dad won the battle. Davis, however, was a self-proclaimed "lousy student," barely managing to pass his classes. He remembers art as an easy subject, but the rest of his courses were of little interest to him. The budding rocker was interested in girls, cars, and sports—in that order, of course. He did manage to graduate on time, but with substandard grades. He went to a community college to redeem his poor high school grades, with the hope of transferring to a four-year university. After a year and a half, he transferred his credits to Wayne State University. Wayne State was considered a big-time university with a well-respected Fine Art department. Davis thrived in the city college environment. The creative environment of art class was easy for him since he had been "through the wringer" at the far tougher Cass. He even enjoyed the academic part of the curriculum. As the folk music and protest movements gained clout, however, and after Davis discovered Bob Dylan, his schoolboy life underwent a rapid transformation. The Beatles, the Rolling Stones, and the Yardbirds had a profound effect on his jazz and baroque tastes, but Dylan captured his young soul altogether. "As a youth," Davis recalls, "at the birth of rock 'n' roll music (*American Bandstand*), I was fascinated by custom cars, juvenile delinquency (*Blackboard Jungle*), teenage fashion, postwar hoodlumism (hanging out with motorcycle gangs), beatniks, modern art, drugs, and so on. Anything of a perverse nature was top priority."

Due to the difference in their ages, while his future bandmates were working on their educations (with varying degrees of success), Davis had other plans. He abandoned his goal of getting a degree and decided to become a full-time layabout. He left Detroit with an accomplice and drove to Florida. He was operating on a typical young man's fantasy, thinking that people didn't really need to earn any money. Instead, he believed he could just go somewhere new and everything would eventually work out. When he got to Florida, it took only a month for his money to run out, ending that particular dream. He decided to sell the Lambretta scooter he'd bought there, buy a car, and drive to Key West with his friend. He had distorted the illusion of survival in his head, now believing that if he changed cities, everything would get better. He got the car, a station wagon, but halfway to Key West the engine blew up, leaving the hapless youths stuck. Davis met a gentleman in a bar who kindly gave him and his friend jobs scraping barnacles off of boats. Both illegally and ingeniously, the boys would go out in the man's boat and poach lobster traps, take the lobsters out of the cages when nobody was watching, boil them in a pot of water, and eat them to keep from going hungry. After a short time, Davis scrounged a ride to New York City, journeying to the Big Apple to find out how people lived in the city that never sleeps (although anybody who has ever been there and tried to find good food after 2:00 a.m. can tell you that Sinatra was lying), hoping to emulate them. The lure of the Motor City was too great, however, and before long he was back in Detroit trying to become a student again. That didn't quite work out, and instead he worked a slew of paltry jobs, including stints as a steelworker, a taxi driver, and a Good Humor Ice Cream man. Still, he'd lived his wild and crazy life, he'd traveled and lived as a hobo, and, at the outset of the MC5, his experience set him apart from his bandmates. The rest of the band looked up to Davis as something of a guru, at least initially. His age and experience were definitely assets in helping him get into the band.

Robin Tyner was born Robert Derminer on December 12, 1944, in Detroit. Davis remembers his first impressions of the future singer:

I used to see Rob. He had a girlfriend who lived across the hall from where I lived, and he would come over. She was friends with my girl, and so we met Rob. He was talking about this rock band he was doing and, to me at the time, rock 'n' roll was not a very serious subject. There were some areas of rock 'n' roll that I really liked; I listened to all kinds of things, like classical, hillbilly music, and rhythm and blues. Rock 'n' roll was, in general, Top 20 music. Mainstream bullshit stuff. Not that I didn't like it—I listened to all those girl groups and the teenage ballads. Ricky Nelson is probably my very first rock 'n' roll star hero. I loved Ricky Nelson. I used to watch him when I was a little kid, on *Ozzie and Harriet,* a TV show. To meet Rob, someone who was in a rock 'n' roll band, I almost didn't believe him. He didn't look like a rock 'n' roll kind of person, plus he was a beer drinker, which I thought was kind of strange. Beer drinking was square, or at least we thought it was back then.

By high school, Dennis Tomich (soon to be rechristened Dennis Thompson) was starting to discover the joys of playing music on a stage in front of an audience that didn't consist solely of family members. He was a self-proclaimed loner in high school, and before hooking up with the MC5, he played in bars with his brother, who was something of a mentor and guardian. The boys filled their set with country and western classics, early instrumentals like "Walk, Don't Run," and music by the Ventures, Johnny and the Hurricanes, and Duane Eddy. They'd play the blues, and classic country music like Merle Haggard and Chet Atkins—anything that would get the small crowds cheering.

It was in ninth or tenth grade that Thompson first met Wayne Kambes, later Kramer, and the pair immediately hit it off. Thompson still thinks that Kramer was and is the best guitarist that he ever had the joy of working with. "I consider him to be a soul brother, then and now," says Thompson.

Kramer was born in Detroit on April 30, 1948. As a child, he moved with his family to the suburb of Lincoln Park, where he would later go to school with Dennis Thompson and Fred Smith. At a young age, Kramer had to go through the ordeal of his parents getting divorced, never an easy thing for a child to experience. Later, however, his mother's boyfriend had a guitar, and the young boy would borrow the six-string while said boyfriend and his bandmates were drinking after rehearsal.

Kramer formed the Bounty Hunters in high school with Dennis Thompson, who he met through the Bounty Hunters' other guitar player, Jimmy Parker. Parker was sort of the leader, simply because the band practiced in his garage. As is so often the case today, real estate equaled power. The band had two guitar players, a sax player, and a drummer. There was no bass player. The Bounty Hunters, at this point, were strictly covering the popular instrumentals of the day. They tried to include a couple of Beach Boys tunes in their set, but that was about as much of a challenge as the band's repertoire could handle. The Bounty Hunters didn't have a large book—maybe eight or nine tunes—all of which were instrumentals. Before long, Thompson quit the Bounty Hunters and got a job with a man who played the electric accordion. To be fair to the drummer, who could resist an offer like that? The pair played weddings, so Thompson was making real money from playing music for the first time. Wanting in on the action, Thompson's brother asked if Dennis could play with him in bars on the weekends.

Thompson left his accordion-wielding buddy to play weddings with the wonderfully named Jeff Warady and the Paramount. By this time, Thompson was about thirteen or fourteen years old. The band played some rock 'n' roll, and mostly classics that were being played on the radio at the time. "The Wedding March," "The Hokey Pokey," standard dancing songs, slow dance songs, and some polkas and songs with lyrics like "I don't want her, you can have her, she's too fat for me." The beer barrel polkas. The classics. As Thompson recalls, "At weddings, you had to play dance music for the bride to dance to. She'd dance with the guys and they'd give her money."

The final piece of the MC5 puzzle, Fred Smith, was born in West Virginia on September 13, 1949. In contrast to his bandmates, particularly Thompson and Davis, Smith had a less than ideal childhood, as Wayne Kramer alleged on page 183 of Victor Bockris's biography of Patti Smith (Fred Smith's future wife), claiming that Smith had been beaten by his father. "That syndrome," Kramer said, "gets passed down generation to generation, unless you interrupt it with a lot of hard work."

Thompson remembers Fred having a striking impact at school because he had extremely long hair, longer than anyone else's. He left in the tenth grade—one rumor suggested he was expelled for not cutting his hair. To an impressionable Thompson, "He had hair like Moulty from the Barbarians—an early [rock] band. Long, long hair down to his shoulders. At that point in the universe, that was just not done at all. You didn't do that. You were really considered a freak if you did. I believe he was expelled or maybe he got tired of the hassle and quit. I didn't like him at first. He seemed just a tad bit rough around the edges. Over the years he truly became, as they say, an acquired taste. We eventually became friends and I considered him like a blood brother."

Kramer had put the Bounty Hunters together by the time he was fifteen. The band was named after a dragster belonging to local hero Connie Kalitta. He was, claims Thompson, "always winning." (The website for the National Hot Rod Association pours more affection on Kalitta, stating that "dogged determination took Kalitta from a beginner like everyone else in the 1950s to a factory-sponsored Top Fuel driver in the 1960s to a self-made multimillionaire in airfreight and championship-winning crew chief for Shirley Muldowney in the 1970s to a satisfied multi-championship-winning car owner in the 1990s who sometimes still drove for the hell of it.")

The future members of the MC5 visited the drag strip often. They loved the excitement, the noise, and the smell. The members of the band all grew up in and around Detroit, and cars are a big part of the city's makeup. The band loved fast cars and custom cars—anything that tore up the track and made a lot of noise. The drag strip was all about dragsters going, at that time, about 200 mph. Drag racing was powerful and high-energy. It was very attractive to young people who were already getting their fill of the opposite sex at their shows—the other part of the high-octane, rock 'n' roll equation. The MC5 and fast cars went together like peanut butter and jelly. The Beach Boys, in California, were all about surfing, fast cars, and custom cars. Back in Detroit, muscle cars with 450-horsepower engines were coming off the production line at an extraordinary rate. Thompson recalls sneaking into the drag strip and watching the races for free: "I think we all went together once or twice, or at least me and Wayne did."

In fact, Kramer even found work at the drag strip. He talks about the experience in Legs McNeil's book, *Please Kill Me*:

We all shared a love of hot rods and big-assed engines. I even took a job at the drag strip selling ice cream—"ICE COLD, ICE COLD ICE CREAM!"—just so I could be there every week. Drag racing was in our blood. I mean, it was so loud and fast, just like the music. It's funny about the cross-pollination between drag racing and rock 'n' roll—my first experience seeing live rock 'n' roll was at the drag strip. It was Del Shannon, backed by this Detroit instrumental band called the Ramrods. They had matching red blazers, all new Fender gear, and they did choreographed moves on the return road at the drag strip. I thought it was the coolest thing I'd ever seen. (35)

Future MC5 poster artist Gary Grimshaw—undoubtedly one of the most important artists of the 1960s and 70s—was another petrol-head, although he had far less idyllic memories of the place:

Lincoln Park, Michigan, is a lower middle-class "bedroom" suburb of Detroit populated by factory workers in the nearby car assembly lines, steel mills, and chemical complexes. It has no industry of its own, unless you count the big cheap liquor warehouse at the northwest corner. The Lincoln Park school system was noted for the lowest pay scale for teachers in the state. We called it "Stinkin' Park." "We" were myself, Rob Tyner, Kelly Martensen and Carl Schigelone. The four of us were the core of a gang of sorts, an art gang, if you will. I was the driver because I was the only one with a car. It was a 1953 Ford Mainline two-door sedan with a flathead V-8 and a stick shift. When I wore out the main bearings on the motor, I upgraded to a 1956 Chevy 283 V-8 automatic four-door hardtop. That was the Cruiser. The most essential hardware on both of these vehicles was the radio. Our station of preference was WCHB-AM, the powerhouse black dynamo, but WJLB (the other black station) and the Top 40 stations such as WJBK, WXYZ, and WKNR, and CKLW out of Windsor, Ontario, were all fair game. This was the time when Motown ("The Sound of Young America") was the new big thing, but there was also Jackie Wilson and a host of great rhythm and blues artists of the late 1950s and early 1960s who were in heavy rotation. My particular favorite was Jimmy Reed.

Having gained some respect locally with the Bounty Hunters by playing at parties and dances, Kramer turned to his old friend Smith, who was initially playing bongos with local band the Vibratones. They joined forces, though they kept the name the Bounty Hunters, deciding that it sounded cool. They continued to gain momentum when the by now inseparable Kramer and Smith found a drunken Rob Derminer hanging around in the parking lot of a White Castle burger restaurant. Derminer had taken to calling himself Robin Tyner after McCoy Tyner, John Coltrane's pianist, due to his passion for jazz. He considered rock 'n' roll music to be nonsensical, and was known in the area as a poet and beatnik. However, that night at White Castle, he was playing the harmonica and professing a newfound love for the Rolling Stones. Shortly afterward, he was installed as the new singer with the Bounty Hunters. Tyner wasn't happy with the moniker, though, and before long the name

Motor City 5 was adopted. The fact that the name could be shortened to MC5 and resemble a car part number appealed to the auto-loving kids.

Following an unsuccessful attempt at teaching Tyner to play bass, Kramer, Smith, and Tyner were joined by a rhythm section comprising of bassist Pat Burrows and drummer Bob Gaspar. As Burrows told Ken Shimamoto of the I-94 Bar, "We played a lot of blues at first, a lot of R&B. The Stones, the early Stones; before they were rock, they were blues . . . 'The Spider and the Fly.' That's what we were doing. Me and Wayne went to watch the *T.A.M.I. Show* one night at the drive-in and that was what we were all about. Old James Brown, blues, rock—everything."

It was around this time that the MC5 introduced an original song into their set of rock 'n' roll covers, a feedback-fueled monster called "Black to Comm." While the song didn't make it onto any of the band's three subsequent albums (although it does pop up on various bootlegs and live albums), it clearly provides the blueprint for the MC5's future sound. It's the sound of a work in progress, but even today it's a thrilling piece of experimental music. The song refers to the fact that, when the 5 were playing regularly at the Grande Ballroom, a lot of bands would use their equipment, and the boys would say something along the lines of "if you break it, we told you . . . black to comm." On a PA, the negative ground connection is commonly referred to as the "comm," and "black" is the wire that connects from the power source. The song served as instructions to other bands: "OK, just be sure you put the black wire into the comm connection here if we trip over it and knock it out again." The fact that there were often wires strewn all across the stage meant that the song title came in handy on many occasions.

Wayne Kramer told Ian Fortnam of music365.com how the sound of the song was achieved:

> We were just trying to find our own sound and so we played the songs that were popular of the day. We played "Louie Louie," "Gloria," "Shake a Tail Feather," and Chuck Berry songs. Those were the sorts of songs that people played in the bars. Detroit, in those days, was a boomtown, and there were a lot of good jobs available in the auto factories, and those guys worked hard and they wanted to play hard. So they'd come out to the clubs and they wanted to hear those songs. But we had an idea that we were trying to find a new sound of our own, and we discovered it accidentally one day when we left a guitar leaning up against an amp and went to make a peanut butter sandwich. And we heard this unholy

noise coming from the other room and went in there, and the vibrations had knocked some stuff off the shelf, and we realized that we had discovered the power to control the universe: feedback. At least we believed we'd discovered it—we found out later that a few other people had discovered it too. Anyway, that's the legend.

"Black to Comm" begins with the simplest of riffs, played so as to sound like the roar of a Chevy engine, and it never lets up. For the ultimate head-fuck version, the eleven-minute therapy-inducer that appears on disc three of Castle's *Are You Ready To Testify?: The Live Bootleg Anthology,* recorded at Detroit's First Unitarian Church in 1968, is a must.

Possibly as a result of this experimental new direction, cracks began to show within the band, emanating from the rhythm section. Rob Tyner told *Creem* magazine in 1969 that Gaspar's frustration with the exploratory arrangement on "Black to Comm" became integral to the song: "Sometimes the song'd go on for ten minutes with no drums. He'd sit there and sit there and get madder and madder because he hated it so much and he couldn't relate to it at all. We're all flipping out, screaming into the mike, and finally he'd go crazy and take out all his frustrations by coming in very strong, maintaining the thing at a very high energy level. Gaspar did not want to play that kind of music 'cause he didn't feel that it was valid. It was just an outburst of energy and noise as far as he was concerned, and in some ways that was exactly what it was."

"An outburst of energy and noise" is just about the perfect description of the song, but more importantly, "Black to Comm" signaled that the MC5 wasn't going to settle for being just another proficient rock 'n' roll cover band clogging up the circuit.

Rob Tyner wanted to continue with the sonic assault until it reached some sort of illogical conclusion. "The first night we did 'Black to Comm,'" he told John Sinclair in *The Warren-Forest Sun* in 1967, "we wrote it down in Kramer's basement, and Fred Smith discovered that you could turn up the Super Beatle amp until it was unbearable, right, and started playing the opening chords to 'Comm' spontaneously and smashed a jar!"

Michael Davis and Dennis Thompson had yet to join. Davis remembers that Rob Tyner invited him to go and see his band in a bar, and that they had surprisingly awful band uniforms on—olive blazers made out of corduroy, shirts, and black ties. Davis was impressed with the band's musicianship; they played R&B material and

Chuck Berry-esque rock 'n' roll. There wasn't anything original in their set, but they had an aura about them that the bassist found captivating. "To me," he says, "they were just kids. Kids with guitars. I liked it, though—they were enjoying themselves and it was fun. I met them after the set and we hit it off."

Pat Burrows was playing bass in the band at that point. Davis remembers him playing an Echo Violin bass, and holding it upright like Bill Wyman holds his instrument. He played well and he seemed like he fit in with them, at least to outsiders. As Davis recalls, "He really wanted to play a Fender Precision bass, because he liked the Motown sound. So he pawned the Echo, which the rest of the guys thought was their ticket to getting popular because they thought it was very British, so they all got pissed off at him."

In truth, Kramer and Tyner really wanted Davis to be in the band and were looking for an excuse to oust Burrows. They would tell Davis that "Burrows is going to be gone," but Davis was skeptical. After all, why would Burrows quit the band? Eventually, somehow, Burrows became a nonmember of the MC5. How it happened isn't entirely clear—the details remain a little fuzzy. What is certain is that Davis had to get a new bass guitar. Initially, he used Rob Tyner's, which was the bass Tyner had tried to use when the band started. Davis used that for a very short while, then he went out and—oddly enough—bought a white Fender Precision bass. The rest of the band had no problem with Davis playing a Precision, despite their issues with Burrows over the same guitar. When they met Davis, he already had steel boots on and had what they considered to be cool hair, so they considered him a much higher draft choice than Burrows.

Davis told *Mojo* in an essay he wrote titled "Ballad of a Bad Man" that

they were stuck between the old and the not yet. I approached them when they had finished a set, and was introduced by Tyner to the rest of the group as his artist buddy from downtown. Such as I was an artist, but in a limbo state from a year of wandering without a cause, I saw what they were about as a direction that was particularly attractive. Unaware of the intrigue or delicate power structure that was taking shape in that earliest of times, I wanted in. It was instant, like mixing chocolate syrup and milk: we became bonded in the new musical express of 1965. I was that art world hipster meeting the ruffians of rock 'n' roll. We recognized a future in each other that couldn't be denied. In early 1966, I joined the band as a member and thus the MC5 took its banner to the battlefield.

In those first days and months as a highly volatile force of pop dreamers, partnerships were formed and deformed within the band to calibrate our chances, and forge the strongest possible assault we could in the exploding market of grassroots bands.

So much time has elapsed that no one is absolutely certain why Burrows parted ways with the band. While it seems unlikely that Burrows was forced out of the band purely because of his appearance, sources agree that Davis had the image the band was looking for, with his greaser hair and heaps of experience, unlike the slight Burrows. After a stint playing a few nights at Detroit's Crystal Bar, Gaspar and Burrows were replaced by Davis and Thompson. To this day, Burrows maintains that the split was amicable, and that he has no regrets, as he told the I-94 Bar:

I was there in the original stages of the band, before everything really happened. I was in it from the beginning. I knew 'em as guys . . . Rob was a good, good guy. So was Fred, he was laid back. Smoked a lot of cigarettes. Always late for everything. Fred always expected people to wait on him, he would always want people to pick him up—he was the quintessential rock star. Always. Wayne was always business-minded. Business-considerate. Wayne always had a business mind, was always polite. Fred never gave a shit whether anybody cared about anything. Fred was Fred. But Wayne always cared. Had a good mind. Didn't try to insult anybody because he knew; shit, we gotta be nice to people. Rob Tyner was a gentleman, total gentleman. The other guys, Michael and Dennis, I knew very little, just as friends. I knew Wayne would always survive as a person, because he was always able to look at you and talk to you and not lie to you, and always be gentle. You could talk to him and tell he wasn't a liar . . . Wayne's not a liar. You're going to get the truth from Wayne, but you'll get it gentle. Hell, I remember him as a kid. There was something inside him . . . I attribute it to his mother. She was a sweet lady, and she brought him up the best she could, and did good. You go back years ago, he treated me like a little brother, although we were the same age. Wayne was the same guy years ago as he is now . . . he's a listener. He's not a bigmouth. He'll listen, and if he has a disagreement with you, he'll let you say what you have to say, and he doesn't get arrogant. He'll say his piece . . . and he was like that at sixteen years old. He used to have a little motorcycle, a little Yamaha, and we used to go all over Detroit on that Yamaha! I reminded him of that, and he laughed . . . he forgot about that. It brought smiles on his face. I said, "Do you remember the summer we cut all the grass?" at some big refinery where he worked, and I painted his mother's house, and it brought back memories. They were good years. He was a positive person then, and he's still a positive person. He wasn't negative, even though a lot of people could look at his message and say, "That's negative," he's not about that. One thing I can say about Wayne is that every time I've talked to Wayne over the years since I left the band in '65, '66, every contact we had was pleasant, was good, he was always, "Come on over. Let's talk. Let's do this, let's do that." He was always good. And Fred was, too, when he was straight. A few times when Fred looked at me, I don't think he knew who I was, but that was 1967, 1968 . . . he was high! And Rob was, too . . . Rob was like a brother.

Burrows would go on to enlist in the Marines and fight in Vietnam, probably completely unaware that his ex-bandmates were actively speaking out against that very same war.

The beginning of Michael Davis's life with the band wasn't without its problems. The new bassist felt as if he had "entered a web of competition that was on one hand, a creative haven," he wrote in an essay for *Mojo* titled "Lil Robin Tyner,"

and on the other, a chess match of personalities, without end. All I know is that after I became a member of the MC5, Rob Tyner was as distant as a black hole galaxy from me. Our conversation was made up of one-liners with very little in the way of real dialogue. Rob once told me that I'd better watch my step with Wayne, because he held me in such high regard, that if I ever blew it, he'd turn his back on me, and it would be all over. I thought he was trying to burst my balloon. It never occurred to me that he was jealous. I was his find, after all, and he may have had a scheme in mind that would create the perfect rock 'n' roll masterpiece. You never know in bands, someone is always thinking they have the winning plan. It can be a nightmare.

Dennis Thompson remembers that Kramer paid him a significant visit one night when he was in the twelfth grade. The guitarist appeared at Thompson's house on his motorcycle. They'd played together in their early teens in the Bounty Hunters. This night Kramer asked Thompson to sit in on a gig with his new band, the Motor City Five. Thompson did, and the rest, as they say, is history.

Dennis Thompson met Michael Davis when the drummer played his first show with the MC5 at the Crystal Bar in Detroit. Thompson enjoyed Davis's company. "I thought he was really cool and handsome," Thompson says, "like Paul McCartney, but with more style. He was older and seemed so sophisticated and world-wise to me."

Thompson also met Rob Tyner at the Crystal Bar, and he liked the singer, too. He thought that he was a rebel and a talented singer. They were roommates on the road, and Thompson learned much from Tyner about life and love: "He helped save my life when I was nasty into drugs. I miss him dearly."

At that point, the MC5 was an accomplished and respected cover band, playing material by the Kinks and the Who. They were also doing songs like "I Can't Explain," "My Generation," Them's "I Can Only Give You Everything" (written by Van Morrison), the Kingsmen's "Louie Louie" and songs by the Yardbirds—songs by a lot of British bands, but some American R&B, too. They did some Motown stuff, due to their location, and some Rolling Stones songs, like "Satisfaction" and "The Last Time." According to Thompson, "What the Brits did was study American R&B, and then they took it from there—they got creative with it. It just took off, and there wasn't anything going on in the U.S. that could compare. Sort of like the Japanese stealing our technology in the auto industry and then refining it. I used to watch the Japanese coming into our factories with cameras. They refined their manufacturing techniques by studying American techniques."

By the time Michael Davis joined the band, its members were already impressively tight and had a formidable Chuck Berry-esque sound. Kramer and Smith had both learned to play guitar by studying all of Chuck Berry's songs. With Davis not being a trained musician, and not having played that kind of music before, the band had a sort of "let's see what happens" attitude. The band had a very liberal and informal approach, throwing things together and seeing what came out in the mix. In this way, by not emulating people who had a precise way of playing, the band developed a sound that was arguably more original. Nothing was set in stone with the MC5. Davis was new to the game, and he relished the cutting-edge, exciting feel to the band. Something was very obviously happening. Davis:

> I'd never heard myself playing with other people at those volumes, and the sound set my
> hairs on end. It was so ripped and powerful. With my rudimentary bass playing and those
> guys just cranking it out with the Chuck Berry stuff, it was an emotional and uplifting
> experience. The sound developed as we went along, because we were all learning all the

time. We'd branch off Chuck Berry and see what the possibilities were. Back in that time, everything was very regular, except for a couple of groups—the Yardbirds, who had a cutting-edge guitar player in Jeff Beck. That was like the Ten Commandments. Like, this is where we start from here. They used a really dynamic approach to playing rock 'n' roll, and we learned from that. So we developed as we went along, but there was something great to begin with.

Over the next couple of years, the band gigged themselves into the ground in order to meld themselves into as tight a unit as humanly possible and to drum up buzz around their hometown. According to Thompson, the band would play anywhere, and they'd play for free. They'd play college parties with local DJs, basement parties, high school dances—anywhere—in order to drum up a following.

Initially, Thompson remained at college, but the band members were becoming increasingly focused on the band. Thompson doesn't remember any of them working during this period. The drummer was going to school and living off-campus with the band, at John Sinclair's Artists Workshop. Through these living arrangements, they formed a relationship with Sinclair. The hippie movement was growing, and 1967 saw the band set up with Sinclair. The police harassed them constantly, due to the fact that the authorities were on edge because of the Vietnam antiwar movement. Becky Tyner told me that the persecution from the police was unrelenting. Their house was raided regularly, the law keeping a closer-than-usual eye on the members of the band and those close to them. The hippies got turned on, tuned in, and dropped out. All across the nation, college kids were protesting about the war in Vietnam and protesting against the establishment's non-acceptance of their new lifestyle, which was loving and peaceful.

John Sinclair was born in Davison, Michigan, on October 2, 1941, and like many people in the area, his father worked in the auto industry, at Flint's Buick assembly plant. He graduated from high school in 1959, and for a short period he was a student at Albion College, but decided that student life wasn't for him, instead gaining a "street education" on Flint's north side, where he was happy to soak up the black culture that was prevalent in that part of the city. "I was just hanging around," he told me, "listening to records, taking pills. Good people—they schooled me in the ways of the streets. We'd hang around barbershops, poolrooms, and fried chicken restaurants in the middle of the night. After-hours gambling spots. Y'know, just street life."

Before long, he was back at the books, gaining a B.A. in American Literature at the University of Michigan. He later attended Detroit's Wayne State University, where he wrote a thesis on William Burroughs's *Naked Lunch* as part of his master's coursework. He developed a passion for blues and jazz music as a teenager, listening to "Frantic" Ernie Durham, a DJ on Flint's WBBC radio station who played records by the likes of Muddy Waters and Howlin' Wolf. In college, he received his musical education from jazz pioneers John Coltrane and Pharoah Sanders. College was also where he met his future wife, Magdalene Arndt (who went by "Leni"), in 1964. In November of that year, John, Leni, and assorted artist types, including Robin Eichele (a poet/filmmaker), Charles Moore (a jazz trumpeter), Martine Algier (a dancer), and eleven others created a collective called the Detroit Artists Workshop (DAW), the idea being that everyone in the group would support each other. Sinclair recalls in David A. Carson's *Grit, Noise, and Revolution* that the basis for the idea of the collective already existed in Detroit when he arrived there: "Back when I first arrived in the area, Leni, George Tysh, and some of the others had been members of a similar group that had a place called the Red Door Gallery over on Second and Willis. It closed in the summer of 1964. We took what they'd been doing and expanded on it. (108)"

More recently, he explained that, following the closure of the Red Door Gallery group,

> there wasn't anything happening in our area, [no one was] trying to do interesting things like people in other places were doing things. New things, modern, y'know. So some of us were poets—there wasn't anywhere that would let us hang around and read our poems or anything. We were too far-out for the venues that existed, as far as musically speaking. They didn't like what we were playing, they didn't want us to sit in and showcase ourselves. So we rented a house, a place of our own. Everybody was united by smoking marijuana, pretty much. I would say that if we had one thing in common, that was it, because some people didn't make anything in art, and others went from making underground films, [which were] in their infancy at that time, to printing poetry magazines and playing the sitar. There were all kinds of people, and we knew each other from getting high together. It was very underground then.

Future White Panther Pun Plamondon would, upon meeting Sinclair, describe him as "a tall cat, six-foot-three and several stones over 200 pounds, which isn't important, except that it seems easier for a large person to be charismatic, and Sinclair is. His bushy hair, just getting long, made his head look like a champagne cork. Wire-rimmed glasses seemed to make his face shine. I liked him immediately."

Part of the philosophy of the DAW was to avoid regular, mainstream life, which Sinclair lovingly referred to as the "death system." The group rented a house to use as their workshop, close to the Wayne State University campus, and all sixteen members chipped in for rent. A year later, the DAW had expanded to six other rented properties and two storefronts. The group was now able to provide space for performances and meetings, plus more living quarters for new members and hangers-on.

Meanwhile, Sinclair was writing more and more. He contributed a regular column to *Fifth Estate* (the longest-running English-language anarchist publication in the U.S., started in 1965 by Detroit resident Harvey Ovshinsky), and also wrote for the jazz magazine *Down Beat*. He also published his own newspaper for a while, with the self-explanatory title *Guerrilla*.

In November 1964, Sinclair was arrested for the sale and possession of marijuana. He received a two-year probationary period and a $250 fine. Less than a year later, however, Sinclair was in trouble again. An undercover police officer named Vahan Kapagian infiltrated the DAW by using the name "Eddie" and posing as a hippie. Sinclair was going straight, but "Eddie" would pester him constantly to help him score some weed. In October of 1965, Sinclair gave in and drove him to a connection. Five minutes after the transaction, the DAW house was raided. In court on February 24, 1966, Sinclair pleaded guilty to possession and was sentenced to six months in the Detroit House of Corrections. Sinclair: "The six months in prison were terrible. There's nothing alright about prison; they're horrible places for people to go. This one's kinda worse, because it was just outside the city of Detroit and it was a farm, and it didn't have walls. So there was a temptation each day to disappear, and you'd have to fight that off because it would just make things worse. You're so close to your life that you'd been taken from, but on the other hand, you're so far away. It's very frustrating."

Upon his release, Leni arranged a party in celebration, and the MC5 was booked to play, though somehow Leni was unaware of this. "At the end of the evening, this band showed up," she told Ken Shimamoto's I-94 Bar. "I really didn't know anything about them, or who said they could play here."

Sinclair himself remembers little of the band from that night: "I didn't really hear them that day. It was about three or four in the morning, and I was upstairs in my apartment, enjoying being at home. Some bands were there from all over, and we were sitting around talking, and whatever we were doing. There was this tremendous noise from downstairs. My wife went down to tell them that this might not go down well with the neighbors or the police. So I didn't really get to hear them then. I think I heard them for the first time at the Michigan State Fair."

Having been fascinated by the beatnik community for some time, Wayne Kramer and Rob Tyner were well aware of John Sinclair. The MC5 were living together, kind of like an anarchist, beatnik version of the Monkees, in the same Cass Corridor apartment in Detroit that Tyner and girlfriend Becky had previously moved into. It was an article Sinclair wrote for *Fifth Estate* that put the wheels of a historic relationship in motion. Sinclair had written that rock 'n' roll music was for children, and that the people who played it were untalented oafs. He further claimed that jazz was a superior use of instruments. Kramer was not about to allow his band and their music to be patronized. An ongoing argument began through the mail, with Kramer letting Sinclair know in no uncertain terms that his band knew exactly who John Coltrane and Miles Davis were, thanks to Tyner's passion for jazz. Sinclair's recollections of his article are hazy: "I'd like to read that. I wonder what I said. I really can't remember. Rob particularly didn't like it, and Frank Bach, his friend. We had this argument via mail, but then they came to kick my ass or whatever they were gonna do. Give me a good talking to or something, and I kinda disarmed them with a joint and some good music. Thank God for that. Frank Bach [Grande Ballroom stage manager, *Fifth Estate* rock columnist, and lead singer of the Up] became one of my closest friends for twenty-five years."

Kramer and Sinclair soon made up over the obligatory joint, when the MC5 were looking for rehearsal space. Sinclair's DAW provided it. Soon Sinclair developed a genuine affinity and passion for the band and what they were setting out to achieve by pushing boundaries and bending genres. Kramer elaborates that

> after we all left home and moved into our own apartments, we all moved down to an area in downtown Detroit near Wayne State University that's kind of like most university neighborhoods—anything goes. It's a kind of [a] cosmopolitan ghettoish kind of thing; they don't care if you look different and dress different or you play music loud at night; it

had a kind of laissez-faire atmosphere. And rents were cheap. So we all got our own apartments down there and we discovered this fellow Sinclair who ran the Artists Workshop. We thought, Well, you know, this is kind of what we're into, and they had a space that they used for rehearsing and we needed a place to rehearse. So we struck up a friendship with them, and it just grew real organically. We found that we were all trying to do the same thing.

"I thought John Sinclair was a pretty good poet, but I didn't like him at first," says Thompson. "I thought he had a big ego, and he didn't like me, either. He called me 'the Polish college drummer.' We just didn't see eye to eye. I think I had a gut feeling about John, that he was good for us at that point when we first met him, because [of] the beatniks and the hippie community—with John's help we could co-opt that audience, which we did."

Davis remembers warmer initial feelings toward his future manager: "Sure, I liked him. The girl I was hanging around with at the time knew John really well. He seemed like an amiable guy, and he was an organizer of arts around campus. He was always the big guy within the people in the underground. I liked him a lot—he was nice. At that stage his politics were about art and free-form thinking, which of course I agreed with."

Sinclair remembers becoming particularly close to Tyner:

He was my kind of people, in many ways. We were very good friends for that year, before I became involved in any of their affairs. I knew Mike because he had married this woman who used to be a friend of mine—Sandy Whitehouse, who lived around the corner from me when I first went [to Detroit] in '64. He was this pretty boy that she had. That's how we thought of him at first, and then he turned up playing bass with Rob, Wayne, and Fred. I loved Wayne's playing—I loved all of their playing. I thought it was the bomb. I didn't know Wayne that well at first, but I loved his playing. They moved into the neighborhood.

A common misconception is that John Sinclair introduced the MC5 to jazz music, and therefore played a prominent part in the development of the band's sound. Tyner was, as has been previously noted, a fan of the genre long before he met Sinclair, and the other members of the band were familiar with jazz in varying degrees. Thompson, for one, was already "semi-interested." As he recalled, "I used to listen to the big bands, which I got from my mom. Glenn Miller and stuff like that. I loved the big band drummers."

Clearly, however, Sinclair fueled their nascent interest considerably, thanks to his unbelievable jazz record collection. A jazz aficionado could listen to all the John Coltrane records, Archie Shepp, Charlie Parker, and Albert Ayler. The MC5 called it a gold mine, and they realized that the legendary jazz musicians were really good players. They had originally thought that rock 'n' roll was pretty simple, but they discovered that it could be infused with a number of different styles. They took in Otis Redding, R&B, John Lee Hooker, Motown, avant-garde and traditional jazz, and the British invasion.

Davis is careful to distance himself from the notion that Sinclair gave him his first taste of jazz:

I think most of the other guys will tell you that that's correct, but he didn't introduce me to it. I used to listen to jazz because my father was a big jazz fan. He had 78 rpm records of jazz at the Philharmonic, and really old bebop jazz types. My dad's from the big band era, and he was a big music fan. Plus, when I was a student in school, jazz was the thing we listened to. Everybody listened to Dave Brubeck and all those early Miles Davis and John Coltrane things. It wasn't the sole domain of John Sinclair. His strategy around the university was to have this art workshop thing, where he knew a lot of jazz people. He gave them a place to play on Sundays. It is true that John had a big record collection—he was a disc jockey to start off with. He'd play a lot of jazz and R&B. I was way into jazz before the rest of the band met John Sinclair.

Still, Sinclair was a self-proclaimed "fiendish collector." He built the foundation of his collection when he was an undergraduate in Flint, working in a record shop. He liked working in record shops, because he could steal records. He was and is fiercely proud of his jazz collection. He recalls that when the MC5 opened at the Grande Ballroom in October 1966, they were billed as "avant-rock," so they had already made some headway out of the realm of conventional rock 'n' roll before crossing paths with him. The fact that their singer had taken McCoy Tyner's last name confirms that he was a jazz aficionado before meeting Sinclair.

Whatever his influence on the band's music, John Sinclair's impact on the MC5 over the coming years would be monumental.

2
Ballrooms and Politics

During the summer of 1966, an English teacher and local radio DJ named Russ Gibb returned to Detroit from San Francisco and, having been inspired by the success Bill Graham (rock concert promoter from the 1960s until his death in 1991) had transforming long-abandoned dance halls into music venues, he took over the Grande Ballroom (pronounced "Gran-dee"). That fall, the MC5 were installed as the house band. Gibb had visited the Artist's Workshop to see the band (plus a light show called "Magic Veil" by an artist named Jerry Younkins), and had been impressed enough to allow them to play on the club's opening night (on October 7, with the Chosen Few), and for the following two weeks. They wouldn't, however, be paid.

The Grande Ballroom was designed and built in 1928 by architect Charles N. Agree and builder E. W. Wood for owner Harry Weitzman. In a 1957 issue of the *Detroit News,* John Finlayson, reporting on an upturn of interest in dance hall music, wrote:

The pace on the ballroom floor has slackened through the years, but a Detroit husband and wife, who have two children and operate the Grande Ballroom at 8952 Grand River near Joy, are doing their best to revive it.

The Grande, which has been operating for twenty-nine years, boasts one of the largest polished hardwood dance floors in the Detroit area, according to Mr. And Mrs. John T. Hayes, of 18911 Greydale, who have been managing it for the last two years.

The Grande boasts more, particularly in the enthusiasm Mrs. Hayes brings to her part-time job. The mother of two children, Jackie, 14, and Shaleen, 11, Mrs. Hayes reflects the concern of a good housekeeper and homemaker anxious to create a wholesome atmosphere for a pleasant activity enjoyed by many.

And because she is a woman and happens to assume the more active role in the managing partnership, her husband works full time at Sears; Mrs. Hayes has a romantic view of the Grande making public dancing available. "We are seeking to make the ballroom the type of place where young people may meet and enjoy dancing in wholesome surroundings."

Mrs. Hayes would prove that she had zero psychic ability later in the article, when she was quoted as saying, "Our patrons are only minorly interested in bebop and rock 'n' roll music. The teenagers now seem to be more interested in learning the more graceful steps that will possibly be an asset for them in the future."

Or maybe not.

Russ Gibb, meanwhile, was described in David A. Carson's *Grit, Noise, and Revolution: The Birth of Detroit Rock 'n' Roll* as "an unlikely rock 'n' roll hero in the fall of 1966. Already in his mid-thirties with short hair and glasses, he was employed as an English teacher at Allen Park Junior High School North [Gibb told me he actually taught at Dearborn Junior High]. A closer look, though, revealed a man who liked to ride motorcycles, take chances, and make money. Away from school, Gibb had been successful promoting dances at a rented union hall he called the Pink Pussycat, fronted by WKNR disc jockey Gary Stevens" (98).

Gibb was born in the Detroit suburb of Dearborn (where he still resides) in 1932, and in 1953 graduated from the University of Michigan with a degree in educational radio and television administration. Keeping plenty of irons in the fire, he found a job teaching in Howell, Michigan, but also worked weekends as a floor manager at Detroit's WWJ-TV; and did some production and DJ work with the Mount Clemens radio station WBRB, and later with the Detroit station WKMH. It was during a trip to see his best friend, Jim Dunbar, that Gibb was exposed to Bill Graham's Fillmore Auditorium.

Jim Dunbar could easily be the subject of his own book. The radio program director, also from Dearborn, is perhaps best known today for his part in the infamous Zodiac murders. Dunbar, who was portrayed in the 2007 movie *Zodiac*, was the DJ the Zodiac killer (whose identity is still unknown) would call while he was live on the air. A huge jazz fanatic, Dunbar met Bill Graham when he appeared on the Dunbar's KGO-TV show, *AM San Francisco*, to promote his ballroom. The seed of an idea was sown.

Gibb remembers his formative years with no small amount of pleasure:

My daddy worked for Ford and my mom was a maid. I was lucky to get through university. I always tell the kids that I taught that I was number three in my graduating class, if you turn the goddamn thing upside down—three from the bottom. I think that gave me a leg up in understanding the MC5, because they were basically what we called "factory rats." That was a slang term. If you didn't come from the upper classes and high society, wealth-wise, you were a factory rat. I worked at the DeSoto plant putting on hubcaps. That was my first experience of finding out that just because a man works with his hands and doesn't have a degree, it doesn't mean he's not smart. That was a big revelation to me—I always assumed that if you worked in a factory, you were a factory rat. That's what I'd always been told—that you weren't very bright. I met an old Italian guy at the plant who would talk about opera on the production line, discussing Verdi and things like that. That blew my mind away. The thing about America that the European Union doesn't understand is that this is still the land of opportunity. Look at me—I was a poor boy. Didn't have a pot to piss in. Worked as a teacher at the beginning for $2000 a year. That was it. I had to put on music to make a buck. I wanted a car. You see that in England now—all the kids want a car and [people] call them babies.

I [later worked] at the White House [as National Director of Youth and Education for the U.S. Bicentennial], and I was brought up [to believe] that the *New York Times* was a great paper. When I got [to the White House], I had dinner with Jimmy Carter. I got to the point where I realized that all my heroes were in the liberal world. [But] what turned me off in Washington was that all the liberals were talking about public schools, and these people all sent their kids to private schools. They all talked about the inner city and how we should all live together, but they all lived across the fucking river in Arlington or [elsewhere in] Virginia. They were "limousine liberals." That was the first time I called my father and told him that I was going to vote for a Republican. He said, "How can you do that? What kind of son have I raised?"

The 5 came out of that environment; most of them came out of Lincoln Park, with Wayne State University close by. Like most university towns, it's a bastion of liberal philosophy. I think Winston Churchill said that if you're not a communist at college, you're a moron. At thirty-five or forty, if you're still playing that game, you're another moron.

Michael Davis considers the relationship between the MC5, the Grande Ballroom, and Russ Gibb as pivotal in the band's success, the milestone in their becoming a real band, in the sense that they had a legitimate venue and an audience that was primed for the "avant-rock" they were honing. As for Russ Gibb, or "Uncle Russ," as he liked to refer to himself, Davis viewed him as a "neo-hipster wannabe":

He was a schoolteacher and a novice entrepreneur. He used underground terminology that were clumsy attempts to sound hip, often using the wrong phrases, such as "going up tight." He came to a rehearsal one night to audition us for his new club, the Grande Ballroom. He was aware of the San Fran ballroom phenomenon, and obviously wanted to be the guy that brought all that to Detroit. The city was [full of] Motown at that time, or bar band types that did R&B, pop hits, or one form of fad or another. The psychedelic sound was the underground hotbed of the near future. Russ was determined to cash in. At first I thought he was a perv, because I couldn't understand why he wanted to be in with all this weird stuff, and he was not what you might call a "cool guy," nor did he seem knowledgeable about music. I didn't know if his thing was guys or girls. Turned out he was just being a businessman. He never hung out with us, or anything. I never knew what he did besides run the Ballroom. He liked what we were doing at the rehearsal. We were working on a new tune called "You Got Me Freakin' Out." So he hired us to be the house band, meaning we would hold down a continuous gig at the Grande. We opened the first night at the Grande with the Chosen Few, an Ann Arbor band that included Scott Richardson [SRC] and Ron Asheton [the Stooges] on bass guitar.

There were only a handful of people at the Grande on opening night, and they showed up out of curiosity more than anything else. The doors opened into a cavernous room with multicolored lights swirling against the walls and floor, where an echoing sound system played an assortment of tunes. People wandered around the perimeter wondering what would happen. Although the first night was sparsely attended, within a few weeks, more and more kids started to show up. A boutique opened in the room at the back of the main room that sold Carnaby Street fashions and assorted hip accessories, which were popular in London at the time. The members of the MC5 started to realize that people knew who they were and respected them as a hot band. As time went on, more like-minded people were moving into their neighborhood, around the university. The MC5 were the regulars at the Grande. The drug underground was growing, and they were a part of it. The Grande was a part of it, too. The venue featured a light show, as well as strobes and odd furniture, like a bathtub in the middle of the room where people could lounge. There was also a raised promenade that circled the room, where people would sit on couches and benches and indulge in their treats. With an underpowered PA and no monitors whatsoever, the MC5 cranked out some of the most audacious music ever experienced on this planet. It was a time of pure growth and experimentation, but all the while eyes were kept firmly on the door in anticipation of a police raid. Local law enforcement regularly planted an undercover agent in the crowd, though most concertgoers claim that the police were easy to pick out.

Dennis Thompson remembers both Gibb and the Grande fondly: "Russ was one of the MC5's best friends and supporters. He stuck by us pretty much through thick and thin. Our involvement with Russ is one of the keystone blocks in the MC5's arc of history. The Grande was like our big living room or, say, garage. We owned the place. It was home. I have many anecdotes, but just suffice to say, it was one of the best periods in my life. I am truly blessed to have been a part of it all."

For Gibb, the MC5 and the Grande were made for each other, thanks to, in his opinion, similar backgrounds:

They were angry, I think. They probably didn't analyze the anger, but there was a time of great union upheaval, the great battles of organizing labor took over, [the authorities were] attacking social situations that they were concerned about. I think it's fair to call them intellectuals, in the sense that they had an intuitive intelligence, in the anger about what they saw going on. The best way to learn about people is to get to know people, and have to live with them, and they did because when you're a factory rat, you didn't have the beauty of coming down to the Grande from the suburbs and being hit [entertained] for a couple of hours. You had to live it for twenty-four hours. I certainly didn't pay them much, maybe twenty-five to fifty dollars per show. Maybe it'd go up to $100.

Gibb first met the MC5 in Wayne, Michigan. They were playing at the Civic Center, and John Sinclair suggested that Gibb come out and see them. Gibb didn't hear them play, but he did get to meet them. Gibb remembers them being dressed in a similar manner to the early Beatles or the Stones, a style commonly referred to as "the mod look." Gibb needed a house band for the Grande, and John Sinclair—who Gibb thought of as the MC5's guiding light and the consummate PR guy—organized the deal, although Gibb doesn't remember ever using the term "house band." Sinclair knew what was going on in San Francisco, so the first time they played for Gibb at the Grande, according to Gibb,

> they had morphed into sort of escapees from the Fillmore. I think that was courtesy of John. He's a bright guy and a very nice guy. It was so funny. When he was head of that mob, I was the promoter so I was the bad guy. Uncle Greed Head, I used to call myself on the air, just to play back on it. [John would] be ranting about charging $2.50 to see the Who—that was outrageous. But privately, we'd break bread together. I knew his wife, Leni, at the time. [John was] totally opposite to his media persona. And I think maybe I was a little as well, I don't know. But the 5, when they played for me, their stage presence was . . . they'd come out at ya. I'm picturing them now. The bottom line is, they just came on and were marvelous. Privately, the one I knew best was Rob Tyner. Great guy. The only thing that age gives you is wisdom. Rob and Michael Davis were the oldest and they had a little more wisdom, I thought. Tyner knew what was going on. When they were being outrageous to the point they were gonna blow the fucking place apart, they were mouthing things that would have got me shut down by the police—I could talk to Tyner and he would moderate. His wife, Becky, was kinda like the mother to the MC5. If there's anybody I'd give a big hug to, it'd be Becky Tyner. She made food for them, she made clothes for them, she was just . . . I don't think Kramer could ever forget what she's done for the group.
>
> Davis always reminded me, when I compare things like one of those overeducated assholes that always makes lists, he was like Harrison in the Beatles to me. I don't know how deep he was—I never really got to know him that well. But he did a great job. He was always there and he was responsible. All the qualities that you would admire, he had. But he never really opened up. Smith was just sort of like a young guy being carried around. I never met Patti after they married. We were all going our separate ways—the whole craziness of that—Davis reminded me of every kid when they first get a guitar and go for it. I don't know this, but I can see him down in his basement where his folks live, banging away, finding the chords.
>
> Wayne was pretty vocal. I think Wayne got caught up in the scene more than the others. But again, these were working-class kids. There were times when they would pass off

things and I would wonder if it was rehearsed or whether it just happened. Sometimes I would think that it was just spontaneous. These incredible sounds coming out of them. So much of that can be put down and rehearsed, but they would throw off chords to one another, and go with it. It was sort of like jazz at times. I think they had an appreciation of jazz, because Sinclair was into jazz. John was deep into jazz. I had been more into blues than jazz, even though Nina Simone and some of those people were heroes of mine. Being in a band is a very tough fucking business, I don't care what anybody says. Even when they make money.

Gibb remembers some animosity directed at the Grande crowd, and particularly the management, who were perceived to be hanging out with hippies. In fact, many people wanted to close the club down because they had decided that rock 'n' roll was the devil's music. Gibb was and is quick to point out that it is the devil's music, and gleefully so. When he started his teaching career, he was making $2200 per year. He swiped a book out of the library called *The Problem Teacher* by A.S. Neill, who wrote about radical approaches to child rearing. Gibb couldn't believe what he was reading because, all through his own education, the kids, not the teachers, were considered the problem. Gibb read all of Neill's material after that, and he even made an appointment to meet him when he went to London. The day of his appointment, Neill was ill, so the meeting never took place. Still, Neill was a great influence on Gibb's business practices, at least within the world of rock 'n' roll, because his philosophy was basically that you take people where they're at and you let them go.

To that end, Gibb never interfered with the music:

There were times when I remember thinking, Oh my god. I would want to break the plaster in the place. But if you have that philosophical understanding . . . that's what's wrong with education today—you try and impose a view of the world. People will come to learn. If you have any faith in humanity, people will come. That served me well in education, and in running the Ballroom. People would say, "Do you know they're smoking dope and having sex?" We had a philosophical understanding to let everything go. And it worked. You have to assume growth, and you have to assume that wisdom comes with its breaks.

Gibb has fond memories of the MC5 blowing visiting major label bands off the stage:

They were the hometown favorites, no question about it. There was glamour when the bands came over from England because it still wasn't that frequent. I remember I had to set up long-distance calls. You couldn't just call. The glamour has diminished today, because you can just do that. I maintain that if the media in Detroit was like they have in New York and L.A., they would have been as big as the Stones. That's my honest opinion. In John Sinclair, they had a genius, in my mind. They had the drive and intensity of being poor boys. I don't know the drive that they had through music but I know what it was to be poor. I wanted to make money because I saw what money did and what it opened up. Gary Grimshaw's art gave substance to the magic of the MC5. But I was a factory rat and they were my kind of people. They're still my kinda people. You don't forget your roots.

Gary Grimshaw's job was to dream up posters to promote the Grande shows, and many of his creations are worth an immense amount of money today. Because Grimshaw was a light show artist as well as a poster artist, he attended and worked at a lot of shows. In the 1980s, when he moved back to Detroit from Ann Arbor, he became more involved in the band scene in Detroit, which was almost raw enough to be termed punk, even though the term was not yet widely recognized as a musical genre. Grimshaw maintains that he doesn't "like the term hippie, I don't like the term punk—they're just words that *Time* magazine makes up to pigeonhole people."

Grimshaw practically lived in the clubs, attending five or six shows a week. He started doing concert posters simply because he adored the music. According to the artist, his posters are inspired specifically by a band's music:

The Detroit Cobras, for instance—I know a couple of members, I have their CDs, and I'm very familiar with them. I knew what they would like. When they appeared in San Francisco, I was living there at the time. I went to that show and it was a great show. I have done posters for bands that I'm not crazy about and in those cases I don't go to the show. Things have changed with regards to doing posters, because it used to be, [from] the 1960s through the 1970s, the promoter would hire you to do a poster, and that's how you got paid—to advertise the show. But when arena rock came and the whole music business expanded, posters were old-fashioned. They were too slow. It took too long to make them. Radio and newspapers—that's how you bang people over the head. During the 1980s it was all flyers, and I worked directly with the bands. Younger artists coming up really loved old posters. They wanted to keep doing them, and the promoters weren't going to pay them to do it, so they would hook up with the bands like I was doing with the flyers, and get permission from the bands, and design and print the posters themselves, mostly with silkscreen. They'd make their living by selling the posters after the show. There's a whole new approach to doing posters, and that's pretty much how it works now.

Chaos followed the MC5 around like a bad smell and, thanks in part to the establishment's blossoming distrust of Sinclair and anyone connected with him and his organizations, their shows were rarely without incident.

On April 30, 1967, John Sinclair's artistic collective, Trans-Love Energies, helped organize an open-air music festival, dubbed a "love-in," on Belle Isle, in the Detroit River (between Detroit and Windsor, Canada). Sinclair had somehow managed to convince the police that this would be a peaceful event, and that "Trans-Love Rangers" would be patrolling the grounds to ensure that the festival was orderly. Before sundown, things moved along exactly as Sinclair had said they would, with an atmosphere of hippie-happy joy hanging over the field. When night arrived, though, events took a dramatic and unpleasant shift. The massive level of alcohol consumed by the partygoers and music lovers didn't help. Problems really started to arise when the Outlaws, a local motorcycle gang not known for being peace-loving, arrived on the scene and started fights with some of the hippies. A local band called the Seventh Seal was urged to halt their set in an attempt to control the escalating carnage, but the group declined, and a mostly oblivious crowd urged them on. Bonfires of garbage were ignited, and the air became thick with unpleasant smoke and fumes. When an ill-advised motorcyclist began riding through the crowd, displaying little control of the vehicle, mounted police brought the rider down and took him into custody. Nothing gets a hippie's hackles up like police aggression, and before long firecrackers and bottles were being thrown at the officers and their horses. Predictably enough, the batons came out, 150 more police officers arrived, and order was eventually restored, but by then Sinclair's reputation with the authorities had taken another pounding. And that was only the beginning.

In early June, the MC5 opened at the Grande for classic British blues-rockers Cream, the supergroup consisting of Eric Clapton, Jack Bruce, and Ginger Baker. Like many bands before and after them (including, notably, Janis Joplin's Big Brother and the Holding Company), Cream failed to match the intensity and showmanship of the Detroit band, their clever riffs simply sounding insipid. On this particular evening, Gibb had heard that the MC5 were planning to burn an American flag on-stage, an act that at the time would have been far more controversial than it would be today, and he threatened to call the police. His remonstrations had little effect, how-ever. Sure enough, while jamming through "Black to Comm," Steve "The Hawk" Harnadek (the band's equipment manager) brought on the Stars and Stripes, which he and Rob Tyner then proceeded to tear apart, while the crowd inside the sold-out venue gleefully cheered them on. The band then raised their own flag, featuring a large cannabis leaf and the word "FREEK." Just to put the icing on the cake, Jerry Younkins of the Magic Veil Light Company appeared onstage toward the end of the evening—stark naked. Gabe Glantz, the son-in-law of the Grande's owner, and the rent collector, was livid, accusing the band of obscenity. He was clued-in enough to realize, however, that to ban the MC5 from his Ballroom would be to outlaw his big-gest draw (no pun intended).

A couple of weeks later, the MC5 were back at the Grande, playing a show with the San Francisco Bay Area band Blue Cheer. The Psychedelic Stooges opened, but before the MC5 were allowed onstage, Glantz threatened to turn off the power unless Sinclair promised that the band wouldn't do anything "un-American." When Blue Cheer retaliated by saying that they wouldn't play if the MC5 didn't, Glantz be-grudgingly backed off.

The drama wasn't confined to the Grande Ballroom, however. A month after the show with Blue Cheer, Fred Smith and John Sinclair were arrested and beaten by police officers while the MC5 was playing at a converted barn. According to Sinclair's testimony, there was a dispute about payment for previous shows at the venue. The money problems had not been resolved when the MC5 arrived to play, so the band played a shortened set.

While the MC5 was onstage, band members encouraged the crowd to stay away from the venue in the future. A worried security officer made a phone call, and the police arrived in full riot gear. When Sinclair stood his ground and demanded to be paid in full, he was clubbed and maced by overzealous and hyped-up police officers. Smith leaped in to help his friend and received a similar punishment. The pair spent the night behind bars. Sinclair later reported in Simmons and Nelson's *The Future is Now!* that "one sister had a camera, and I told her to get pictures of the shit, but the pigs spotted her and grabbed her camera and broke it before they pushed her down the stairs too" (43).

Such an overreaction by the powers that be wasn't uncommon; the band's reputation as commie, hippie troublemakers preceded them, and police everywhere seemed to want to let their own feelings be known in return. A perfect example of this over-aggression occurred at the Festival of Life in Chicago, organized by the Youth International Party, in August of 1968. Members of the group were known as "yippies," and their numbers included Abbie Hoffman, a political activist, his wife Anita, and journalist Paul Krassner. The yippies stood firmly to the left, though they're remembered as much for their crazy theater and satirical pranks as for their more serious statements. One communist paper once referred to them as "Groucho Marxists." The YIP made a statement to announce the fact that "the life of the American spirit is being torn asunder by the forces of violence, decay, and the napalm-cancer fiend. We demand the politics of ecstasy. We are the delicate spores of the new fierceness that will change America. We will create our own reality. We are Free America. And we will not accept the false theater of the Death Convention. We will be in Chicago. Begin preparations now! Chicago is yours! Do it!"

The "Death Convention" is a reference to the 1968 Democratic National Convention, which was scheduled to take place the day after the Festival of Life. The yippies' timing was no coincidence.

Before the big day, rumors flew. Bands thought to be appearing included the Grateful Dead, Big Brother and the Holding Company, Country Joe and the Fish, the Rolling Stones, the Beatles, and Bob Dylan. Not one of them would play—in fact, the MC5 were the only band that played that day. There were also whispers that the yippies were planning to pop a load of LSD into the Chicago water supply. Needless to say, that didn't happen, either (although that stunt would have resulted in some fantastic anecdotes). Drugs, nakedness, and some revolutionary violence were reportedly the order of the day, but for most, it was just a quiet afternoon in a park. The MC5 were, predictably, excellent, and the band received some rare positive words from the straight press as a result, with Norman Mailer reporting on the convention for *Harpers*. In his study of the *Kick Out the Jams* album, Don McLeese remembered the event thus: "I can still see the orb-like Afro of the lead singer as he badgered the crowd, pointing his finger, thrusting his fist, working his feet like a speed-freak James Brown. I would later know him as Rob Tyner, but all I knew at the time was that he was crazy. But not as crazy as the two guitarists, the ones I would later know as Wayne Kramer and Fred 'Sonic' Smith, both brandishing their instruments as if they were lethal weapons while swiveling their hips, arching their backs, flailing their arms, kicking their legs" (11).

McLeese wasn't the only person there to have such a strong reaction; it was many people's first exposure to the band, which, before this point, had barely ventured outside of Michigan, and only a handful of music lovers with their ears close to the ground had even heard of them. Their performance that day in Chicago did their reputation a world of good. Of course, trouble wasn't far behind, but at least it would wait until they were gone. The police duly enforced the 11:00 p.m. curfew, when all of the musical acts (namely, the MC5) had to be finished. Unfortunately, because of the rules against camping, a few thousand angry protesters now found themselves on the street with no place to sleep the night before the Democratic National Convention. Predictably, they didn't behave themselves, and many gas-induced tears followed. For the MC5, it was just another weekend, but they would get high praise from their fans, from the press, and from the organizers, both for their performance and for showing up when so many others had decided not to. Davis has mixed feeling about the day:

Ah, the Lincoln Park massacre of 1968. Sinclair had determined that our role was to be the "people's band." He had a clear vision that the MC5 would be the flag-bearer of the revolution. Wherever radicals were staging an event of political rebellion, the MC5 was available to take up the cause. These events were seen as the ultimate publicity we could get. Opening for popular groups had become chances to ambush the more popular band and blow them off the stage. I think the word was out and a lot of touring bands refused to play with us. We were badasses and proud of it. So the political outlaw thing was also a good fit. It was appealing to play at the Democratic Convention in Chicago, even though it was for no money. Aligning with radicals made us irreverent and reckless. Our real relationships with these people were more simply about getting stoned and partying than anything political, although Tim Leary was a great person to hang out with.

　　　The riot in the park started while we were playing. I remember the crowd moving in a panic toward the stage, a makeshift flatbed truck or wagon of some kind. Overhead a helicopter was circling. At the top of a rise, mounted police were riding through the crowd with batons waving. It didn't seem that anything in particular had set off this harsh reaction, but it was in full swing and coming our way. We had been through one of these affairs before and knew it was time to pull the plug. We got our gear together and drove out of there in the fastest possible time. Later, we heard that Country Joe McDonald had been assaulted in an elevator by some redneck Dems, but who knows what really happened. We could always say we were the only band to show up and play at Lincoln Park that day. That turned out to be only a minor skirmish. Later that evening, the cops literally busted heads for virtually no reason just because people were there. It was a disgrace.

Thompson, meanwhile, remembers little of the day: "I was pretty stoned on hash that day. To me it was, simply put, surreal." That winter, the MC5 entered the United Sound and Terra Firma recording studios and laid down the tracks "I Can Only Give You Everything," "I Just Don't Know," and "One of the Guys" for their debut single. "I Can Only Give You Everything" was originally recorded by Them, Van Morrison's hard-edged former band. Thompson recalls it was a staple of the MC5 set when he joined, but that it wasn't the band's first choice for their debut single: "They were doing 'Gloria,' another Van Morrison tune. That was the first record that we were going to release as a single, but a band out of Chicago called the Shadows of Knight beat us to it. The very same week we were going to go into the studio to record it, it came on the radio. We were pretty shook up over that. We did 'I Can Only Give You Everything' instead, but 'Gloria' was our first choice. They beat us by a couple of months, which is a bitch. We could have been off and running really early."

The single "I Can Only Give You Everything"/"One of the Guys" was released in the U.S. in March 1967 on AMG Records and received a fairly indifferent response. A world that held the Dave Clark Five and Phil Spector's "wall of sound" in high regard wasn't ready for the rough, minimalist approach of the MC5, but heard today, the single benefits from the zero-production it received. The fact that it captured the live energy of the band meant little to a general public who, for the most part, hadn't seen them. "I Can Only Give You Everything" features a groove that stays consistent throughout, while Tyner is uncharacteristically restrained. The B-side, "One of the Guys," is the first recorded example of the band's original work. Sadly, it's now hard to find, rarely popping up even on compilation albums. The lyrics are a joy. Centered around drinking, fighting, and cars, they provide glorious insight into where the boys' heads were at the time.

"We used to have the first MC5 single on the jukebox at the Artist's Workshop," John Sinclair remembers. "That would have been the spring of 1967." The band was billed as the "MC-5" on the vinyl's label, and the few copies still in existence fetch a pretty penny on Internet auction sites.

Between the single's recording and its release, Sinclair, along with Gary Grimshaw, Rob Tyner, and others, formed the 1967 Steering Committee, a short-lived project geared toward getting artists more exposure by linking them with journalists. The "sleeping with the enemy" idea didn't last, however, because by the end of January 1967, Sinclair had been arrested and detained once again for possession of marijuana (In total, fifty-six arrests were made at the Artist's Workshop, the local "LEgalise MARijana" movement, *Guerrilla*, and in the local artistic community, but only Sinclair remained in custody. His case did not go to trial for two and a half years. In response to the charges, he formed the Legal Self-Defense (LSD) group.

Possibly realizing that he was beginning to collect organizations, groups, and committees, Sinclair, his wife Leni, and Gary Grimshaw combined the Artist's Workshop and the 1967 Steering Committee into one collective, known as Trans-Love Energies Unlimited, which took its name from a line in the Donovan song "The Fat Angel." Dennis Thompson remembers Trans-Love as being a consortium of artists: "There were people who made posters, people making clothes, writers from the alternative press, all different artists."

According to Sinclair, many of the people who worked at the Artist's Workshop stuck around for the Trans-Love Party: "A lot of the same people were involved. I don't really know what the difference was. I hate to say it, but I think it was an organic change. Some people moved on to different things, new people came in, people started taking LSD, wanting to save the world . . . things of this nature. So we evolved from a place where you could do work and art into trying to deal with the new people that were turning up, called hippies, from the suburbs."

By now, the MC5 had developed a genuinely impressive fan base, the most devoted of whom John Sinclair tagged "the Stompers." Included in the group was Debby Pietruska-Nathan:

The Stompers wasn't an official name, because in those days everything was on the catch and the fly. The Stompers were named that by John Sinclair, and basically they were a group of between fifteen and twenty [people], and we came from all parts of Detroit. When I think back, what's interesting with the Stompers is that we were from all different financial strata, backgrounds, and education, and yet the one thing we had in common was that we were very much devoted to the MC5 and the success of the MC5. And other Detroit bands as well. The 5 were the priority, but we also supported the Scott Richard Case, the Rationals, Iggy and the Psychedelic Stooges, Bob Seger, Ted Nugent and the Amboy Dukes—all the big Detroit rock bands of that time. We set up big love-ins, like free concerts. What we would do was show up and support [the bands], and little by little we would play more of an active role in helping out with organizing political material, promotional material; sometimes we would help out with the light show at the Grande Ballroom if somebody needed to take a break.

We were all very young. I met them when I was fifteen, at a place called Massimino music studio in Detroit, on Seven Mile road. It was a wonderful mom-and-pop family-owned place. It was where everybody shopped for their musical instruments on the East Side. I think I met them in April of 1967, and I had a band called the Children of Darkness, and we were in there shopping for instruments. I was shopping for a new PA system, and I was looking around, and there was one room devoted to classical music when you first walked in, and the next room was all electric, rock 'n' roll. I was in the rock 'n' roll room, and this guy walked up to me and started chatting me up, and it was Fred Smith. We were talking, and the next person that came into the room, as I recall, was John Sinclair. So then we started talking, and John asked me which sign I was, which is classic. I told him I was a Leo, and John said, "Don't you know how wonderful that is?" So that's how it started, and then I started going to gigs and so on. The first time I saw them, I believe, was at a free concert, because a lot of the antiwar stuff was starting up then. I believe it was at Wayne State University on the football field, they had a huge concert. A love-in, as they called it. Or a be-in, as it was also called.

I was really into the Stones, the Who, and the Beatles, and they were all fabulous. But there was something that was so intrinsically Detroit about the MC5, and the fact that their music had a drive and energy to it that was just so much edgier. I think they raised the bar, or they were the earliest of bands to raise the bar, in terms of rock 'n' roll bands transforming into something much more powerful. It wasn't just dance music anymore. It was politically driven—I think a lot of it came out of the politics of the time and the hard-edged reality of what it was to live in Detroit. The city has a very tough history. From 1701 onward, it's always been a tough city. I think we grew up in Detroit at a time when it was the most magnificent time to [be brought] up there. Post-wartime, there was prosperity because they had done all the ammunitions and stuff there, and the car industry was flourishing. A golden age of Detroit. The MC5's sound nailed down the experience of growing up in Detroit, being working-class. And it somehow spoke on some soul level about the frustrations of the time, to the ambitions of the kids of the time, and it inspired me in numerous ways. It was really important to my development as a person.

While she was mainly driven by the music, Pietruska-Nathan, like so many of the MC5's fans, was also inspired by their message:

I was raised with politics. My parents were Democrats, and they were very liberal. I was already very politically inclined, so the marriage of politics and music, which is what I grew up with, was reinterpreted in a progressive way that was kismet for me. I pretty much agreed with them, but I was also taught to question everything. Any political agenda has to be questioned, reanalyzed, and debated. It wasn't automatic acceptance . . . y'know, like a cult thing. It was subject for debate. To think politically and to think analytically, and to think about how your actions have consequences. I became a little disenchanted in the early 1970s when some of the associates, even some of the Stompers, started talking about picking up guns. You say guns, I'm out of the room. It was becoming very fear-based rather than affirmative action-based.

Within the group, there was a range like there always is in politics. There was the unholy trinity of sex, drugs, and rock 'n' roll. Depending on whom you were and what you aspired to, you were going to respond to one or two of them. I think politics is the fourth thing, and I was always into the rock 'n' roll and the politics. As for sex, you were gonna grow up anyway. Sex didn't need an explanation, but let me tell some tales out of school. Among the Stompers, there were certain girls that had their favorite, and Michael seemed to be the favorite of favorites, because he was, quite frankly, the pretty one. Even though I loved all of them, he was gorgeous. What was interesting was that about every other week, one of the Stompers would claim that she was his particular woman. We had this one girl, who was a very nice woman, but she said that she was engaged, and she had this idea that she was gonna run off and marry Michael. Very funny. Others just aspired to having good healthy sex . . . free love—not getting attached. When you stop and think of the ages we were all at, at this point, we were all trying to grow up too soon. Everybody shared and shared alike. Everything got passed around. You never held on too long to a joint, and you never held on too long to a particular person. It was all part of the learning process.

When I started hanging out with the group in 1967, Rob and Becky were already together [they married in 1966], Wayne had a girlfriend, and Fred too [Fred's first wife was Sigrid Dobat, with whom he would remain until 1980]. They seemed to be the ones that were committed. I was about ten years younger than Michael, but I was very excited about hanging with people that were older, because I was in such a big hurry to grow up. It was like I led a double life at that point. There was my life at high school and at home with my family, and then there was my adventure life, running with the wolves. It was great because it facilitated my growing up in a very interesting way, which was a good thing. I was talking to a friend of mine about this period in time. She was like, "How did you meet these people?" At first she thought it was a little bit of bullshit that I knew these people and partied with these people. She was like, "How is that possible?" You have to remember that at that time, everyone was more accessible. At the Grande Ballroom, I became acquainted with members of the Who, who were a huge band. I had conversations with Janis Joplin. I ran into Jim Morrison, physically. We didn't have much of a conversation, but I ran into him. It was exciting and there was a fame aspect to it, but there was accessibility—that's a key thing. Unfortunately, as rock 'n' roll started going into bigger venues and then, of course, the assassination of John Lennon, that slammed the door on a lot of that, which is so sad because I don't think kids get to experience what we experienced.

We had some fabulous aftershow parties. This was Stomper territory. Always after the show, there'd be a party at somebody's house somewhere. It was done on a very spontaneous basis. Everybody would just show up at whoever's house. I only had one at my house, when my folks were not there. There was rotation in the various bedrooms. People would make love under the peach tree in the backyard. They totally raided the refrigerator, although we did do a big cleanup. When mom came home, there was a funny moment where she thought the place was a little too clean. Unfortunately, we had forgotten to restock the fridge. We were telling her that we were so hungry and had done it ourselves.

In July of that year, events unfolded in Detroit that either put the work of Sinclair and his colleagues into perspective or highlighted the necessity for it to continue, depending on whom you asked. When police officers raided an after-hours drinking establishment in a black neighborhood, they found eighty-two people celebrating the return of two soldiers from Vietnam. The police, perhaps unwisely, decided that the best course of action would be to arrest everyone in the building, a decision that provoked unrest among the locals. A crowd gathered to protest, and, as the last police car left the scene, the windows of a nearby store were smashed. The acts of vandalism snowballed into looting and fires across northwest Detroit and the East side, and within forty-eight hours, the National Guard had been mobilized. The violence escalated over four days, at which point the 82nd Airborne was brought in. After five days, the riots reached a conclusion but not without casualties. Tragically, 43 people were killed, 1189 more were injured, and there were over 7000 arrests. Sinclair remembers the events vividly:

> We were in the middle of it by choice. There's a sequence in my movie, *Twenty to Life: The Life and Times of John Sinclair* [directed by Steve Gebhardt], where footage from the riots is cut to "Motor City is Burning." Oh man, it's exhilarating. It was an exhilarating experience. For a while we thought that the police and the government were going to be overthrown right there, which was what we wanted to happen. We weren't scared. We wanted a confrontation with the authorities, and we wanted them to lose, so this was exciting because it was happening.

Pun Plamondon concurs:

> It's one of my favorite chapters in my book [*Lost from the Ottawa: The Story of the Journey Back*, Plamondon's 2004 memoir]. These black folks were getting ripped off for years and years by all these stores and institutions in the inner cities. For instance, the grocery stores, when they got their produce, it all came from the suburbs. They'd try and sell it there for three or four days. When the lettuce started to wilt, the tomatoes started to get soft, and the various other things, then they'd bring them down into the black communities. They were all getting secondhand, inferior goods, and they were all getting ripped off, because if you don't have a car in Detroit, you've gotta shop at the corner grocery store. They had all these people by the shorthairs and without any options. So when this riot broke out, you could just see all these grandmothers and grandpas, and all these beautiful people just saying, "Fuck you, man! We're taking it now, you son of a bitch. You've fucked us over for long enough." It was exhilarating, and I thank God every day that I witnessed it. It was people rising up.

Thompson remembers the riots being a far nastier business than Sinclair and Plamondon's warm tales of uprising imply:

I was visiting my parents. When the riots happened, I stayed [with them]. It wasn't a good idea to go home, but some of the guys were at the Artists Workshop. John especially, he stayed. He got to get involved with the police. I think the actual action, the burning and the shooting, was less than a week. But the occupation, with the National Guard, was longer. It was scary, very much so. Bullets were flying and tanks were driving down the street in Detroit. There were guys on every corner with their M13s or M15s, whatever they were. It was actually an occupied city. It was dangerous—people died. Black people didn't have much to lose because they lived in the ghetto. So when their places burned down, they were like "OK, what are you gonna do now?" That was their way of saying, "We're tired," y'know? The black people were smoking pot too.

The rest of the guys in the band may not agree with my philosophy on this—my theories are my own. Most of what I tell you is my own personal opinion and not the opinion of the MC5. But I believe that the drug of choice powered the whole revolution. In the early days, it was smoking pot and [taking] LSD. There was opium and hash like in Amsterdam, but mostly people were smoking pot and dropping LSD and rebelling against the alcohol-soaked generation before them. We saw alcohol as a death drug. It made people violent and stupid. It made them closed-minded and closed up. LSD and marijuana make you open up and, for the most part, become far friendly and outgoing. That's how people would bond; they'd sit around the campfire like a bunch of Indians smoking a peace pipe. The thing that happened as time went on was that the government realized that this was a drug-propelled movement, so all they had to do was change the drug. They used this chemical substance called paraquat to kill a lot of the marijuana fields, and [then] all you could get on the street was speed, amphetamines and heroin, and this other drug [they were calling] THC, which, in effect, was animal tranquillizers. PCP was the actual chemical.

They're all death drugs. Those drugs will kill you, they're all about becoming alienated and separate. You do heroin, you don't want to get involved with anybody. You want to be by yourself, stare at your hand, and nod off. The same thing happened in England to Jimi and everybody. People were doing hallucinogenic drugs, then all of a sudden the drugs of choice (orchestrated by the government) changed, and the movement disappeared. We were young and we weren't experienced. We were idealistic, and that's the way it should be. You start off believing that Santa Claus is real, and then you want to know that the people that live around you are all good and want the right things.

In his book *Lost from the Ottawa*, Pun Plamondon recalls taking a risky drive through the carnage:

As we eased down Clairmont toward 12th, we began to see more cops in heavy riot gear: black jumpsuits and boots, dull black helmets and face shields, carrying carbines and pump shotguns and wearing ammo harnesses across their chests. Their teargas canisters clanked together as they marched in formation.

For the last half of the block, traffic was directed between a gauntlet of cops, badges taped over with black tape so the number couldn't be read. They poked their guns with their white porcine faces through the windows of cars with black occupants to snarl and ask where they lived and their destination. The whites, of course, were just waved through.

While they were going on, I saw the riots as a big party—a people's festival and a chance to show our ass to the man, to shatter the nerves and dreams of the complacent and to piss in the face of the long-absent landlords. However, the aftermath was sobering. Seeing citizens—all poor, mostly black—in shock, some wailing by a smoldering pile of bricks, others picking through the rubble for anything of value, a memory perhaps—this gave me pause. Seeing people who had lost their homes and every earthly belonging, some of whom had barely escaped with their lives, made it all real and compelled me to look at the situation though others' eyes. (78)

Over the course of the riots, Kramer was mistakenly arrested, but police officers quickly realized their error and released him. Trans-Love, reveling in revolution, gave out clothes and food to people who were injured or had been made homeless. A month later the streets had—on the surface at least—calmed down. Within the MC5 camp, however, one of the biggest decisions of the band's career—one that would affect them until they broke up and beyond—was made sort of by accident. John Sinclair became the band's manager, although today nobody seems to be quite sure how. Even Sinclair's recollections are patchy: "Boy, that's one thing I can never put my finger on. One day, it just seemed like it was time to do something—to solve some of their problems as a performing unit. Getting gigs, getting them to the gigs, making sure the equipment was working when the gig was on, making sure they got paid—all that kind of stuff."

Sinclair had already been giving the band advice, and making him the manager was the next logical step for a band with no organizational skills. When the Grateful Dead had paid a visit to Detroit, Sinclair had spent time with their managers, Rock Scully and Danny Rifkin, who, in Sinclair's affectionate words, were "as nuts as I am." He decided that he wouldn't mind doing the same job.

Thompson doesn't recall a band meeting or any discussion about the matter: "There wasn't a discussion—it just happened. Wayne and Rob got together and thought that it would be a really good idea to meet John Sinclair and form a relationship with him. They forged ahead and did that. One thing led to another, and John became our manager."

It seems plausible that the band, which was already working with Sinclair's Trans-Love Energies, would have allowed Sinclair to slide into the manager's seat without kicking up any fuss. It seems certain that they would have needed a manager around that time; none of them had any experience with business dealings, while Sinclair had a bucketful of connections. Everyone knew him.

Nineteen sixty-eight began with another visit to Detroit's United Sound Studio, this time so the MC5 could record the tracks "Borderline" and "Looking at You" for their second single. The session was financed by Russ Gibb. This time, Sinclair handled the production duties himself, a fact that becomes very obvious when listening to the finished product. Sinclair later admitted that "it was really a non-existent production job, since I 'produced' it and didn't have any idea what I was doing. I just knew that the music was killer and that we had to get it down."

While the MC5 had yet to set the world on fire, Sinclair's involvement resulted in the single faring significantly better than its predecessor, in terms of raising the band's profile. Kramer and Davis collaborated on "Borderline," and it remained a part of their live set throughout the band's career. A primal song built on pure sexual energy, the lyrics forgo double entendres and aim directly at the main vein, while Smith and Kramer create sonic filth with their guitars. It's psychedelia for street kids—a hippie versus hoodlum paradox that would stick with the band throughout their relationship with Sinclair.

"Looking at You" was penned by Smith, Tyner, and Davis, and it's perhaps the band's first true classic. A strong Davis bass line kicks off the song and drives it forward, only varying when the two guitarists veer off the beaten track with a sonic onslaught that, thanks to Sinclair's self-admitted lack of experience behind the mixing desk, sounds like it was recorded in an echo chamber—though the song doesn't suffer for it. "Polish" wasn't a word that would apply to the MC5 until their second album.

With an unmistakable air of tension looming over the very heart of Detroit, news came through on April 4 that Dr. Martin Luther King Jr. had been assassinated. The civil rights leader was shot in the back of the neck while standing on a Memphis hotel balcony. King was in the city preparing to lead a group of sanitation workers in a protest against poor wages and working conditions. James Earl Ray was charged with the shooting in June of that year, and the following March, he was sentenced to life imprisonment. Of course, by then, the subsequent riots had caused untold damage across the United States, and conspiracy theories abounded. Detroit suffered more damage than any other city, and a protective curfew enforced on the day of the shooting and lasting fifteen days ensured that the MC5 and the Trans-Love collective were very restricted, and therefore couldn't earn any money during this period. On top of it all, somebody set Sinclair's Artist Workshop house on fire.

Understandably, Sinclair, Trans-Love, and the MC5 had had enough, so they all moved to nearby Ann Arbor, into two turn-of-the-century mansions at 1510 and 1520 Hill Street. Little changed, though, and within days, Trans-Love members Pun Plamondon and Gary Grimshaw were arrested for possession of marijuana in northern Michigan. Grimshaw fled the state for two years, while Plamondon served three months in Grand Traverse County Jail. While in jail, he learned about the Black Panthers, the radical group aimed at gaining equal rights for the black community through whatever means necessary. The Black Panthers were part political party and part army, and they scoffed at the idea of nonviolence. Their methods were the polar opposite of Martin Luther King Jr.'s.

Sinclair remembers Plamondon planting the seed of an idea: "Pun Plamondon came back [from] doing ninety days in jail that summer and he had this preachment about the Black Panthers, and I said, 'We should have the White Panthers, and why don't we be it?' That's the way I remember it, and it seemed like a great idea to us."

"I was in jail way up north in Michigan, and there's very few people of color up there," Plamondon told me of his time behind bars.

I was preparing for trial, and our attorney spoke to the judge, saying that I had to have access to the underground press, the alternative press, because that was one of the tools we were using to prepare for trial. So that was the context for which I had all these underground papers. I came across this interview with Huey P. Newton. You must understand that, up until that time, we considered ourselves cultural revolutionaries. We didn't really involve ourselves in the political dialogue; we were against the war, we were for the liberation of marijuana smokers, and we were for the personal liberation of human beings. But as far as developing a political line and getting into the debates of the day, about socialism, communism, capitalism, Trotskyism, Leninism, or any of that stuff, we avoided all that. We just focused all of our attention on the creative arts and used that to further our goals of freedom. So this was a big move, when I came out and we formed the White Panther party, because we jumped in with both feet into the political melee.

In his thesis, "Total Assault on the Culture," Jeff A. Hale, PhD, wrote:

The selection of the name "White Panthers," which demonstrated a close identification with the Black Panthers, might appear as something of a contradiction, considering TLE's (Trans-Love Energy's) mostly white membership and sparse record of attention to black causes in Detroit. However, Sinclair never strayed from his close identification with black culture (especially its music), and the Artists Workshop had been a multiracial organization. Most TLE members envied and respected the Black Panthers' armed self-defense strategy and disciplined organizational model. Yet, the most influential Black Panther advocate within the collective was Pun Plamondon. At this time, the Black Panthers were actively seeking alliances with "white mother country radicals" in the New Left, counterculture, and peace movements. For Plamondon, the Black Panthers' call for white allies, essentially white Black Panthers, was a revelation. (makemyday.free.fr)

Pun Plamondon was born in 1945 to mixed-blood American Indian parents in a psychiatric hospital (his father was incarcerated for being an alcoholic and his mother was being treated for syphilis). Plamondon would go on to live an extraordinary life, filled with incidents both amusing and outrageous, which seems befitting for a man who had such a bizarre introduction to the world. According to his website, in 1947 he was adopted by a "dysfunctional white Catholic family." As a result, his childhood was less than ideal, and at the age of fifteen he found himself shut away in a Catholic reform school. Five years later, Plamondon's left-wing lean-ings manifested themselves in the form of organizing a union for migrant farm workers.

By 1967, he was living on the streets of Detroit, making sandals during the day in order to finance the pot he was smoking at night. Before long, he was mixing with radicals like Allen Ginsberg, journalist Peter Werbe, the artist Gary Grimshaw and, of course, John Sinclair. In his book, Plamondon recalls meeting Grimshaw: "Grim-shaw was the artistic genius of the *Warren-Forest Sun*. Quiet, slim, and fine-featured, with the delicate, tapered fingers of an artist and long, straight, thick black hair hanging to the middle of his back, Grimshaw was a museum-quality example of a hippie" (60).

Grimshaw, who would play a key role in the White Panthers, was already inter-twined with the MC5. In high school, Grimshaw was friends with Rob Tyner. The two of them were half of the aforementioned street cruisin' gang with friends Kelly Martensen and Carl Schigelone. After school, his life had taken him away from Detroit and the MC5:

> I went working in a steel mill then I went in the service. I'm a Vietnam veteran. I was gone for about two years, and it was during that period that Rob met Fred and Wayne, and put the band together. So they were a band and were just putting out the AMG single ["I Can Only Give You Everything"] when I got back. We always wanted to be beatniks. We always used to come down to the Cass Corridor neighborhood all the time. We'd go to jazz clubs, like Mr. Kelly's over on the East Side, and we'd go to parties around Wayne State. So we loved this neighborhood, first of all.
>
> I was stationed in San Francisco, which was the home base. My ship came back from Vietnam, and I was in San Francisco for about six months before I got discharged. I got to know the whole Haight-Ashbury, Fillmore Avalon thing out there. When I came back, Rob had a band together and he was living in this neighborhood. I had met Becky [Tyner's wife], and I actually stayed with them for a few weeks. That was right around the time that Russ was getting the Grande Ballroom together, and Russ was looking for a band that played original music. He heard about the MC5 and called Rob. I was sleeping on his living room floor at the time, and Russ asked him if he knew anybody that could design a poster. I'd been telling Rob stories about all these posters I saw in San Francisco, and he knew I

could draw and stuff. He handed the phone to me and said, "This call's for you." That very night, I did the first Grande poster. I got the copy over the phone. Through the MC5 I met John Sinclair. That turned into Trans-Love Energies, and through police harassment, that turned into the White Panther Party. In a nutshell, that's how it happened.

Grimshaw remembers his exposure to the hugely influential psychedelia posters in San Francisco:

I'd get on the bus, and that's where they'd put the early Fillmore Avalon posters, right behind the driver there. You couldn't miss 'em. San Francisco is a great walking town. It's a tough driving town but a great walking town. Posters are very effective, and they were all over the place. You could go into a record shop the week before the show, and there'd be a stack of the posters, and you could take a dozen. Now they go for $150—it's unbelievable. I know I can't afford my Grande posters. I know the collectors that have 'em, and if I need to reprint the image I can. But I don't have 'em. Because of my political activity during the early 1970s, I was moving around a lot, and I spent two years with a warrant hanging over my head, so I couldn't drag around a pile of posters. It wasn't till the late 1970s that I started to save things.

Prior to that trip, Grimshaw had been painting and drawing for as long as he can remember:

Art's a family thing. My father was a mechanical engineer and he'd bring home his drafting equipment. I had a big drawing table when I was a little kid. My uncle was a printer and he [did] all the Grande posters. My aunt was a staff artist at Kresge's, which is now Kmart. My grandfather was a stylist for General Motors. Everybody in my family was into art, and every little picture that I drew, they'd all say, "Oh yeah, that's great, do more," ever since I was little. I remember my mother bought me a set of books called *The Wonder-Story Books.* There's like sixteen of them, and they were numbered to correspond with an age. They were very simple at the beginning with big type, but as you went up the numbers, the type got smaller and the stories got longer. But they had beautiful full-color illustrations all the way through. I love that set of books. It was all like fairy tales and really great illustrations. I wish I could find one of those sets.

The trio of Grimshaw, Plamondon, and Sinclair formed the backbone of the White Panthers, a party of sorts modeled on the Black Panthers, a group that Plamondon had had limited exposure to while imprisoned. Grimshaw:

> I took it very seriously. Pun was the Minister of Defense; I was the Minister of Art. In 1969, there was a warrant out for my arrest in Michigan. I'd left in 1968, first going to Boston, then to California. I was hooked up with the Black Panther party there, with Emory Douglas, the artist who did all the magazine covers for them. I hung out with them. I did the layout for *Berkeley Tribe* [a newspaper then based in Berkeley, California], and they'd interview members of the Black Panther party on a weekly basis. I would go to those interviews and got to meet them all. Pun had a warrant out for his arrest [too]. Mine was for intent to sell two joints. His was for conspiracy to destroy government property, namely a secret CIA office which he allegedly [tried to blow] up.

Grimshaw admits that he was guilty of possessing marijuana, though as was often the case around that time, a drug possession charge was merely a tool the police used to control the people associated with the revolution:

> It was right after the Detroit riots, the police riots. We were all living at Trans-Love, which was right down the other side of the freeway. We stuck it out for like six days. Most white people just took off, but we stuck it out. On the sixth day, the National Guard broke down our door and pointed guns at us. They said they had reports of a sniper on the roof. Yeah, right. We didn't have any guns. So we decided it was time to leave. We went to Traverse City, which is [in] the northern part of Michigan, a resort city there. We just had a party there and somebody brought a bag of weed. I was the expert roller, and I'm sitting there rolling joints and rolling joints. Well, one of the people at the party was an informant for the state police. He took two of the joints and held on to them. This all came out in the pre-trial. He held on to them for a week before he informed the state police that he had them and that he had gotten them from me. Also, it turns out the guy had a motorcycle accident before he went to the state police, and he had a metal plate in his head. He was going through treatment for loss of memory. He was not a credible witness as it turns out, but it was enough for them to issue a warrant for me.
>
> I was living in Ann Arbor then; I had moved out of the White Panther house on Hill Street, just for personal reasons. There was like thirty people in the house and it was

like living on the street. Me and my girlfriend Judy just wanted our own place. I was still working with them full time, but I wasn't living in the house. [The police] came to the house with the warrant. John's brother Dave, who was the chief operating officer of the White Panther Party, told me about it. We moved to Boston and stayed there for most of 1968. Then Judy's parent's died and she came into a ton of money, so she decided to move to California. When I was in California, that was when I working on the *Berkeley Tribe* and all that. They came to the *Tribe* office for my arrest. I wasn't there at the time; they missed me. So I got the phone call, and all this time I was talking to David Sinclair and doing artwork for the party. When I couldn't work at the *Tribe* anymore, we started making arrangements for me to come back. He got a bondsman, an attorney and all that. I took the train back to Michigan and surrendered, and posted bond. I moved into the White Panther house and worked full time on the party for the next three years.

Before any of this happened, I was very much inspired by the civil rights movement. My family [members] are all liberals. Not activists so much as sympathizers. I was predisposed toward this liberal, democratic mindset anyway. Then when I saw firsthand how the police treated black people from living in the neighborhood, just seeing how brutal it was, it radicalizes you pretty quick.

Grimshaw remembers his first impressions of the MC5 and John Sinclair:

I thought John was great. I still do. The thing about John was, I was just a levelheaded kid. I think I was twenty when I met him, and I didn't know what to do. I tried going to college; I tried working in a factory; I tried the military—I hated it all. It all sucked. John showed me how to do something, how to write and publish, and use my artwork to do something, and do it along with people that I liked. That to me was a big lightbulb going on over my head. I worked with John from 1966 to 1987—twenty-one years.

As for the MC5, Rob was my best friend, always. I didn't know the others very well, and by the time I got to meet them, even though they were also from Lincoln Park, they were just a lot younger than me by two or three years, which is a lot when you're a teenager. I liked them and everything, but I didn't hang around with them too much, and by the time I got to know them, the band was this all-consuming thing they were involved in. I was working with John, and I had my own all-consuming thing. So I did a lot of work for them, but it wasn't like I was hanging out at their house every day. So I didn't know the other members anywhere near as well as I knew Rob. The music was great. It was right in the pocket of the music we listened to growing up—rock 'n' roll, Motown, jazz.

Way before the band, Rob played the flute. He'd make his own flutes. And he had bongo drums, and he'd sing to the radio. He was very musical from the beginning. He even encouraged me to sing, but you don't want to hear it. I sort of sound like Mark Murphy, the jazz singer. I'm a huge fan of the band itself. I was their roadie for a while. I was their substitute roadie—when one of the roadies couldn't make the gig, I would fill in. Live, they were loud. It was like baseball, when you go and play another team in their stadium. It's their house. That's what the Grande Ballroom was for the MC5, because they also used it as a rehearsal hall every week, besides being booked there almost every weekend. They were fine-tuned to that place. Everybody in town knew them. Cream would come in, and people would only know them from the records. I was doing the light show that whole time. I was at the back of the hall, in this booth. I heard all the music. When Cream first played, they were awful. They were having a bad night. And they're a good band—I like Cream a lot. But they weren't up to it, and the MC5 had just blown everybody away like they usually did, and then Cream turned in a half-assed set. It wasn't even good for them. After a while, touring bands realized that if they played the Grande, they had to put on a good show because the opening bands were really good.

The Black Panthers were formed in 1966 when, following the assassination of black leader Malcolm X, Huey P. Newton organized his friends Bobby Seale and David Hilliard into a group originally called "the Black Panthers for Self-Defense." The group quickly created a ten-point program that outlined the issues the group felt needed to be addressed in order to end the oppression of black people in the United States:

1. We want freedom. We want power to determine the destiny of our black and oppressed communities.
2. We want full employment for our people.
3. We want an end to the robbery by the capitalists of our black and oppressed communities.
4. We want decent housing, fit for the shelter of human beings.
5. We want decent education for our people that exposes the true nature of this decadent American society. We want education that teaches us our true history and our role in the present-day society.

6. We want completely free health care for all black and oppressed people.

7. We want an immediate end to police brutality and murder of black people, other people of color, all oppressed people inside the United States.

8. We want an immediate end to all wars of aggression.

9. We want freedom for all black and oppressed people now held in U.S. federal, state, county, city and military prisons and jails. We want trials by a jury of peers for all persons charged with so-called crimes under the laws of this country.

10. We want land, bread, housing, education, clothing, justice, peace, and people's community control of modern technology.

These ideals would prove controversial enough to prompt the director of the FBI, J. Edgar Hoover, to say that the Black Panthers presented "the greatest threat to the internal security of the United States." Eager to latch on to the slightest sign of a revolution, Sinclair, Plamondon, and friends were immediately attracted to the terror that the Black Panthers seemed to strike into the hearts of conservative Americans. The group conceived the idea for the imaginatively named "White Panther Party." Moving quickly to dispel any notion that they were a white supremacist organization (as their party name might suggest), the White Panthers devised their own ten-point program:

1. Full endorsement and support of the Black Panther Party's 10-Point Program.

2. Total assault on the culture by any means necessary, including rock 'n' roll, dope, and fucking in the streets.

3. Free exchange of energy and materials—we demand the end of money!

4. Free food, clothes, housing, dope, music, bodies, medical care—everything free for everybody!

5. Free access to information media—free the technology from the greed creeps!

6. Free time and space for all humans—dissolve all unnatural boundaries.

7. Free all schools and all structures from corporate rule—turn the buildings over to the people at once!

8. Free all prisoners everywhere—they are our brothers.

9. Free all soldiers at once—no more conscripted armies.

10. Free the people from their "leaders"—leaders suck—all power to all the people, freedom means free everyone!

Jeff A. Hale, PhD, defined The White Panthers on the makemyday.free.fr website as:

> a professedly political organization that was dedicated to the confrontational strategy of "a total assault on the culture by any means necessary." Its formation during the fall of 1968 owed much to both local and national influences. On the local front, Detroit and Michigan State Police surveillance, harassment, and intimidation of left-wing activists reached unprecedented levels in the wake of the Detroit Riots of 1967, as well as in reaction to the popular success of the WPP's "house band," the MC-5. National influences, especially the allure of the Black Panthers and the Yippies, also played an important role in the politicization of the group. The dynamics of, and interplay between, these (and other) influences are of critical importance because the existing historiography of the 1960s, still dominated by former participants in the various struggles, offers no useful model for explaining the White Panthers' progression toward radical extremism. To cite just one example, former SDS [Students for a Democratic Society] leader Todd Gitlin explains the New Left's step-by-step evolution from "protest" to "resistance" and ultimately "Revolution" as emanating largely from the Movement's impatience and frustration with the continuing Vietnam War. In dramatic contrast, the Vietnam issue was inconsequential to the evolution of the White Panthers; the forces and motivations underlying the group's "radicalization" are to be found elsewhere.

While the MC5 were happy to go along with the Panthers' political stance, Thompson remembers starting to get riled by the sheer number of people that were benefiting from his band's work. "We supported the White Panther Party and supported fifty people, and we never made much money," he says. "The reason I joined the band was the same reason everybody does—to play rock 'n' roll music, to enjoy the experience, to get laid, and to be a pop star. Personally, if I wanted to be a political person, I would go back to college. I'd finish my degree and do my protesting on campus. The MC5 were like a drug, and I couldn't pull myself away. I wanted to quit a couple of times, but I couldn't do it."

The MC5 was the perfect vehicle for the White Panther Party's message, and the party's members were eager to make the most of that fact. "Not just the MC5, but music and culture were the principal tools that we were using," says Plamondon. "Revolutionaries use what they have to get what they need, and so what we had were writers, musicians, and filmmakers, and we were going to use that creativity to bring down the government. The MC5 were just perfect, because they were eager, they were good, they had a tremendous following, and they were pretty much as militant as the rest of us. They didn't speak militantly so much, although their music of course was, but they were eager to support whatever lunacy I would put forward, I know. I just loved them."

Thompson's opinion is that the White Panthers' politics were little more than student scribblings set to a soundtrack of good music in an atmosphere of pot smoke:

I would say that, in essence, the politics were genuine as a thought model, as a thought paradigm. I think it was correct and I think it was genuine. But as far as backing it up, we started drawing the line there. We were getting thrown in jail for obscenity. The cops were out to get us. The FBI were tapping our phone. They had a dossier on the MC5 that was about a foot and a half tall. They were following us around, mainly because of our association with the White Panthers. Abbie Hoffman and the Chicago Seven [defendants charged with conspiracy, incitement to riot, and other charges relating to protests in that city during the 1968 Democratic Convention]—we aligned ourselves with these people. We gave them our support. Abbie Hoffman, mainly, was trying to end the Vietnam War. It was a confusing time in America because half of the country wanted Vietnam and the other half said, "No, we don't belong there." There was almost a fifty-fifty polarity, like father versus mother and sister versus brother—where do you stand about the war? That movement grew and grew, and eventually the combined efforts of everyone involved came through. It took a while, but I think we did it. We stood our ground.

There was racism going on too; we grew up in a very racist time. Blacks were segregated. All these changes were taking place with Martin Luther King. There was the peaceful approach of Martin Luther King, or there was the more aggressive approach of the Black Panthers. We aligned ourselves and said that change had to take place. People had to give themselves the opportunity to find out who they were. Part of our policy platform was peace and love, but we didn't deliver it with flowers in our hair. We were aggressive— aggressively preaching peace. In other words, you had to stand your ground. You couldn't waffle. You're either for this or you're against it, one way or the other. You can't be in the middle. There was no middle ground—it wasn't accepted. Don't argue with me— you're either for or against this war, and if you're for this war, get the fuck out of my face. The bottom line was, boys are dying left and right, and no one could see the reason. It was a confusing time. It was all hype about the communist baloney. We did it, we all sat around and came up with the ideas, but it . . . was more for PR. It wasn't a hoax, but it was intended to show that the white kids would back up the Black Panthers with what they were trying to communicate. So it was more like a paper tiger.

Davis concurs, saying, "I always thought these things were tongue-in-cheek, like political satire. To me, it wasn't real politics. It was making fun of politics that we didn't like. For us to enter into it on that level, it didn't make any sense. I think it changed over time into actual politics rather than critical politics, though."

Davis maintains that young Americans had a lot to be angry about in the late 1960s, however:

The whole notion that the government controlled society, and that we could be suppressed at any moment . . . we were at a point when the people were realizing that the government lied to you. We were in the middle of a war, and there was great debate over what was communism anyway? What was socialism? What is capitalism? These are really big terms, but at that time, with drugs coming into it, all of a sudden everything became really clear—the people that have the money are the enemy and we're the good guys. All we wanted to do was play rock 'n' roll music, and make our statement with the music.

Still, he stops short of referring to the White Panthers as a "real" political party: "It was a party in the sense that we smoked a lot of dope. It was that kind of a party—smoking and laughing. It was real for us in that it was a way to bring people together to have a good time and play rock 'n' roll music. It was really a satirical statement, but I never thought of it as a political party."

If there was one person within the White Panthers' ranks who was really taking things seriously, it was Plamondon:

I was probably a little more strident in the political line than the others. I came out of the labor movement. At nineteen and twenty years old, I was a labor organizer for migrant farm workers, [and read about people like] César Chávez, the famous Mexican organizer, so I have some indoctrination into a labor movement and the difference between the right and the left. I came into the situation with slightly more sophistication than most; not [more than] Sinclair, though. Sinclair is quite a genius. I carried the political line, and I was pretty strident about it once we formed the party and the organization. Although, neither Dennis's vision [of satire] nor John's vision [of the party as a group of well-meaning pot smokers] are wrong. We had all those visions. I had a vision very much of Jerry Rubin, Abbie Hoffman, and the yippie movement—a decentralized, amorphous, no-leadership sort of an organization. But it was pretty clear early on that that wouldn't work because we really wanted to do stuff. We wanted to start free health clinics, and we wanted to start community organizing and community control of police, and other things that required some centralization, required some discipline, and required some continuity. The thing about Rubin, Hoffman, and the yippies is that they had no continuity. They had no office that you could call and talk to someone about anything. They had no letterhead, they had no phones . . . which was one of their strengths. But for a long-term project, it was also a weakness because you couldn't do business. I'm sure everyone would agree that of all of us, I was the most strident in the militant political line.

Plamondon claims today, however, that the title of Minister of Defense bestowed upon him was part of the joke:

I was raised in the country, did a lot of hunting, and I've been around guns all my life, so therefore I was the Minister of Defense. Most of the other city boys, like Kramer and the MC5 and John Sinclair, they all grew up in the city, as did most of our followers. Plus, I was quite a violent young person. I used to get in fights all the time. Every weekend, we'd go out looking for fights, get drunk, and rumble. I kinda had that militant, arrogant attitude about me. Plus, I admired Huey Newton so much. A lot of it was hero worship, you know?

Thompson is happy to admit that at first he believed in the politics the White Panthers were preaching:

For a period I agreed with the ethic one hundred percent. But as time progressed, I realized that John Sinclair . . . [due to] going to jail because of his possession charges, he became more radically politicized. He took that and imprinted it on the band, and that's what the media picked up on. We should have just stuck to playing rock 'n' roll, and maybe we could've looked at the revolution as "yeah, we believe in ending the war; we believe in equality for women and equality for people of color," but not to go around flipping the middle finger at the police, saying "Fuck you!"

Eventually, links would develop between the two sets of Panthers. Although the official line from the Black Panthers was that Sinclair's group were "psychedelic clowns," Kramer is quoted in Legs McNeil's *Please Kill Me* as saying,

> We got along well with the Ann Arbor chapter of the Black Panthers. They were neighborhood guys and they used to come to the house to hang out, and then we'd go have shooting practice. We had all these M1s and pistols and sawn-off shotguns, so everyone would set up in the woods behind our house and blow the shit out of everything imaginable. *Bla-bla-bla-bla-bla-pow-pow-pow-pow-pow-pow-bam-bam-bam-bam.*
>
> Then we'd drink this concoction the Black Panthers called the Bitter Motherfucker. It was half a bottle of Rose's lime juice poured into a bottle of Gallo port. So we'd sit down, smoke reefer, drink that, and shoot guns. I guess we thought, We're all gonna end up in a shoot-out with the Man, you know, we'll shoot it out with the pigs. (49)

For John Sinclair, the links between the White and Black Panther groups were tenuous at best: "We just idolized them. We had no more idea what was a political organization than the man on the moon. We just wanted to say something and we had a national record contract, and we thought if we said something, people would listen. We came up with our own crazy shit, y'know. We believed in all that, and also we were setting out to shock [*laughs*]. It's all part of the same thing. 'Fuck you' was our bottom-line political stance."

Still, Kramer told writer Ian Fortnam that there wasn't much more to the White Panther party manifesto than "dope, guns, and fucking in the street."

> You know, in the beginning, we were just frustrated with the pace of change. The principles of patriotism were actually very important to us: justice and self-determination, freedom of speech, freedom of expression, peace and harmony. We took those things to be real, and what we saw all around us was injustice, intolerance, lack of freedom of speech, and American aggression around the world, and we felt that we had to do something. We were young, powerful, headstrong and [so when] Huey Newton and Eldridge Cleaver [a prominent American civil rights leader and activist] of the Black Panthers said that there needed to be a White Panther Party to do the parallel work that the Black Panthers were doing, we said, "Here we are, we're ready."

Plamondon maintains to this very day that the White Panthers achieved much during their four years in existence, and, what's more, he's very proud of the work they did:

> The ramifications are still being felt today. When I speak with young people, so many things that are taken for granted today were real battles back in those days. Just as simple a thing as growing your hair long could get you beat up, thrown in jail, could get your head shaved, could get you all sorts of attacks from right-wing rednecks because "you look like a girl." Those were real battles. People paid real prices and shed real blood. The movement, for instance, for organic food. Those [battles] were all brought forward by the hippie and the yippie movement, in an effort to get back to something that was real. People seem to forget the incredible plastic nature of the culture at that time. Everything was phony. Women throwing their bras away, people wanting to eat real food, looking for new ways to educate children—these were all things that we were involved in. In Ann Arbor, we helped organize what we called the Children's Community Center, which was an alternative school for children. Free health clinics, shelters for runaways—none of those things existed. Today, thirty years later, many of those things are supported by the major charities. I mean, I don't take credit for all of those things, but I do take credit for being part of that movement that brought those changes and expanded people's consciousness, and opened their eyes and their minds to be able to accept this stuff. So I think we were tremendously successful. It was only lack of finances, and to some our extent our lack of experience and training that it all fell apart. Somebody had to do something.

Though they weren't part of the Trans-Love/White Panther collective, future Stooges Ron and Scott Asheton and their sister Kathy moved in some of the same circles on the local band circuit. Sinclair once described the brothers as "just two dead-end kids. Rock 'n' roll kids without a thought in their mind, watching goofy shit on TV."

However, things would change when the Asheton brothers hooked up with Jim Osterberg, soon to be known as Iggy Pop. Though he had been playing the circuit for some time, first as a drummer with the Prime Movers and later with the Iguanas (the reason he became known as "Iggy"), when the bright and razor-sharp Pop started making music with the previously docile Ashetons, magic happened. In Joe Ambrose's biography of Iggy Pop, *Gimme Danger*, John Sinclair recalled seeing the Stooges (originally called the Psychedelic Stooges) for the first time on Halloween night in 1967: "I don't know if there were twenty people there. It certainly wasn't a big house and there wasn't a big crowd. I can't imagine what the neighbors made of it but me, I got the fuck out of there! I was terrified! I just thought, Jesus, they can hear this all the way downtown. Of course, my senses were enhanced, it was loud anyway and I was probably hearing it two or three times louder than it was."

Wayne Kramer continued: "Iggy was sitting on the floor and he had a steel guitar with some modal tuning and he was bashing away on it. He had this vacuum cleaner too. He held it in front of the mike and made different noises with it. The whole thing was tremendously abstract and avant-garde. People didn't know what to make of it. They didn't know to laugh and they didn't know to take it seriously."

Grande Ballroom manager Russ Gibb has mixed memories of the Stooges and Iggy Pop, and his opinion is that the MC5 were pivotal in Pop's success. "Iggy played off of the 5," Gibb says. "His father taught with me, by the way. [Iggy's] real name is Jimmy Osterberg. The kids called his dad Iggy's Pop. Iggy was brought to me through the courtesy of John Sinclair. I remember the first time he played for me, he made a suit out of aluminum wrap and he proceeded to strip on stage. And by the way, when he was hanging with the MC5, he was working at the YMCA as a boy's counselor, which appealed to my sense of the absurd."

Kathy Asheton had become enamored with the scene after seeing Iggy's Prime Movers and the MC5 on consecutive nights when she was fourteen. She was particularly partial to Fred Smith's long hair, which was unusual for a man at the time. Much later, Kathy Asheton and Fred Smith would begin a relationship of sorts.

Wayne Kramer admits in Legs McNeil's *Please Kill Me* that there was perhaps a certain amount of contradiction with regards to the politics of the band: "We were sexist bastards. We were not politically correct at all. We had all this rhetoric of being revolutionary and new and different, but really what it was, was the boys get to go fuck and the girls can't complain about it. And if the girls did complain, they were being bourgeois bitches—counterrevolutionary. Yep, we were really shitty about it" (47).

The two bands became close friends, with the MC5 often referring to the Stooges as their "little brother band." Indeed, the Stooges signed a booking deal with Trans-Love Energies early on. Thompson certainly enjoyed spending time with them:

I liked them. I hung out with them. They had a place that they lived in called the Funhouse. Rather than hanging out at our house in Ann Arbor, I'd go and drink beers with them. We'd watch TV and screw around. I like Ron and Scotty, and Iggy too. At the beginning, I thought they were god-awful musicians. I thought they sucked and they should all get a different job. But they were determined to come up with their own sound and, as we know, Iggy and the boys developed performance art. They were the first band to really do that, whereas we were the first band to infuse many different musical styles. Personally, I was friends with them. I liked to hang out with them because they were more fun. We both knew our time was coming, but we [the MC5] didn't know that we'd be so politically attached—that the media would make us the political poster boys. That's not what we wanted, or at least, that's not what I wanted. The Stooges totally avoided that. They just went up there and played their tunes, which have now become classics. I give them an A plus for determination, to start from scratch. Scotty had never played drums before. He just started playing, at first, on these big fifty-gallon oil drums. Iggy would do his wild stage show with self-abuse, and they would play these simple songs. The reason they were so simple was because that's all they could play.

"They were like fish out of water. They didn't really know anything," says Michael Davis, on the Stooges' limited musical ability.

All they knew what to do was get on stage and be very interesting. When we listened to them playing, we were like, "What are these guys doing? They really don't have the songs, and the music they're playing is so ridiculously simple." But there was something really charming and straight to the point about it. It was so rudimentary that it was great. We really loved what they were doing, and they were totally satirical and sarcastic people, and really motivated. Even back in the very beginning, Iggy was the king of outrageousness. He would do anything to get attention and shock people. Not in the way that Arthur Brown would—it was theatrical, but there was something so raw and brutal about those guys, and they were cute too. They looked really cool. They had the right attitude—they weren't full of themselves and they weren't trying to blow you over with anything. They were like homeless dogs or something. The first time they played with us, we were just gawking at them because it was so charming. We invited them to come over and party with us, and we found out that we were like-minded. We were on the same page, but the MC5 were more about playing hard, tight rock 'n' roll music. The Stooges were kinda lackadaisical and very intense about it. We became really good friends, and when the MC5 went to Ann Arbor, we were in the same town and we'd hang out together.

The admiration was mutual, with Ron Asheton once quoted as saying, "I always admired them because I loved the big sound. I would learn things by watching them: How do they do that Chuck Berry, regular rock 'n' roll thing? I learned from them, being around the dressing room."

The two bands would go on to have uncannily parallel careers, both releasing three classic albums before they called it a day. And even then, members of both bands would join forces to create whole new groups. But all that's for another chapter.

3
Kick Out the Jams, Motherfuckers!

At this point in the tale, the MC5 was a regionally renowned band, politicized, notorious, and with a following to match. The stakes, however, were about to get considerably higher. During the fall of 1968, two journalists from the New York magazine *East Village Other* by the names of Bob Rudnick and Dennis Frawley convinced Danny Fields to travel to Detroit to check out the MC5. Fields held the official title of A&R man at Elektra Records, but in fact he was the label's token hippie—the corporate suits' way of reaching out to America's pot smokers and war protesters, and raking in their dollars. Fields had previously persuaded Elektra to sign the Doors, so in the eyes of the Big Cheeses, he was earning his keep and proving his worth. Eager to grab the opportunity for a record deal with both hands, both the MC5 and John Sinclair pulled out all the stops when news of Fields's impending arrival filtered through. In the band's eyes, this was their chance to become the rock stars that they had dreamed of becoming since hearing their first Chuck Berry lick. For Sinclair, a major label deal for his band was an opportunity to send his message across the nation, perhaps even the globe. And so Fields was met at the airport by the MC5 and driven to the Ann Arbor Hill Street house, where he was made to feel welcome by the assorted artists, militants, and girlfriends who resided there. Fields' first impressions were positive—and lasting: "Of course I was just stunned. I'd never seen anything like it. John Sinclair, the MC5's manager, was bursting with charm, vigor, and intellect. Just the look and the size of him—he was one of the most impressive people I had ever met—and that house!"

Of the house, Fields recalls that "it was sort of a Viking commune on Fraternity Row. Each place had hundreds of bedrooms, and each bedroom was decorated by its inhabitants, sort of psychedelically. A lot of beds on the floor, draperies hanging from the ceiling, the typical 1960s stuff."

Aesthetics aside, Fields was fascinated by the printing presses, design studios, workshops, and darkrooms in the basement, and by the number of copies of Chairman Mao's *Little Red Book* spread around the place, one for each inhabitant. Less impressive to the Elektra man was the blatant sexism that the pseudoliberal men of the house displayed:

> On the one hand you had the politics of revolution and equality and liberation, and on the other hand you had silent women in long dresses, gathered in the kitchen, preparing great meals of meat, which were brought out and served to the men—who ate alone.
>
> Of course, I thought all that male bonding was sexy. It was a world I never knew . . . I just thought it was quaint! I mean, there was a Minister of Defense carrying a rifle! Wearing one of those bullet things—a cartridge belt! With real bullets in it! I never saw a man wearing a cartridge belt. Even the girls were wearing these things. And they were serious!

If Sinclair and the band had intended to make an indelible impression on Fields, and to appeal to his sense of the bizarre, they had certainly achieved their goals. If Fields wasn't sold yet, he was, at the very least, intrigued to find out more, starting with what the band sounded like. He was given his chance when the band played the Grande Ballroom on Saturday, September 21, 1968. The venue was sold out, and the band put on their best satin suits for the occasion. Fields was impressed, if not completely blown away, calling it "finely tuned rock 'n' roll."

Michael Davis remembers in David A. Carson's *Grit, Noise, and Revolution* that "Wayne did a lot of dancing and gyrating. Rob would do the pony . . . Wayne and Fred got into choreography, backbends . . . Fred did a lot of dramatic, bravado moves. He'd bend his knees and lean back" (177).

Adhering to the Trans-Love philosophy of giving fellow local artists a leg-up, Kramer told Fields, "If you liked us, you will really love our little brother band, Iggy and the Stooges." Fields didn't have to wait long to see them, because the Stooges were playing the following afternoon at the Union Ballroom in Ann Arbor (festivals aside, the Stooges playing on a Sunday afternoon seems a little odd, but they played whatever they were offered back then). "I can't minimize what I saw on stage," said a still excited Fields. "I never saw anyone dance or move like Iggy. I'd never seen such high atomic energy coming from one person. It was the music I'd been waiting to hear all my life."

Fields introduced himself to an unimpressed Iggy, who passed the record exec on to his manager, Jim Silver. Understandably, Silver was much more excited. The very next day, Danny Fields and the two managers, John Sinclair and Jim Silver, gathered around a table in the Hill Street house while Fields made a call to his bosses, recommending that Elektra sign both bands. Speaking with head honcho Jac Holzman, Fields said, "I'm in Ann Arbor looking at that group the MC5 I told you about. Well, they're going to be big. They sold out four thousand tickets on Saturday night; the crowd went wild, and there were crowds around the street. They're also the most professional and ready-to-go act I've ever seen. And what's more, they have a baby brother group called Iggy and the Stooges, which is the most incredibly advanced music I've ever heard. And the lead singer is a star—he's really mesmerizing."

Holzman instructed Fields to offer the MC5 ("the big group") $20,000 and the Stooges ("the little group") $5,000. Both managers accepted. Through one awesome twist of fate, thanks in no small part to Rudnick and Frawley, the MC5 and the Stooges had record deals.

Elektra had no idea what they'd gotten themselves into, but Davis, for one, was delighted:

> That was surely a no-brainer. In spite of all the rhetoric and righteousness, signing with a record label was everything the MC5 wanted, above all else. From the earliest times, getting signed was the ultimate goal. It was even more appealing that the label was Elektra. A not-so-big corporate label with a trace of independence of their own. I was familiar with their Nonesuch catalog that was the realm of classical music, particularly baroque, my favorite. Also, their roster had some very interesting bands. David Peel and the Lower East Side were very much in tune with our point of view. I loved Love and Arthur Lee, and the Doors were somewhat like us, in a different way. So, no problem, it was as good a match as you could ask for. Their representative, Danny Fields, certainly was an indication that we were in the right company, and we got on really well with him. We also led him to the Stooges, and it all seemed so perfect. When we met Holzman, it was more of a business deal, but things appeared to be quite cozy between Elektra and the MC5. I was completely happy.

Dennis Thompson was similarly elated, though as he says now, "I don't remember thinking too hard. Today in perfect twenty-twenty hindsight, I think we were young and naïve and probably could have held out for a better deal. The band might have been able to overrule Holzman and Sinclair, but *que sera, sera*. All in all, you can't change the past, so it was, and is, what it was."

Davis has vague memories of meeting Holzman, the man who would later be credited as joint producer on their debut album:

> I didn't know him very well. This was different for us. We'd go to New York, and we'd go into Jac's office, where it was all carpeted and mellow. He'd sit at this big desk on this big, tall back leather chair, and he looked kind of sophisticated. He was kind of a young-to-middle-aged guy. He seemed nice enough to me. We had the groundwork for something really creative, but I don't think that Jac was prepared for how deep he was going to have to get into it with us. He wasn't prepared for our unprofessionalism, which we were very proud of. We were like forces working against each other instead of with each other. It worked up to a point, and then after that, it was too risky for him and it wasn't risky enough for us.

The deal with Elektra was just reward for the fact that the MC5 had been working so hard on honing their live show, particularly since Russ Gibb had taken over the Grande Ballroom and given the band, and many others in the area, some much needed focus.

Throughout this time, the band had their steady gig at the Grande Ballroom, and though Glantz continued to make disgruntled noises toward them, he was happy that his venue was full. As time went on, the line outside the venue lengthened, so great was the buzz surrounding the band. It was onto this unsteady, but at least forward-moving, ship that Brothers J.C. Crawford and Panther White would step. The two announced themselves as the High Priests of the Church of Zanta, which was true. It was also true, however, that they were the only parishioners. Exactly what the Church of Zanta was remains something of a mystery.

Crawford, a huge James Brown fan who took great pleasure in reciting the late Godfather of Soul's evangelical rants, would prove to be the perfect Master of Ceremonies for the MC5, who were on the lookout for a way to give their show a rousing introduction. Hands aloft, his thin blond hair parted to the side, and wearing dark glasses, Crawford looked like the love child of Andy Warhol and Jim Morrison as he preached the gospel of the revolution to the kids who gathered at the Grande, most of whom were there simply to listen to rock 'n' roll and had no idea what the strange man was talking about. By all accounts, however, Crawford's rants were always entertaining and achieved their goal of warming up the crowd for the main event.

Davis has contrasting memories of Crawford and White:

We saw Panther White in Boston recently while on tour. He was hanging out in the dressing room. Nothing like what I remembered. They used to come around to the house in Ann Arbor, and we'd get together to smoke a lot of weed, drink our beers and whatnot. We'd party together. Crawford was really inspired. He had the gift of the gab. He was like a carnival barker or something. He could just carry on a show: He did a lot of W.C. Fields impersonations, and he was just a really good, funny guy. He told a lot of stories and jokes. Just a great guy to be around. It was unusual to find someone that sophisticated and hilarious, and of the same frame of mind as us. We got along really well, so we decided to have J.C. Crawford introduce the band, like a James Brown kind of thing. He kind of roused up the crowd, like an old showbiz trick. Get the crowd all excited, then you bring the band on and it's pandemonium. I don't think J.C. really gets enough credit for what he contributed to the total spectacle of the MC5. He was a wonderful person, he hung out with us, we had a lot of laughs, and he was just a great human being. I sometimes wish that J.C. would get more attention, but the fact is that he doesn't want it. At some point in time, he just disappeared, and he doesn't want people to contact him; he doesn't want anything to do with us; he doesn't want to be interviewed; he doesn't want to talk about it. He wants to leave all that in his past. We didn't know too much about Panther. He was a real geek. He wasn't a deep guy like J.C. was. He kinda got lost in the shuffle. But he had this crazy name, Panther White, and we were forming the White Panther party, so I think we made him the chairman. It was all tongue in cheek.

With a deal with Elektra secured, it was time to start thinking about the first album. The label came up with the idea of recording a live album for the debut, a bold move considering that conventionally bands release a handful of studio albums before releasing a live record. Still, this was never a band that liked to do things by the book, and the live arena was where their raw rock 'n' roll really shone. Sinclair's memories of the decision to record the debut live are hazy: "I've read in recent years that the fellas maybe thought that wasn't the best way to go. I don't remember them being opposed to it at the time, although they could've been. We were bold—we just wanted to do things that nobody else did. That's what I liked about the Clash when they came out. They presented themselves boldly, with that Elvis Presley-looking cover. They believed in themselves the way the MC5 did. It was exhilarating, for me."

Kramer has a more specific, cash-related theory, which he told Ian Fortnam of music365.com:

> It was cheaper. Well, actually, it's a two-part answer. One is, everything that the MC5 had done up to that point was focused on live performance—all our work went into perfecting the ultimate live performance that would just destroy an audience, would leave them not knowing what hit them. We didn't really put any work into the recording studio, because our experience in the studio at that point had been limited to a few single recording sessions where you go in and in three hours you record, overdub, and mix two songs. Real old-school-style recording. And it was kind of an exciting concept in its day, a debut album that would be a live album and . . . it was cheaper.

Michael Davis feels that the album perfectly showcased the band's ability to explode in a live setting:

> Basically, the album was intended to be a replication of our live performance. We were well aware that our strength was largely centered in the interaction and involvement of the audience with the band. We wanted to represent that on the record. For us, as the performers, feeling the audience's exhilaration was what gave us satisfaction. Knowing that a studio setting would eliminate that aspect entirely, it was the best way to go at the time. Our show had evolved to a point that, with a large content of cover material, we needed to stage the event with a minimal amount of covers, and present our original material as the featured aspect of the band. Some, if not all, of these songs were improvisations from start to finish. So, it was a we'll-see-what-happens situation in many ways.

The twenty-thousand-dollar advance was quickly spent, paying off a few bills and purchasing some new equipment. Sinclair also recalls that the band "headed right downtown and bought some expensive leather coats from Louis the Hatter." Between Sinclair, Gibb. and Elektra main man Jac Holzman, the decision was made that the MC5 would play two nights at the Grande Ballroom over Halloween (Wednesday,

October 30, and Thursday, October 31), and the shows would be recorded for the live debut album. The Psychedelic Stooges would provide the support, and there would be no entrance fee, virtually guaranteeing a full house and a good, buzzing atmosphere. For Davis, it was the perfect venue to make the record: "I remember how odd it was to be recording our first album on our own turf, right in the middle of the house that we had built. The room was packed from front to rear. The air was electrified. You knew history was being made."

Holzman assigned Bruce Botnick with the responsibility of ensuring that the shows were captured and the album was cut without a hitch. Botnick had previously engineered the Doors' classic debut and had therefore proved himself capable of finding the magic within the chaos. Holzman also came up with the idea of recording the tracks in the empty Grande on the Thursday afternoon, in addition to the two concerts, to ensure that there were plenty of choices with regards to takes when the time came to pick and choose what would make it onto the final album. Davis denies that any of that material was used on the album, though: "When we were setting up, getting all the levels right, the label or Bruce Botnick asked us to run through some of the songs, one of which was 'Kick Out the Jams,' and to do the 'Brothers and Sisters' speech for the single. Yeah, it was to an empty room, but I don't think we used any of that stuff."

That Wednesday, as the time approached to begin recording, the Grande was, as expected, filled to the brim with excited fans. Brother J.C. Crawford took to the stage: "Brothers and sisters, the time has come for each and every one of you to decide whether you are going to be the problem, or whether you are gonna be the solution! You must choose, brothers, you must choose. It takes five seconds, five seconds of decision. Five seconds to realize your purpose here on the planet. It takes five seconds to realize that it's time to move. It's time to get down with it! Brothers, it's time to testify, and I want to know, are you ready to testify? I give you a testimonial: THE MC5!"

As discussed earlier, opinions vary about how genuine the revolutionary rhetoric surrounding the 5 was. But when listening to the opening seconds of "Kick Out the Jams," those opinions are irrelevant. It's a stunning way to begin both a record and a concert, and those words have since passed into rock 'n' roll folklore, even if they're usually recited with a heavy dose of irony (just as Crawford originally did with James Brown's sermons).

Journalist Ian Fines, writing for the online magazine *Perfect Sound Forever*, described perfectly the sense of excitement in the air that night:

> The thunder of primal rage bursts from the guitars of Wayne Kramer and Fred "Sonic" Smith, while vocalist Rob Tyner squirms and leaps like a dispossessed demon, and the rhythm of a million discontented youths is kept constant by drummer Dennis Thompson and bassist Michael Davis. This is the night the MC5 are recording their first-ever album, live in front of a jam-packed audience. As a result of this night, the nation and the rest of the world would be exposed to the force of the MC5, along with their revolutionary aims . . . at this point in time . . . it seems almost possible that the MC5 and the Revolution could take over the nation.

Davis believes that the bulk of the album was recorded on the first night:

> I'm sure we sat down and chose which version of each song to use. But from my personal view, the first night's performance was the most frightening. I probably did the best performance on that first night. The energy was just so right there. It was so immediate. I'm sure we mixed it up. I was happy with the performance, but I didn't know what it would sound like. Everything was on the line, so it was more intense than anything else that I'd ever done. It was so frightening and intense in the moment—the energy was just unbelievable. It was like an orgasm. You can't control it, but you were right in the middle of it. You couldn't stop and decide what to do next; you had to keep it going. I was happy with it, but I had no idea how it would turn out.

Following an all too obvious switch between shows after Crawford's intro, the album kicks off with a cover of Ted Taylor's "Ramblin' Rose," a mainstay of the band's set at this point. Taylor was a soul/blues singer who released a string of gospel-influenced singles over the 1950s, 60s and 70s. Sadly, a car wreck claimed his life in 1987. Back in 1968, however, Wayne Kramer's falsetto vocals and Fred Smith's buzzing Mosrite guitar were doing Taylor's song justice. No double entendres here—Kramer blatantly grabbed his crotch as he reached the end of the line "Love is like a ramblin' rose, the more you feed it, the more it grows."

Kramer clearly enjoyed himself as he tore through the song, as he recalled in Carson's *Grit, Noise, and Revolution*:

I'm flying on pure adrenaline now, and I'm dancing my best James Brown through the first eight bars of the tune. Trouble strikes almost immediately. My low E string has slipped out of its saddle on the bridge, and it's about nine steps out of tune. But there's not a damn thing I can do about it now. I finish singing the first two verses and tear into the solo. Everyone in the band is looking great. We're all dancing, grooving, and—except for the tuning problems—it's all perfect. We finish the song with a big fanfare and perfectly timed leaps, landing on the final chord. The fans are crazed, jumping up and down. They're yelling out political slogans, song titles, rhetoric, and good old-fashioned whoops and hollers. (180)

Observers recall Kramer leaping about and spinning around during the opening song, determined to keep the energy level high and the atmosphere charged. As the song reached its climax, Rob Tyner emerged from backstage, and, as Kramer remembers, was "sweating, screaming and dancing like a man possessed by forces you don't even know about."

With Tyner on stage, it was time for the band's anthem, their call to arms. "And right now," crooned the singer, "right now, right now, it's time to—*kick out the jams, motherfuckers!*" The room predictably explodes as the riff kicks in to the song that would become the band's signature tune, a song covered again and again as the decades rolled on by a succession of darling rock bands, all of which have made a hell of a lot more money than the MC5 ever did.

The song is about sex with a dose of pot smoking thrown in for good measure. The term "kick out the jams" was born when bands from outside of Detroit would play the city, often with the MC5 on the same bill, and the hometown band would shout the phrase from the side of the stage or from the crowd. "Being hormonally driven and arrogant," says Kramer, "we used to fuck with them and yell at them, 'Kick out the jams or get off the stage!'" The phrase was an alternative to shouting "Is that the best you can do?" and the four words that were most associated with the band.

At Elektra's insistence, the song, originally called "Kick Out the Jams, Motherfuckers!" would lose the expletive from its title by the time it reached the record sleeve. In this case, Elektra was probably wise. "Kick Out the Jams" is a far punchier title, even if it is less shocking. Still, the song is one of the most powerful pieces of rock 'n' roll ever recorded, and it benefits massively from having been captured live.

"Come Together" is next, the third song on the record and the third song to have sex at its core—it perhaps remains unique in its description of stiff nipples. A theme was certainly beginning to develop at this point. If the band had the White Panthers' politics on their minds at all while driving through the incredible first three songs on the album, it was the "fucking in the street" area of the ten-point program, and little else. This was the sound of a band laying bullshit rhetoric to one side and simply singing about the subjects that affect any young man in a band; namely, girls and drugs.

Keeping the momentum motoring along, "Rocket Reducer No. 62 (Rama Lama Fa, Fa, Fa)" is the fourth song on the record—to many, the highlight of the band's live set. In his study of the album, Don McLeese wrote, "This is the supercharged 5 in all their garage-band glory, with pedal to the metal and flight plan to the stars. Between the way the verses lurch and the choruses soar, the band generates so much kinetic energy that it fulfills the most grandiose claims ever made for the music" (76).

"'Rocket Reducer' was our party song," recalls Michael Davis, "and was a good way to get into the middle of the show. That song is about a very bad substance abuse activity that we adopted. I mean BAAAAD! Tyner never refers to the actual substance Rocket Reducer #62 [a highly toxic solvent used in removing paint from engine blocks]. The gist of the song is about getting fucked up and acting recklessly, and gets to the core of what the MC5 held as sacred. Wayne's high regard for soul/ R&B guitar licks and Tyner's regard for community make up the music and lyrics, while the band shapes it into a raucous party anthem. I think it's a silly song, but [it] has an effective role in the MC5's stage show."

Unsurprisingly, the song is about sex and drugs. Anyone could be forgiven for thinking that this album was being made by five men with permanent hard-ons, and the band members were driving themselves into such a frenzy by this point in the set that that wasn't far from the truth.

Passing the halfway point, "Borderline" is the fifth song on the record, the only song to have been previously released (on the single with "Looking at You"), and therefore recorded in a studio. As Davis recalls, "Wayne and I started writing that song in the very early days of the band. It was completed at band rehearsal, with Fred adding the conspicuous three-four time middle section, and Tyner adding the inexplicable lyrics, 'I'm at my borderline.' Because it was an original MC5 song, it made the cut."

J.C. Crawford reappears onstage to preach, screaming out: "Brothers and sisters, I wanna tell you something. I hear a lot of talk from a lot of honkeys, sitting on a lot of money, saying they're the high society. But if you ask me, this is the high society, this is the high society—you!"

It's an apt introduction to "Motor City Is Burning," a song about the Detroit race riots of 1967, originally written and recorded by Detroit's own blues hero John Lee Hooker. There's a common misconception that the second side of the record (in the days before CDs) is a comedown and something of a disappointment. The truth is that on the second side the band cease to sing about their carnal desires and start to get serious. That the songs, particularly the final three, are less frenzied and rabid is undeniable. But to suggest that, with the slower pace and—with the exception of "Starship"—more disciplined song structure, the band lost its buzz and momentum is nonsensical. Michael Davis:

> "Motor City Is Burning" was not only about Detroit and personal for us as an experience, it showed our roots as a blues-oriented band. We played many a blues song in our early days, and regarded the blues as the sacred starting point of all rock 'n' roll. Plus, the performance of that song that night was extremely well done. The next song was "I Want You Right Now." This song represented the MC5's roots as a rock band, both as a solid straight-ahead rock tune and also as a tune we could do in a dynamic arrangement. However, this, too, is a cover.

"I Want You Right Now" is the proverbial post-sex cigarette. Originally recorded by early British rockers the Troggs (of "Wild Thing" fame) as "I Want You," the song is a slow burner and, as Davis suggested, a demonstration of just how solid this band could be.

The album concludes with a scorching musical tribute to Sun Ra, one of the band's heroes. "We had recorded our usual finale of 'Believe It to My Soul' [Ray Charles] and 'Black to Comm' as the climax of the show, but for reasons of time and/or performance quality, it was decided that 'Starship' was the best option for the record," recalls Davis.

> "Starship" touched all the bases for the MC5. It was paying homage to our musical guru, Sun Ra, and it was futuristic and highly dramatic. I think had we included "Black to Comm" as a finishing cut, it would have helped the record, but that's my opinion. I do

think "Starship" is a brilliant piece, and in many ways my personal favorite. To my knowledge, no one has ever attempted or come close to recording anything so inventive or original in all of rock 'n' roll. So that is the whole of the record; five originals and three covers. Since our set was largely three- to four-minute cover songs and undetermined-length originals, it was a problem making it work as a forty-minute album. We really wanted "Black to Comm" on the record, but we thought we could save it for the next record, which of course never happened on Elektra.

Although they have met him many times over the years, Davis and the band have never found out what Sun Ra's thinks of "Starship": "Really, I have no idea what Sun Ra thought," Davis says. "I don't know if he ever even heard it. I don't think I ever had a conversation with him. He and his band stayed with us in Ann Arbor for a short time. It was like having a saint in your midst. I only recall having brief eye contact with him, and that was very reassuring and empowering. It was like being touched and given a blessing. He had omnipresence. If he did listen to 'Starship' I'm certain he would have nodded his head in approval."

Thompson is justifiably proud of the album. "These songs were all written as a synergistic effort," he says. "The writing took place over a few years, and basically these eight tunes were our strongest set. They edified, at best, the diversification of our abilities. I still have mixed emotions about it. Truth be told, it does stand up to the test of time and that is just fine with me."

He does concede, however, that he was less enamored with the idea of releasing the live album, having heard the finished results: "To the best of my recollection, we all made the decision together. By 'we,' I refer to Sinclair, Danny Fields, Holzman, and the MC5. After we heard the live recordings, the band wished to redo the album in a recording studio." Holzman and Sinclair disagreed, and with some tension in the MC5 camp, the first album to be released was recorded live.

The album would be released in February of the following year, preceded by the "Kick Out the Jams"/"Motor City Is Burning" single. Both Bruce Botnick and Jac Holzman are credited as producers on the sleeve. Davis feels that Holzman was somewhat more removed from this specific role, but that "Bruce Botnik, on the other hand, deserves to be credited as the hands-on producer of the record, since he directed the mechanical aspects of the recording. In truth, I think we—the band—should have been also been given a production credit."

Thompson is slightly more diplomatic when considering the roles played by the two men:

> Holzman was essentially the corporate director of our recording business affairs, and as a producer, he was the guy who fronted the money to launch the regime. I must commend him for his wise choice in taking on the speeding train named MC5, as we were rather volatile and unpredictable, sort of like handling a pound of unstable nitroglycerin. Bruce Botnick was the on-site recording engineer at the Grande Ballroom. Calling him a producer is just that—calling him a producer. He was really the recording engineer and mixologist. He did a fine job, considering the primitive state of the technology in 1968.

The front of the sleeve features a collage of pictures of the band performing live that soon became an iconic piece of rock 'n' roll imagery. Inside the re-released CD, there's one of Gary Grimshaw's painted flags, complete with a cannabis leaf. Grimshaw's image was originally intended to be the front cover, but the blatant advocation of drugs was too much for Elektra. as Along with Botnick and Holzman, John Sinclair is credited as "Guidance," Brother J.C. Crawford as "religious leader and spiritual advisor," and the members of Trans-Love Energies were also listed.

With the album out, reviews started to appear in the press. Famously, the legendary rock journalist Lester Bangs didn't like the album when he first heard it, and he said so in *Rolling Stone*, then later in his book *Mainlines, Blood Feasts, and Bad Taste*. He compared the album to the 1960s movie *Wild in the Streets,* a tale of rock 'n' roll, LSD, and homemade explosives. He went on to say, "About a month ago, the MC5 received a cover article in *Rolling Stone* proclaiming them to be the 'new Sensation,' a group to break all barriers, kick out all jams, total energy thing, etc., etc., etc. Never mind that they came on like a bunch of sixteen-year-old punks on a meth power trip—these boys, so the line ran, could play their guitars like John Coltrane and Pharoah Sanders played sax" (33).

He would later conclude that

> "Kick Out the Jams!" sounds like Barrett Strong's "Money" as recorded by the Kingsmen. The lead on "Come Together" is stolen note-for-note from the Who's "I Can See for Miles." "I Want You Right Now" sounds *exactly* (down to the lyrics) like a song called "I Want You" by the Troggs, a British group who came out with a similar, sex-and-raw-sound image a

couple of years ago (Remember "Wild Thing"?) and promptly disappeared into oblivion, where I imagine they are laughing at the MC5.

Aside from the fact the band never tried to hide the fact that "I Want You Right Now" was a cover of a Troggs song, Bangs would later do an about-face and proclaim his love for the 5, writing in *Creem* magazine, "They weren't just fantastic, they wuz cataclysmic, and it's only now I completely and finally understand why so many people lose their cool and objectivity over this band."

Michael Davis perversely enjoyed the original review:

Frankly, it's the only one I remember. When I met Lester some years later, I was in another band called Destroy All Monsters. We got on really well, being hearty drinkers, and he started off by apologizing for trashing the *Kick Out the Jams* album in his original review. He had been very descriptive in his derogatory review of the record . . . When he presented his head for the axe, I bade him to rise. I actually liked the review, the vivid analogy, and thought it was totally accurate. It was without doubt a noble image to live up to. We laughed, hugged, and cracked open another beer.

In response to Bangs's criticism of "I Want You Right Now," Davis says, "Tyner used to sing the line that way, but it was maybe a mistake. It might be just a typing mistake. We weren't very fastidious about doing things correctly. It might very well be that the "Right Now" got added as an error. The lapse even confused Lester Bangs. We did a worthwhile interpretation of it, but we weren't saying that we wrote the song." Recalling the Bangs review, Thompson simply says, "At that point in his life, the poor soul just didn't get it. Bless him."

Looking back on the album, Davis is still satisfied:

I like it alright. It's withstood the test of time, for one thing, but now I hear it objectively. I have heard many people tell me about how great this stuff is, and have wondered a lot what it is that sends them over the top. I ask them what makes it for them, and mostly they tell me it's the energy between the band and the crowd. Nothing else compares to the MC5 for audience and band interaction. I still have iffy opinions about the sound, but that's what you have to expect with a live record, especially one from 1968. That was truly a ballsy thing to try. All things considered, it does tell the MC5 story in a raw setting. For me, it's not my ideal, but it is what it is, and history has proven [the album's] merit. You have to remember that we viewed this record as an introduction to the band. We had no idea our contract would be terminated . . . within a few months. Had we continued to grow and develop a good relationship with Elektra, we might have become a much more successful band, but that's speculation.

Bangs aside, the reviews were consistently glowing. However, Detroit's largest department store, Hudson's, took exception to the use of the word "motherfuckers" on the record and refused to stock it. Instead of taking yet another slap in the face from the establishment in stride, the MC5 decided to run a full-page ad in the *Ann Arbor Argus,* stating, "KICK OUT THE JAMS, MOTHERFUCKER! And kick in the door if the store won't sell you the album on Elektra. FUCK HUDSON'S!" The ad might have been dismissed with little more than a snigger, if not for the fact that it carried the Elektra logo. Holzman was less than impressed, telling Sinclair in no uncertain terms that the band didn't have the right to use the company logo in a political statement. Sinclair fired back that Elektra "needed to support the revolution." An angry Holzman replied that he "supported their music, but not their revolution." Davis feels that the band could have handled things differently:

I'm not so sure that I'm glad we did that. If it was Hudson's decision not to stock the album, then we should have been able to just accept that. We were creating a really controversial product. Once that establishment tried to resist the MC5, the more it worked to our advantage. For young people to be denied access to something that they were curious about, the natural reaction is to want more of it. I don't think we should have confronted anybody about that. I think we should have let it happen. That's my thing about it. If Hudson's refused to stock the album, that shows where they're coming from. That would demonstrate our point precisely. I don't think we needed to go up against them at all.

Kramer, on the other hand, is unrepentant: "Oh, that was our decision, absolutely. Did we stand behind it? Of course. What else could we do? We couldn't say somebody else did it. There wasn't anybody else. That was a good move to make. I'd do it again, sure."

Those are bold words, considering the stunt irreversibly damaged the band's relationship with their label. Holzman knew he had taken on a lively, controversial band, but he hadn't been aware of just how far these five men were prepared to go in order to make a point. When Hudson's refused to stock any Elektra products (including mainstream artists like Judy Collins, Phil Ochs, and the Doors), Holzman tried to make amends by replacing the word "motherfuckers" on *Kick Out the Jams* with the phrase "brothers and sisters." But before the edited versions were ready, the label recalled the "offensive" copies of the record, and so, for a short but important period, there wasn't a single record on the shelves for eager fans to buy, a situation that benefited no one, although the band remained unflinching.

On the surface, at least, the MC5 were fearless. And that fact put the fear of God into Elektra.

4
Back in the USA

With the album getting heavy rotation in Detroit, Elektra organized a tour, so that the band could become equally adored elsewhere in the United States. In December of 1968, they shared a bill for three nights at the Boston Tea Party with the Velvet Underground, a band that shares many qualities with the MC5, few of them musical. The first two nights passed without incident (save for the fact that audiences were seeing two of the most groundbreaking bands ever to hit a stage together), but on the third night, a gang called—oddly enough—the Motherfuckers made themselves horribly visible.

The group, whose full name was the Up Against the Wall Motherfuckers, was from New York's Lower East Side, and they took the term "radical" to a whole new level. In fact, according to legend, Abbie Hoffman was refused membership to the group because he wasn't radical enough. These guys didn't mess around. To the MC5, who had been a "radical" group for the past couple of years and saw the whole thing as a great way of stirring up some controversy and publicity, the idea of allowing the Motherfuckers to say a few words before their set was little more than an afterthought. What harm could it do? However, these tough New Yorkers had been known to cause huge amounts of damage at their demonstrations, and would usually arrive equipped with knives, chains, and anything else that might make people realize they weren't playing. At the Fillmore East in New York, Bill Graham allowed the Motherfuckers to use the venue for free on Wednesday evenings, after they persuaded him that he should support the Lower East Side community. As a result, many people avoided the Fillmore on Wednesday nights.

Founding member Ben Morea had been arrested for knifing a serviceman, and it was in Boston, following the MC5's first set, that a Motherfucker spokesman made a plea for defense funds. He then began ranting about how the Tea Party was ripping off the people, and that music should be free. The power was cut, and club owner Don

Law banned the band from ever appearing at the venue again. Law was also part of a group of concert promoters and had considerable influence over venues across the country. The story was far from over, though.

The following Monday, the band arrived in New York and, after visiting the Elektra offices, visited the Motherfuckers' headquarters and agreed to play a free, unannounced show for them at the Fillmore East on Wednesday, their community night. The band arrived late for the gig, which angered a few, but the show went down well enough with most. However, just after Christmas, when the MC5 returned to New York to play a highly publicized Fillmore show, the Motherfuckers were even more fired up than usual. After disagreements about ticket allocations flared, five hundred or so angry Motherfuckers were pounding on the Fillmore door. Adding fuel to the fire, they had seen the MC5 stepping out of a limo Danny Fields had rented for them. Suddenly, in the eyes of the radicals, the band had gone from friends to traitors. When Rob Tyner told the audience that the MC5 were there for rock 'n' roll, not politics, that only pumped up the Motherfuckers more, and before long, a riot began. A lot of the band's equipment was destroyed, as was a fair amount of the Fillmore's furnishings.

Dennis Thompson recalls feelings of panic as the hall went mad around him:

I remember that Wayne almost got stabbed. Jesse [J.C.] Crawford and Wayne and I were surrounded by about fifty to sixty crazed MF's in the seating area of the Fillmore. They were debating with manic, intense zeal about the revolution with Wayne. They were speed-freak crazies. They started shouting, and it felt like it was going to get out of hand, and it did. One guy brandished a knife and came at Wayne, and Jesse knocked him over and I grabbed Wayne and the three of us pushed our way through the crowd to the limousines waiting outside, where they were throwing bottles and shouting "sellouts" and other rude epithets. They trashed the Fillmore's stage curtain and our equipment. A scary and spooky moment in time.

Michael Davis doesn't remember the evening fondly:

First off, that show came on the heels of a failed attempt to create a soundtrack for a New York indie theatre company that specialized in impromptu guerrilla theatre. They were called the Living Theater. They had filmed one of their performances and asked us to create a soundtrack for the film. We assembled in a small Midtown recording studio with all the participants as audience and proceeded to hack out spontaneous *musique de chaos*. The end result was uninspired noise. Next up on the Manhattan carnival ride was Bill Graham's Fillmore East and that blind date with the East Side Motherfuckers, who were at war with Graham and his establishment. In an unusual act of disrespect for etiquette, we spent an enormous amount of time in the dressing room preparing for the performance by drinking and smoking pot beyond reasonable standards, even those of the day . . . I was checking my wristwatch, it was that bad. I sensed that we were fucking up. Thus, when we condescended to make an appearance, I was actually feeling guilty for making the audience wait [ninety minutes] for us to show up. The first thing I heard anyone say as we took the stage was "Where the hell were ya?" People were yelling and throwing things; it was downright hostile. This was supposed to be a showcase gig for the New York media, and maybe that's why the dressing room atmosphere had been so unprofessional, with us having no concept of the impending confrontation. We were dressed in colorful spangly outfits, sequined and satined to the tens. Most un-revolutionary in every respect, we must have appeared to be a huge target to the rabble that called themselves Motherfuckers, much like the aristocrats appeared to the revolutionary rabble that stormed the Bastille in 1779 . . . the MC5 [were] the symbolic accused.

Actually, there was not a riot. The show went off without interruption. I felt it lacked a certain intensity that we were capable of. There were some testy moments, but no riot. In the end, we found ourselves in the alley behind the Fillmore, attempting to explain our position and predicament to a group of angry street people while limos waited to take us out of the turmoil. The revolution that we held in such precious naïve esteem ended that night as knives appeared in my peripheral vision and we retreated to the open doors of the two black limos provided by our record company. It was a collision of forces whose impact was felt at once . . . we were banned from ever playing [certain] venues again, cursed by the underground, and rejected by the music industry, all in one fell swoop. Maybe it would have helped if we actually had real management, but then in those days we were probably unmanageable.

In the midst of it, somebody hit Bill Graham on the nose with a chain. He blamed the band for what had happened and vowed that the MC5 would never play the Fillmore again. The band's chances of playing the country's best venues had just become considerably slimmer, whether it was entirely their fault or not. To many, rightly or wrongly, this was the night that the MC5 signed the death certificate for their career.

When the MC5 visited the Elektra distribution center, they found a pile of re-designed *Kick Out the Jams* sleeves. John Sinclair's "offensive" liner notes had been removed, and the title song had been replaced with the version released as a single, with the line "Kick Out the Jams, Motherfuckers" replaced with "Kick Out the Jams, brothers and sisters." An incensed Sinclair traveled to New York to meet with Holzman, but the only thing he returned home with was a terminated contract. The combination of the Hudson's store fiasco and now the Motherfucker riots was just too much for a label still recovering from the bad publicity caused by Jim Morrison's antics. The Doors had made Elektra's trouble worthwhile in the form of sales, but the MC5 were not nearly as commercially viable. Davis remembers the kick in the stomach of being dropped: "It was like being dumped by your girlfriend or something, when your girlfriend tells you that she just wants to be friends. I wasn't prepared for that. But I'm like a tough guy and I let things roll off my back. I was thinking that if we weren't with Elektra then we'd just keep doing what we were doing and see what happens."

When old friend Danny Fields learned that the MC5's relationship with Elektra Records had come to an end, he gave critic Jon Landau a call and recommended that he give the band a push with Jerry Wexler at Atlantic Records. Landau had been Wexler's guide to the youth and underground music scenes for some time, and Wexler held his opinion in high regard. A recommendation from Landau would go a long way, especially with Landau goading Wexler that Atlantic could succeed when Elektra failed. In May of 1969, John Sinclair met with Wexler and Fields and agreed on a deal, complete with an advance worth $50,000. "Danny Fields and I went to talk to Jerry Wexler and made the deal," recalls Sinclair. "Then they arranged for Jon Landau to come and produce the record . . . [an accountant] and Landau were living with the band in this house they'd gotten in Hamburg [Michigan]. We thought it'd be good for him to be there, and they could rehearse and work out the record and all that."

Davis remembers feeling as if his band had finally landed on their feet: "It seemed too easy. It was like somebody made a telephone call, and they said, 'Come over here, we'll be glad to help you out.' I think Atlantic saw that we had a lot of potential, and they would set us up and give us all the right actions, so we'd all make a lot of money."

After being given a second bite at the cherry with the Atlantic deal, the band was determined to hold on to it. Various theories abound as to how the decision was first mooted—personnel within the record company are usually mentioned—but the decision was made to fire John Sinclair. Sinclair still gnashes his teeth when recalling the experience now: "Evidently [other parties expressed to the MC5] a stream of criticism of myself and my people and what we were doing and how we were ripping them off. How they could never go anywhere with this kind of approach, blah, blah, blah. The next thing you know, they called me, [publicist] Bob 'Righteous' Rudnick, and J.C. Crawford [road manager] in and fired us."

Of course, there are always various opinions about events such as these. The fact that Sinclair was about to be locked up was key, as Davis attests:

It wasn't really a decision. John was going to prison for marijuana [offenses]. He was going to get locked up, so in our minds, we didn't have a manager anymore . . . everything was starting to look very promising for the band, so why did we want to go back to the ragtag political thing? We were in a state of kind of chaos, because our revolutionary agenda was really being shaken. When Atlantic sent John Landau out, his job was to clean us up and make us a good recording studio band. He started questioning the politics, like, "What do you mean, you're gonna be taking over?" and "Are you guys serious about this or what?" . . . we were feeling insecure about what our position was. We did not want to abandon our appetite for change in society. We still believed in what we were doing, and Landau was convincing us that we needed to change our way of talking about it—that we would be laughed off the planet. We needed to sell records to make records—that was number one. With regards to change, we needed to speak to people in a more . . . well, talking about having shoot-outs with the police was not [ideal]. This was really an upheaval for us. We were trying to write songs that are marketable and good, and not offend our original foundation.

Naturally, Sinclair disagrees:

I wasn't on trial then. I'd just got them a record contract that was about five times better than the first one. Our first record had hit the charts at number thirty. I think I did a pretty good job, and if you look at what happened to them afterward, I think I did a hell of a job. Nobody else could come anywhere close to it. I'll stand by my record, Jesus Christ. Plus, what could have been more spectacular than to have your manager in prison. Jesus Christ! You couldn't pay for fucking publicity like that. About that time, it became clear [that we had different agendas]. Until that time, we appeared to be on the same track. I wanted them to be unprecedented. to have political impact. to take rock 'n' roll to the next level, to shake the walls of the city, y'know? Why not?

"I could not wait to be free of all the political bondage," says Thompson.

That element of our persona was straining us as a musical entity. I believe that John knew he was going to jail and had nothing to lose by turning up the heat on the radical political rhetoric, whereas we had plenty to lose. How could he manage us from prison? We could not support a whole movement on our meager income. I wanted a paycheck, not rice and beans for God's sake! . . . John was *good* for us in many ways and *not so good* in others.

John Sinclair maintains that the band was, in fact, making $125 per night from 1967 into the fall of 1968 and that they were being carried, in his words, by the "hippies in Trans-Love Energies, who loved the band more than anything."

For John's then-wife Leni, her husband's ousting from the MC5's ranks was the beginning of some tough times. "It was like the Saturday night massacre," she says. "It started not with John, but it started out when they fired J.C. Crawford. When J.C. Crawford came to the band, it pushed them a notch higher in terms of getting people excited and to the gigs . . . it was a slap in the face, but it's happened to many people, over and over. At the time, we were devastated. We never expected that. It was hard. Phones got cut off, no money for food with two babies—it was horrible."

For Michael Davis, the decision to fire Sinclair wasn't entirely profitable either:

We weren't free of Sinclair's politics at all. That's the rub. We had to defend ourselves permanently about all the abrupt changes in our game. It was weird, weird, weird. Poor Tyner was up there trying to be natural and himself, with all these conflicting ideas flying around in his head. The new big-time MC5 was not acting like the people's band any longer. Tyner had done the major rapping about our (or John's) political messages, and now he was doing some serious backpedaling, trying not to contradict himself. Kramer, too, was telling the press we had modified our stance, but it still was basically the same as always. Meanwhile, Sinclair was writing articles from prison denouncing the band . . . the idea of the revolution wasn't what was important, it was our integrity. I always felt like we were on the verge of being tarred and feathered, or lynched. No one had the right swagger to get us out of that muck.

On July 22, 1969, the trial against Sinclair for possession of two joints finally began. A witch hunt from the beginning, officers were alleged to have destroyed case notes and failed to record conversations with Sinclair. A chemist testified that there was no proof that Sinclair had even been in possession of marijuana. Regardless, the jury found him guilty, and the judge sentenced him to a minimum sentence of *nine and a half years.* For two joints. During sentencing, Judge Robert J. Columbo told the Court that

Mr. Sinclair is not on trial and never was on trial in this courtroom because of his beliefs. He represents a person who has deliberately flaunted and scoffed at the law. He may think that there is nothing wrong with the use of narcotics, as many people think that there is nothing wrong with the use of narcotics. Although, enlightened and intelligent people think to the contrary and otherwise. And medical studies back them up far more completely than they do the people on his side of this particular question. The public has recognized that the use of narcotics is dangerous to the people that use it. The public, through its legislature, has set penalties for those who violate and traffic narcotics. Now, this man started in 1964, in which he first came to the attention of this Court and upon the offense of Possession of Narcotics, on a plea of guilty, was placed upon probation. We have tried to understand John Sinclair, we have tried to reform and rehabilitate John Sinclair. In 1966, while still on probation for that offense, he committed another offense for which he pleaded guilty. And this Court again showed supreme leniency to John Sinclair, placing him on probation again while ordering him to serve the first six months thereof in the Detroit House of Correction. This placed him in violation of his other probation, which resulted in the Judge extending that probation on again, so that for you [defense lawyer Justin C. Ravitz] or for John Sinclair to assert that the law has been out to get him is sheer nonsense. John Sinclair has been out to show that the law means nothing to him and to his ilk, and that they can violate the law with impunity and the law can't do anything about it. (Sinclair 168)

He concluded by telling Sinclair that

the time has come. The day has come. And you may laugh, Mr. Sinclair, but you will have a long time to laugh about it. Because it is the judgment of this Court that you, John Sinclair, stand committed to the State Prison of Southern Michigan in Jackson or other such institutions as the Michigan Corrections Commission may designate for a minimum term of not less than nine and a half nor more than ten years.

Sinclair was understandably upset, and he let the court know that he considered the whole thing to be a scam and a set up: "You just exposed yourself even more. And the people know that."

Later, Sinclair would note, "When the jury came back and said guilty, I went straight to jail and I didn't come out for two and a half years. There was no chance to straighten my affairs or anything. My wife was pregnant, I had a two-year-old girl, and I was just taken away . . . they kinda just left me in prison." Famously, Sinclair sent Wayne Kramer a fiery letter, saying, "You guys wanted to be bigger than the Beatles, and I wanted you to be bigger than Chairman Mao."

In July of that same year, shortly after arriving at Wayne County Jail, Sinclair wrote in a letter to his wife, Leni, that

the greatest thing though—as usual—is the people. It's like being in a large youth camp, with all kinds of different people around. There is a pretty large contingent of stomp-down freeks [sic] here who relate to the WPP [White Panther Party], and they're really happy to have me with them, which makes me very excited. Everyone seems to know about my case, and the sympathy is really overwhelming. It's really exciting for me, considering the circumstances. Brothers have been giving me packs of cigarettes every time I turn around, a pad of writing paper, this pen, food, soap, books, newspapers, and keep asking me if there's anything I need so they can bring it to me. It's really far-out and not at all like I expected, y'know?

Of course, any man would want to soften the truth when communicating with his wife so she could sleep at night (Sinclair told me that all prisons are horrible places to be), but it does seem plausible that a man who stood for the working man, for power to the people, would be treated relatively well in jail by the inmates (although that's not belittling his undoubtedly difficult experience).

In May of 1970, Sinclair told Peter Steinberger of *Big Fat* magazine that

> I get most of the books I need, with some exceptions of course. The thing about the penitentiary is that when you're on the street it's terrifying to think about going there, because you don't know anything about it. Black people, though, have fathers and brothers (and often sisters and mothers) who've been in prison—for them, it's no kind of frightening thing like it is for our people. But the penitentiary ain't shit to be afraid of. It's like being a straight person for a while: You get up at seven, eat, work, have a lunch break, go back to work, and then at four o'clock you go off work, and go eat dinner at five. Or, if you're lucky, you don't have to have a job you can stay in your cell and read and write all day. But they found out I liked being in my cell, so they made me take a job.

It is clear that Sinclair's time in prison wasn't spent fishing glass out of his food or avoiding a man named Mary during shower time. Sinclair maintains today that he "didn't have any trouble with the inmates. I was a hero to them. That was very good. I was particularly respected by the black inmates, which was what most white people had to worry about. I was just afraid of the administration. At worst, the guards, if they were given orders to do something bad."

Still, Sinclair's situation had the MC5 a little spooked, as Wayne Kramer recalled in 2000: "We were all scared. They were scary, dangerous, and romantic times. And you've got to always be vigilant because those times could return. Listen, if George W. Bush gets into the White House, those times will be back. The cost of liberty is eternal vigilance, if the World Trade Organization gets their way, those times will be back. That stuff doesn't go away."

While the American people went for Bush anyway (let's save the "actually, Gore was elected" argument for another time), it's still unthinkable that a man could be sentenced to nine and a half years imprisonment for possession of two joints, even if the offense was a parole violation. Thankfully, even the God-fearing right have moved on from there. Back in 1970, however, the MC5 were quite right to be scared.

Thanks to the Freedom of Information Act, we are now able to see the file that the FBI opened on the MC5 on December 3 of that year. While most of the text has been blacked out (so much for freedom of information), the band is described as "a rock-and-roll band of the Trans-Love Energies, Ann Arbor, Michigan, the parent organization of the WPP."

Another description later in the document states that "the MC-Five is a musical group headed by John Sinclair, an Ann Arbor, Mich., hippie leader."

An attached memorandum, which, at the time of this printing, is no longer available on foia.fbi.gov, gives a good indication how the authorities felt about the band at the time:

> The article (in *Time* magazine) states that the most violent expression of revolutionary rock so far comes from a Detroit quintet called MC5 (for Motor City) 5. After months of rumbling about them in the pop underground, they erupted at Manhattan's Fillmore East. Their performance was less revolutionary than revolting. The group performed John Lee Hooker's "Motor City Is Burning," and there was no mistaking the message: "All the cities will burn, you are the people who will build up the ashes." John Sinclair, 26 years old, manager and mentor of the MC5, who runs the group's hippie-style communal household in Ann Arbor, Michigan, stated the MC5 are a free, high-energy source that will drive us wild into the streets of America, yelling and screaming and tearing down everything that would keep people slaves. The article states that Sinclair and the MC5 are self-styled "musical guerrillas," who flaunt their membership in a miniscule left-wing organization called the White Panther Party (WPP). The article states that the MC5 now favor outrageous onstage stunts such as removing their clothes and burning the United States flag, and that the MC5 are taking protest one step further to get attention by practicing what they preach, as is shown by their string of arrests on charges of noisemaking, obscenity, and possession of marijuana.

Also attached is a letter sent to the president of the University of Michigan from a worried parent:

> My chief complaint is with the amoral tone of this trash. If this is part of the educational experience for our children, or even relaxation, God help this country. Of course, there is the question of free speech involved. Your attention is called to Chaplinsky vs. State of

New Hampshire, 315 U.S. 568: "Certain forms of speech have been considered outside the perimeter of First Amendment protection. These include the lewd and obscene, the profane, the libelous, and the insulting or "fighting" words.

Also included are a string of quotes from the group and the White Panther Party, assembling in one tidy file the reasons why the band and the party were to be considered, not entirely unjustly, troublemakers. Now that the two entities were separate, the MC5 could perhaps have thought that this sort of unwanted attention would go away. Unfortunately for them, they would soon realize that they were, in fact, their own worst enemies. The government was merely watching from the sidelines.

With a new record deal in place and Jon Landau installed as producer, the MC5 were able to start recording *Back in the USA,* their second album, but their debut studio record. The band had recently acquired a new house in Hamburg, Michigan, and Landau moved in for four months with the band and their families. Michael Davis remembers that the band had already been writing throughout the period immediately following the recording of *Kick Out the Jams*:

> We'd already started writing new songs, because we knew that the *Kick Out the Jams* record was now done, and it was history in a way. We had been fluctuating between covers and a few original songs, and now we had to be a completely original band, and we had to grow all the time. We were in the process of writing songs that we could add into the set, and move on to the next record. It started right away. As soon as *Kick Out the Jams* came out, we were starting to put together new musical ideas. We were coming up with "Teenage Lust" and "High School," just the natural progression of what we wanted to talk about next.

Back in the USA was Landau's first major production job, and though he would go on to receive great acclaim for his work with Bruce Springsteen, many felt—and still feel—that it was a big leap when he took on the MC5. Landau hated the "freeform" feel on *Kick Out the Jams,* and in his alter ego as a music critic, he would often make a point of shredding artists who he felt were taking expressionism into tedious territory. With the MC5, Landau realized that he had a great rock 'n' roll band on his hands, and he felt that the way to make an historic record with them would be to strip away all of the fluff and release eleven short and to the point cuts. Unfortunately, popular opinion suggests that the man who once gave the Rolling Stones' *Sticky Fingers* a zero-star review in *Rolling Stone* magazine also stripped away much of the MC5's spirit. That isn't to say that *Back in the USA* is a bad album; on the contrary, the songwriting is strong enough to see the band through a few not-so-great decisions, and the final results, while not as strong as it perhaps could have been, is still spectacular. "[Landau] was definitely a mental and emotional challenge to me," says Dennis Thompson.

To be honest, at that point in time, I really resented him as our producer. With the second album, the entity known as the sophomore jinx comes clearly to my mind. This was an extremely pivotal moment in our blossoming journey. I thought we needed a tried and true producer like Andrew Loog Oldham or some such. Jon had only produced one album by a chap named Livingston Taylor, Jonathan Taylor's kid brother. Jon had become close friends with John Sinclair and Wayne Kramer. I do believe Wayne's agenda was correct, that the rhythm section needed to tighten it up to a level of precision that we had earlier in our band's career. But at that time, I begrudgingly accepted Jon's authority and went along with his program. In retrospect, he actually helped me a great deal.

As a person, I truly liked and admired Jon. He was a true believer in our potential. All he ever wanted was to make the best possible record he was capable of. Christ, he would have the daily *New York Times* crossword puzzle finished before I woke up in the morning! He remained with us [at the band's house] during the entire recording process. At that time, John Sinclair had gone to prison and we were without a manager, so Jon kind of held down the fort as our interim manager and mentor as well. God bless him. We were a rough bunch to have to contend with.

My basic concern with Jon was his lack of professional recording experience. To me the album tracks sounded tinny and thin, and lacked bass, punch, and drive. All the tunes were three minutes or less. No free playing. I felt somewhat castrated. I had to play the entire album to a click track in my headphones. I am well aware of the fact that today *Back in the USA* is considered an excellent piece of musical work, and to many of our fans, it is their favorite album of the three. Many people have told me personally that they feel this album is highly seminal for punk and metal bands of the future. Today, I look at this record as a necessary and important part of the band's evolution. Some of those tunes will stand the test of time. "American Ruse" comes to mind. "Tonight" is a great tune as well.

As the pressure of recording their second album began to mount, tensions within the previously tight band began to surface, as Michael Davis recalls:

You know, everything was getting kind of testy, because everybody was starting to feel insecure. The pressure was getting really intense, and relationships were starting to fall apart. Things that we had made assumptions [about] and took for granted were starting to become bigger issues. The band morale started to become a little more insecure, and it was just reinforced by the fact that we were going out to play shows and they weren't being received with the same kind of fervor as the *Kick Out the Jams* show was. Our audience was confused and so were we. There were cliques going on. I think some people were putting on a stiffer face than they really were feeling. We were trying to act like we knew what we were doing, and some people were acting more like they knew what they were doing than they really did. I think this is the point where a lot of mistakes started being made, and a lot of people started to feel insecure. It really disrupted the backbone of the band. People started assuming to take charge of things that we really should have sat around and discussed a lot more. A couple of them felt like they knew what was best for the band, and they took it upon themselves to be spokespersons for the whole band, when they were actually only speaking for themselves. We didn't discuss it. That was not good, because we prided ourselves on being a unit, and as soon as people stepped up and took charge, it just didn't work well. Everybody was just as important as everybody else. For one person to assume the lead was kind of counter to the way we wanted to be.

Landau quickly realized that working with this band would be no picnic:

About the second or third day, you know, I realized we hadn't done anything yet musically. We just rapped . . . So I was there for two weeks at first and I concentrated almost entirely on just building rapport with the band and gradually making my feelings known. And we practiced and practiced for three, four, or five days. And we weren't ready for making records but decided that we weren't gonna go anywhere until we went to a studio and everybody heard the results and could decide for themselves whether the way things were was the way things should be. And of course we went in and it was fairly disastrous, in the sense that it was not musically good and we came out of that, and they were leaving to go on a two- or three-week tour and I was going to go home. They were coming to Boston and we were going to have a big meeting in Boston to discuss it. So that's what happened.

Still, Kramer recalls a real sense of purpose as they stepped into the studio:

We really wanted to prove we were a great rock 'n' roll band. You know; when you're young and you've put your first album out and you've opened your heart and soul for the whole world to see, and you get criticized the way we got criticized. And they came down on us with a sledgehammer. Not only were we too revolutionary for the straight world, we weren't revolutionary enough for the revolutionary world. So we got it from both sides. That we could handle, but when we were criticized for our musicianship, that really hurt us; that got us where we lived and damaged our little egos. So we really wanted to prove ourselves—because we knew we could play and that we were a great rock 'n' roll band. So the second album was designed to win over all those people that said that we were revolutionary hype or that we couldn't tune our guitars. The funny thing is that we put out an album of two and a half minute, highly focused, content-heavy political rock songs in a day when [albums were usually] featuring fifteen-minute guitar solos.

"There was an immense amount of rehearsal and a severe, almost anal, attention to detail and military-like precision," says Thompson.

I think what we gained in trying to be exact, we lost some punch in the swagger department. Our approach was like the early AM radio format. Three minutes per tune or less. At that time, bands like Journey and such were playing six- to nine-minute songs. To me, the recording process was actually quite demanding—physically, emotionally, and mentally. We had to do so many damned takes per tune. When someone would make a mistake, we would literally stop and take it from the top again. The music was built from the ground up with guitar, bass, and drums as a foundation. The rest of the guitar parts, solos, vocals, etc., were then stacked on top of that foundation. We were used to playing as an entire ensemble, and this technique was a little awkward and foreign to me. I played every song with a click track in my headphones and that was difficult, believe me. Sort of like serving two masters. One was time, the other the arrangement. I think we did about thirty takes on "Tutti Frutti." Whew!

Like Davis, Thompson also recalls a huge amount of tension within the band's ranks as they came together in the studio:

Landau's desire for the near-perfect record, coupled with the rigorous rehearsals and recording sessions, created some thick air at times. The band's relationship to each other became testy and tentative. The decision we all made for Wayne to play bass on a couple of tunes [instead of Michael Davis] may have not been a good one. To this day, that decision may have become one of the initial factors in the ultimate breakdown of the band's spiritual connection. I don't really know for sure. I am not condemning anyone here. We did need to tighten it up. The first record was live, and this was our first studio album. Call them growing pains. Egos got hurt in this process, and some of that peace and love ethic diminished quite a bit. It was time to get real. Get real good. All in all, I now think it is a fine record, and I am very proud to have been able to play with these gentlemen, no matter what situations presented themselves.

Landau sandwiched the nine band-penned songs between two (eventually perfectly executed) 1950s covers, namely Little Richard's "Tutti Frutti" and Chuck Berry's "Back in the USA." Just as Landau had set out to achieve, ten out of the album's eleven songs clocked in at under three minutes, and there were certainly no "Starship"-style space jams or J.C. Crawford introductions. From the first moment, the album resonates with an almost absurd, tinny sound, although that doesn't detract from the energy of the Little Richard cover. As rock critic Dave Marsh wrote on the reissued album's sleeve notes:

Back in the USA sounds like it was played out on high-tension wires, as if the treble clef has asserted dictatorship over the bass. This is primarily the product of a production accident: Landau wanted the hottest equalization that engineer Jim Bruzzese could give him, and he kept pushing until he wound up with a sound that was at times (especially on "Tutti Frutti" and "Back in the USA") virtually bottomless. This thin, edgy sound doesn't have much relationship to what the Five sounded like live, nor to anything Landau ever crafted again. But its very thinness gives it a manic force that, converted to punk and power pop, became one of the driving forces of the musically, if not socially, revolutionary bands of the late 1970s.

Marsh is right; opinions are divided about the sound on *Back in the USA,* but whether you like it or not, the one thing that's certain is that Landau arrived at it almost by accident. He was a writer who happened to be producing, stepping into

Detroit's G.M. Studios and behind the desk without any prior experience. He also had to deal with the problem that Michael Davis and—to a lesser extent—Dennis Thompson were having trouble nailing their parts. The recording process was, says Michael Davis, a very difficult period:

> [It] couldn't have been harder. Dennis could not keep time, I could not play through a song without flubbing a note or missing a change, Wayne and Fred could not tune their guitars or decide how long a solo should be, and Rob could not sing on key. So everyone's part was isolated and scrutinized. I hated hearing my bass with no other sounds accompanying it. It was embarrassing. That's what we had to get over and deal with correcting. It's like on any team, when a guy keeps fucking up, soon people start talking about him and thinking he's a liability. Everybody had their turn, but I probably got the most scorn. Then on top of it all, my Fender Jazz Bass was deemed defective because of a fucking ground noise and I was presented with a totally unfamiliar bass guitar. It was a Framus Star Bass; large semi-hollow body, and very thin necked. A complete pain in the ass. So, it even got worse. Every night or day for a month, we would ride in the station wagon clear to the east side of Detroit to lay down tracks. It was a brand new studio, sporting a small eight-track facility on one level, and a whole sixteen tracks in the main room. The atmosphere was bright white light, and spacious. You might think it was a good place to record commercials or an orchestra. Piece by piece, we assembled the record for Atlantic. I never got the feeling we were doing the record for us. It was for the record company.

Low on confidence, Davis sought solace in drugs. With Landau demanding take after take, the experience was difficult for everyone. "Landau was really inflexible because he had never produced a record before so he was learning, too," Davis says.

Davis also recalls being ignorant about what employing a producer might entail:

> We took ourselves rather seriously in those days, so the idea of a producer was a vague one. If we thought someone was coming to reshape our musical identity, we might have been one hundred percent resistant. That never occurred to us, and we met Landau with a happy welcome to MC5 land, and with an eager sense of anticipation. It was when we started filling the studio with abstract noise and fragmented arrangements of songs that frowns took the place of peace. When a band begins to work in the studio, you expect things to be disorganized, but it didn't take long to see that this band was not hitting on

all cylinders. Landau was himself a [relative] rookie as a producer, and the MC5 was anything but professional. A major task was staring everyone in the face, and I mean everyone. The engineer, a very big guy named Jim, was also a drummer, and he helped Landau tremendously with the technical as well as musical aspects. What I'm saying is Jon was not a musician . . . I think without Jim Bruzzese, that album might never have come out . . . or at least come out the way it did.

I don't hold any bad feelings toward Jon Landau about *Back in the USA*. What's done is done, and it had to be that way to get it done. I only wish we had communicated better as a band, and gotten closer as a band instead of farther apart . . . I know what all of those songs sounded like in the practice room. In my opinion, we failed to transfer the power to tape. Music is a very fragile medium. It can be uninspiring or it can be magical. Sometimes the magic is contained in a single moment, or in a section. If the entire song is magic, it's a masterpiece. It cannot be described in words. You know it when you hear it. Like "Looking at You," the A-Square Records single; from start to finish, a trip. If we had to pick a Berry tune, "Back in the USA" was everybody's favorite. Same for "Tutti-Frutti"; we'd been playing that one for quite a while.

"Tutti-Frutti" was, of course, one of Little Richard's signature tunes, and the band perhaps felt an affinity with the controversial, cross-dressing rocker. Certainly Tyner was one of the only performers able to do Richard's song justice. Following "Tutti-Frutti" is "Tonight," the first single from the album. It's an obvious choice for a single, because "Tonight" is the closest the MC5 ever got to the Beatles. Very clean sounding with an ultracatchy chorus, this is the band at their most mainstream. "Teenage Lust" continues the theme by filling the chorus with shouts of "Ooooh waa," though the lyrics hark back to the first side of the *Kick Out the Jams* album. This is the sound of a band on a mission to prove that they've lost none of their libido. Pure raunch 'n' roll, "Teenage Lust" is one of the stronger songs on the album.

"Let Me Try" is, on the surface, a ballad worthy of radio play and school dances. Typical of the MC5, however, the lyrics reveal ulterior sexual motives. The song plays out like a young boy's plea for sex, which is very likely exactly what it is. This is the band saying, "Don't feel down sweetheart, I'll fuck ya," but creating a paradox by putting those words within a song that parents would like—a musical Trojan horse.

"Looking at You" predated "Kick Out the Jams" and was the second single of the band's career. The band found a home for it on *Back in the USA,* and it was also the

B-side to the "Tonight" single. "High School" is the MC5's version of Alice Cooper's "School's Out"; a simple tale of student rebellion over a backdrop of buzz saw guitar and a ludicrously prominent tambourine. Still, nothing is cooler than telling kids that they know more than their teacher, and the MC5 and Alice Cooper are just two of many bands that have played on that particular theme. The band members themselves were only a few years out of their school uniforms too, so they could still relate.

"Call Me Animal" is another one of the album's better songs, and it's certainly the heaviest. Tyner attacks the lyrics like a man possessed by the spirit of Screamin' Jay Hawkins, while primal riffs and bass lines pulse over it. According to the Oxford dictionary, Tyner is screaming the music of the "first epoch of the Quaternary period" just because it's got a good beat. It's unlikely that they pulled out the word "pleistocene" by accident; this is the band yelling out that they're loud and heavy, and sometimes primal to the point of prehistoric.

"American Ruse" is the band at their authority-riling best. A protest against both the Vietnam War and the state of their own country, the song has some of the most intelligent lyrics the band ever wrote. A cry of "Rock 'em back, Sonic" from Tyner to Smith introduces one verse—a less than subtle dig at the police force.

Both the lyrics and the music of "Shakin' Street" were written by Fred Smith, and it serves as something of a precursor to what Smith would come up with on the next record, when he would really step up to the plate. On this song, the lyrics play out like a story, rather than—as with "Call Me Animal"—a series of psychedelic sound bites. Who the characters "Streetlight Sammy" and "Skinny Leg Pete" were based on remains a mystery, but the story gives way to a typical MC5 chant-along chorus.

"The Human Being Lawnmower," as well as having the greatest title the band ever came up with, builds from a fairly low-key introduction to a relentless blues jam that wouldn't have sounded out of place on *Kick Out the Jams.* Another gibe aimed squarely at the American government for its war-mongering activities, "The Human Being Lawnmower" proved that, despite Landau aiming at the mainstream market, the band was still anti-authoritarian and could still raise the eyebrows of middle America. Despite the fact that he hated the production job, Sinclair would surely have approved of the questions that his old band was still asking.

A faithful rendering of Chuck Berry's "Back in the USA" gives the album a solid end and reaffirms the fact that there isn't a single bad song on *Back in the USA,* just debatable production. Even those involved in the record's creation were split. As

Michael Davis recalls, "That record was DOA for me. The strange thing about *Back in the USA* is all those songs are great to play and I still hear that power when I play them today. But that record is just bland. To people who never heard what things sounded like before the record, they can't compare it to anything besides the record. So, I see why *they* like it. Should I be grateful?"

Not if the initial sales are anything to go by—the album peaked at number 137 on the Billboard chart. Reviewing the record for the May 1970 edition of *Rolling Stone*, Greil Marcus said:

> There are some first-rate songs on the album, some good musical ideas, and the musicianship is competent throughout, often fun, sometimes exciting. "Musicianship," here, is used as a *concept*—the *idea* of a "solid, clean, tight, and together" sound is as self-conscious as the total freak-out the first LP was. Chuck Berry simply oozes from the album. A group of teenage consciousness numbers fill out the album—a reworking of themes from the Beach Boys, Chuck Berry, Gene Vincent, old South Philly street music, and the like. Then there are the cuts that make it, make it all the way, that show the real talent and special gifts of this band.

Obviously a fan of the band who felt slightly let down and, echoing the thoughts of the majority of people who have assessed the album since (including the MC5), Marcus went on: "The music, the sound, and, in the end, the care with which these themes have been shaped drags it down, save for two or three fine numbers that deserve to be played on every jukebox in the land . . . Phil Spector once talked about the difference between 'records' and 'ideas'—'The man who can make a disc that's a record *and* an idea will rule the world.' The MC5 album, for the most part, remains an idea."

However, when revisiting the album for *Flash* in 1972, Davis was not only more positive about the record and its sound, he seemed to be seething that it had sold so badly:

> It doesn't help, really, that most of the critics who literally blasted the shit out of this album have come back to it now. Now it's a bargain bin oldie, when it could have been a real landmark record. It got the shaft for all kinds of reasons, all of which had one thing in common: None of them had anything to do with the music contained on the album . . . I

mean people were criticizing this record because it signified that the MC5 wanted to be pop stars, because the MC5 deserted John Sinclair, because the lyrics contained no revolutionary rhetoric, because Jon Landau was producing it (rock critic envy on that one) and because—this one floors me—*it was pretentious*. Pretentious? What on earth is pretentious about a great rock 'n' roll band trying to make a great rock and roll album? It might be pretentious for Simon & Garfunkel or James Taylor to try it, *but the MC5? What else could they do?*

Interestingly, Davis doesn't mention Landau, except to accuse other critics of being jealous of the fact that he was producing the MC5, which may or may not be true. What has never been questioned is the quality of the songs on *Back in the USA*. Rather, the main criticism has always been that these great songs deserved to sound better on a record. Such issues are moot now, because *Back in the USA* sounds the way it sounds, and people can choose to listen to it or not. The validity of the production is, at the end of the day, subjective. For most, the production isn't so bad that it makes the album unlistenable, and modern garage bands have even been known to *aim* for the *Back in the USA* sound. If anything, history has been kind to *Back in the USA*, something that the band couldn't possibly have anticipated when it was released.

MC5 at the Grande Ballroom, October 30, 1968, recording *Kick Out the Jams. Leni Sinclair*

John Sinclair in 1967. *Leni Sinclair*

The MC5 at the Hill Street house in Ann Arbor, Michigan, 1968. *Leni Sinclair*

Fred "Sonic" Smith in East Lansing, Michigan, 1968. *Leni Sinclair*

MC5 concert in West Park, Ann Arbor, Michigan, 1969. *Leni Sinclair*

Fred "Sonic" Smith, taken in 1968, to be used as a passport photo. *Leni Sinclair*

Sirius Trixon and the Motor City Bad Boys, 1977. Dennis Thompson is behind the kit. *Sue Rynski*

Fred "Sonic" Smith and Patti Smith in 1978. *Sue Rynski*

Destroy All Monsters, 1978, featuring Michael Davis, far right. *Sue Rynski*

Ron Asheton and Dennis "Machine Gun" Thompson, 1977. *Sue Rynski*

The Rob Tyner Band (aka the New MC5), 1977. *Sue Rynski*

Wayne Kramer and Johnny Thunders, Gang War, 1980. *Sue Rynski*

D KT/MC5 with their 2004 *Kerrang!* Icon Award. *Brian Rasic/Rex Features*

D KT/MC5 at the Reading Festival in 2004. *EMPICS*

Dennis Thompson outside the MC5's old Hill Street house in Ann Arbor, taken winter 2006 by the author.

Dennis Thompson of the MC5 with Niagara of Destroy All Monsters and her manager/husband Colonel Galaxy at the author's wedding. *Richard Peardon*

5
High (and Low) Times

With Sinclair locked away, it was only a matter of time before the White Panther party became inactive and eventually dissolved, but before they did, they shunned the MC5, as Kramer told Legs McNeil in *Please Kill Me*:

> We were purged from the White Panther party for counterrevolutionary ideals, because we bought sports cars that our parents signed for. I got a Jaguar XKE. Yeah, man, it was about the coolest thing I've ever had from playing rock 'n' roll. I still have dreams about that car. Oh, it was sweet. Fred Smith bought a used Corvette. Dennis bought a Corvette Stingray—a big 427 muscle car. Michael Davis bought a Riviera. And Rob Tyner got the band station wagon. We were awful. Not long after Rob got the station wagon, he came out of the supermarket with his arms loaded down with groceries, and the car was gone. Nobody had made any of the payments on it, so they had repossessed it. (73)

The boys who grew up on the drag strips understandably wanted their toys. Kramer still feels disappointed that they were condemned for fulfilling one of their rock 'n' roll fantasies: "Well, it's never nice to have your homeboys jump all over your case when you finally get some reward for all the work you'd put in. But they were dangerous days, and there was no way you could not make a mistake. And fuck it, I love those cars. They were the only things I really got out of rock 'n' roll, the only material things."

With Sinclair in jail and a distance growing between him and the band, Kramer recalls that the MC5 were in a difficult position: "The White Panthers don't exist any more. I think they realize that the 'White' had racist overtones and the 'Panthers' had violent overtones, so overall it didn't work because they weren't racist or really violent. All that is essentially John Sinclair's organization—it's his house and all the people stay with him there." The White Panther Party officially dissolved in April 1971.

During the summer of 1970, British writer and musician Mick Farren persuaded the band to come over to England to play his free Phun City festival. The fact that William Burroughs would be reading at the festival convinced them to make the trip, as they considered the writer to be something of a guiding light. In his book *Give the Anarchist a Cigarette,* Farren, who was completely new to organizing festivals, recalls telling the bands that they wouldn't get paid as they arrived on site:

> When the bands show up they're going to be presented with an ultimatum. There's no money; except to cover their expenses, but there's a good time to be had, so they can either stay and play or fuck off. That should separate the sheep from the goats." With some irony, the only "sheep" were the band called Free, who heard the deal and fucked off without even getting out of the car. All the other performers had a look around and decided that, if they were looking for trouble, they'd come to the right place. Unfortunately, it fell to r.e to explain the situation to each band in turn. It was something I obviously couldn't delegate, and it quite spoiled the first night of the festival for me, until someone noticed I'd started walking in small circles, muttering how all this bloody stress wasn't worth it and wondering if I should kill myself. (70)

The MC5 certainly weren't happy with the situation; they'd just flown thousands of miles, only to be told upon arrival that there was no money. Still, the band had always dreamed of playing in England and, in Kramer's words, "showing 'em how it's done."

Other bands on the bill that weekend, not including the fleet-footed Free, included the Pink Fairies, the Pretty Things, and Mungo Jerry. Taking place in Ecclesden Common near Worthing in Sussex, the festival would pass into 1970s folklore as something of a legend, not least because the MC5 were smoking on the day. The Pink Fairies may have been rolling around the stage naked, but the 5 were used to having to compete with Iggy Pop, and no amount of bare skin was going to steal their weekend. Playing two songs from their forthcoming third record ("Miss X" and "Sister Anne"), the full set list that day in a muddy English field was:

"Ramblin' Rose"
"Tonight"

"Rama Lama (Fa, Fa, Fa)"
"Miss X"
"Looking at You"
"I Want You"
"Sister Anne"
"Kick Out the Jams"/"Black to Comm"

An August review of the set in *Grass Eye* said, "Until you actually see the MC5 live, it's impossible to guess at the energy they send out in their music. The LP sounds so pseudo, so overemotional somehow, that it's not until you see them doing it that you realize what an amazing band they are. Guitarist Wayne Kramer, ass-wiggling across the stage, jumping up in three foot leaps and spinning around in the air; Tyner, sweat pouring from him, rocking through 'Kick Out the Jams,' 'I Want You Right Now,' 'Rama Lama (Fa, Fa, Fa),' screaming at the audience to go with him; Fred Smith, on his knees, his feet, his back, jumping, leaping through the air, firing his gun at the audience machine-fast."

After a quick call to Atlantic Records, the band was put up in a hotel for a couple of nights. The label also decided to use the time wisely, and some studio time was booked for the band to lay down their new track, "Sister Anne." This signaled the beginning of the recording of album number three, *High Time*.

While talking to Caroline Boucher of UK magazine *Disc and Music Echo,* Wayne Kramer dropped hints about the next album, saying, "We've already put one track down—'Sister Anne'—it's about a nymphomaniac nun. And we have four worked out onstage now; we always think it's best to work it out onstage first and see if it fits and what the response is like. I think our second album is perfect. We wanted to make a perfect one and I think we did. We're not so interested in making a perfect one this time, though.

It seems funny to me to hear people like the [Jefferson] Airplane who are semi into jazz, really old style jazz. We've been through all that, further than they could ever go. With us, our music is just a constant process of reevaluation."

Jon Landau was not asked back for their third vinyl outing. Instead, the band chose to self-produce with the help of engineer Geoffrey Haslam. Fred Smith wrote four out of the eight songs (Haslam described Smith as the MC5's "shining light"), and the result—*High Time*—is widely considered to be the band's best album.

Bizarrely, Landau predicted as much when he spoke to *Fusion* magazine in 1970: "I think that Sinclair was very involved and had a large role in the statement they made on their first album . . . I think that my influence is unmistakable on the second album and I think that left a lot of things to be desired, and I think that on the third album they're gonna have to stand on their own. It's gonna be their statement and there isn't going to be any strong influence from any outside sources—you know, they're gonna put up or shut up. I think they're gonna put up." All credit to him.

Put up they did. *High Time* is an extraordinary album, the sound that they were aiming for, and while it's sad that it would prove to be their last, it was as fitting an end as the circumstances could afford. Dennis Thompson remembers the band being in relatively good spirits as they recorded the album: "The interpersonal dynamics of the MC5 during and before recording *High Time* were actually in a delicately good balance. There were no cliques and very little bickering amongst the members of the group, which quite honestly happens with all bands at one time or another. This record we were in hi-def work ethic mode. We were ready to do a proper album on our own, and I have no doubt in my mind that we did accomplish that goal. *High Time* is my favorite MC5 record of the three. Special props to Geoffrey Haslam, our astute co-producer."

Michael Davis recalls starting the recording process in England:

We were still on Atlantic and we were gonna make a new record, so we did the first track at Pickwick Studios in London. We laid the band track down for "Sister Anne." My bass guitar was a problem again—the instrument. There was something, I don't remember what. I don't even remember what I was using at that point. We had a really nice welcome from Atlantic in London. They had a little party for us in the offices, ordered us some drinks and things like that. Then they set up some studio time for us to record. My bass was a problem, and the label called up Chris Squire and asked him if he'd bring his Rickenbacker down, and he did. That's the bass that was used on the band track on "Sister Anne," and a fine bass it was. The track came out really well, and now [that] we had *Back in the USA* under our belt, we knew what we needed to do in the studio.

We had a better grasp of the process of putting together and coming up with a tune, a real song. It wasn't like we'd just start jamming. It was actually an arranged piece of music, and Fred had written this song. It was a great song, a real exciting piece. So all we had time for was to do the music, the band, and when Fred and Rob did the harmonica duet, it was magic. It was a miraculous take, I thought. It was one of those things that, when you're playing music, you're out there on a limb and when you hear these two guys weaving their notes and their parts, and it just came to this climax note at the end of it, it was just beautiful, like "Fuck yeah!" So we got off on a good foot with that, but that was all there was time to do, which was really too bad because I liked that studio a lot. It was small and really cozy. I liked the feeling in there. But that was all there was time to do, so we came back to the States. I think [some of the band members] were starting to mess around with hard drugs, just a little bit. It wasn't serious, it wasn't an issue yet, but it was becoming [one].

We found a studio in Detroit, some place downtown belonging to some old bandleader guy from the 1940s called Artie Fields. He had a little recording studio, and it had a nice feeling in there. There was one big room, and there might have been little side rooms for a drummer or whatever, and there was a pretty good size tracking room like an old-style studio. Large space with a kinda high ceiling, wood floors, a grand piano and stuff around. You got the feeling you were in a recording studio like RCA or something.

We had this English guy, Geoff Haslam . . . he was a more experienced, laid-back, easygoing, easy to work with personality than Jon Landau, who was probably a laid-back enough type of person if he hadn't had the stress of trying to produce the MC5! He just went into outer space when he started working with us. Haslam was the opposite. A real armchair guy, he'd sit rocking in that chair and he'd be like, "You have an idea? Let's listen to it. Let's see what it sounds like." We were more organized, more confident, but our personalities were starting to . . . it was like the big bang. The universe was expanding, and everyone was getting a little further away from everybody else, and in some ways that worked better because each individual could develop their ideas instead of having to share with the group, having to have this group input. If Wayne or Fred had a tune, then they would direct the band how it was to be done. Not this kinda potpourri of throwing everything into the mixer and seeing what came out. So that was better, but on the other hand, we lost a lot of the previous spirit of what the MC5 was, or what our idea of what the MC5 represented. But that's all part of growing. The things that work you keep and the things that don't work get pushed to the side. So we started doing the songs, and immediately I felt that these songs were more direct. They weren't like Play-Doh, they were like a construction of real parts and clever arrangements. The licks were more sophisticated, so it was gonna be a better record—we knew that. The producer was giving us the wheel and telling us to steer where we wanted to go. He would tell us if something wasn't working right, and he'd help us achieve what we wanted to do, work through the problems that way.

There was a problem that comes to mind of vocal phrasing. Phrasing could be a problem if things were moving at a million miles an hour and we had to fit all these words in, like [in] "Gotta Keep Movin'." We must have tossed that one around for days. How to fit all these words. We made the phrasing more syncopated and rhythmic. They're the kind of things you have to do, and be able to not destroy somebody and deflate them by making them feel that just because they couldn't do it one way, they didn't deserve to be in the band anymore. There's a way to do it, and you don't have to carry some grudge off. Things really went well in that studio: Geoff was great, the songs were great, everybody played well, we got Bob Seger down to play some percussion, the horn guys were around—it was a good vibe. The record was cool.

He refers to management issues but says:

I don't know, maybe the seeds of destruction were too planted in the ground by then. It should have worked, but it really wasn't the MC5. Not the MC5 that did *Kick Out the Jams.* We were kinda compromised and desperate at that point. Whatever we had been to get signed onto Elektra was something that we couldn't do any more. Kinda tough squeezing out of that one. The bottom line was that we all wanted to play music, we wanted to be in a band, we wanted to be great, and we wanted to be successful. If we could help the planet, the world, and the population of Earth realize a better life, we'll bring that too. I think we were just a bit ignorant in the late 1960s, but everyone was on this big change thing. The big thing that changed everything was the assassination of Robert Kennedy and Martin Luther King. Those assassinations took the piss right out of it. That was our bridge to the real political establishment—Robert Kennedy. When he was assassinated, it was heartbreaking. Martin Luther King, too. In the years before that, we had seen JFK assassinated. It was like, you try to do anything, if anybody stands up and has the charisma to put your ideas into real life, they get offed. They get bumped off. If it isn't by a conspiracy, it's by some nut—it doesn't matter. They ain't gonna last. It's just like Jesus Christ. You've got somebody that's got the strength and the ability to articulate the truth, somebody's gonna fuckin' take 'em out. So we got really discouraged there, but we never disavowed ourselves from wanting to change what we thought was bad thinking and dishonest behavior. Everybody can look around and see that only a small percentage of people have a prosperous life. People that live in poverty, and not just the U.S., but Africa, South America, Third World countries—they're human beings. So anyway, we would like to have effected a change.

Regarding the new album, he continued:

With *High Time,* nobody could really decide what the concept of the record should be, and Fred had an idea. He had [the cover] all worked out in his head. The broken clock, and this very colorful, kindergartenish look about it. Inside the fold would have the photographs—it looks kind of scrapbookish. We gave Fred control—art direction and co-producer or something like that. It was OK. I think it was the best we could come up with at the time, considering we had left our political persona a couple of records previous to that, and then we still didn't know how to transport who we were to who we wanted to be. So we made our own management decisions. I guess that's what the bottom line is. When you're making your own management decisions, not everybody's going to happy about this. You can't go to another band member and say, "I never agreed with this." If you have a manager, then you go to the manager because they're not part of the creative end. It was pretty false, but that was the way it was.

The first of Smith's compositions, "Sister Anne" kicks off the album in spectacular style, Telling the story of a revolutionary nun, the song is a furious statement of intent, and a middle finger in the face of anyone who thought the 5 were finished after *Back in the USA* (even if they would be soon enough).

The song features a simple Check Berry riff, brought to life by a band fighting to stay alive. Longtime cohort of the band and friend of John Sinclair, Charles Moore—the jazz trumpet player from the Trans-Love days—popped up to add some backing vocals and flügelhorn. Meanwhile, Pete Kelly's piano can be heard plinking throughout the song. The band had been playing the song live for some time, and they transferred the energy seamlessly into the studio environment. It is, in short, the perfect album opener.

"Baby Won't Ya," another Smith song, is pure Motown. Concentrating on the band's favorite subject, namely, sex, the song has a huge, anthemic chorus that harks back to 1960s soul music from their hometown. Whether the song is based on reality or is purely derived from fantasy remains unclear, but the imagery Smith invokes when he has Tyner sing the words "tipsy gypsies" is magical.

Wayne Kramer's "Miss X," another song that they'd been playing live for some time, comes blasting out next. Starting off with a funeral march intro, played on the organ by one Skip "Van Winkle" Knapp, the song has the band up to their old trick of writing a song that sounds like a ballad, but has fiery lyrics. The words to "Miss X" have little to do with romance.

Tyner really seems to enjoy the opportunity to croon rather than scream, and his voice is wonderfully suited to the more subtle approach.

"Gotta Keep Movin'" is a Dennis Thompson composition, and it opens with a traditional blues riff, complete with Rob Tyner's harmonica. The song then opens out into Tyner's manic delivery of Thompson's angry lyrics. The song couldn't be more different from the one that precedes it.

Thompson is understandably proud of this song: "To me, 'Gotta Keep Movin" is synonymous with the band's lives and careers both separately and apart. We kept changing up, and re-creating ourselves. I wrote it primarily to showcase the thirty-second note virtuosity of our excellent guitar players. Take that, Alvin Lee, Eric Clapton, and Jimmy Page! It still feels topical and wicked today. 'Movin" . . . is a tune that I hoped could show other musicians that we really could play well. Hell, the instrumental section ought to be the background theme for a NASCAR racing movie!"

Tyner's own "Future/Now" finds the singer turning into a kind of anti-preacher and screaming about the hypocrisy of religion. It's an intelligently written piece of work that features some of the band's best ever lyrics, and it's no surprise that the uniquely talented Tyner wrote them.

Kramer's "Poison" is perhaps the weakest song on the album, but that's only because the standard is so high. While the melody is there, it feels unfinished somehow. The song that Tyner belts out next is, in the opinion of many (including the author), the best song the band ever recorded. Fred Smith's "Over and Over" is perfect in every way. The unobtrusive guitar that opens the song soon gives way to Tyner at his soul-fueled best, screaming through verses that build up to the nerve-tingling chorus. This is the band capturing on record what everyone always knew they were capable of. This is the power of the MC5, preserved for posterity, singing about Vietnam, whores, pimps and Uncle Sam.

It's almost mind-numbing; Smith manages to crowbar revolution, Vietnam, and the band's blue-collar beginnings into one verse, but without it sounding the slightest bit forced. Smith closes the album with his blues/jazz workout, "Skunk (Sonicly

Speaking)." The song starts out simply enough, with Tyner singing over a blues riff; by the end, however, the track has escalated into muso-heaven, with a full brass section (including Charles Moore on trumpet) coming in, and Bob Seger adding percussion. The Detroit hero may not have made the most notable contribution to *High Time,* but for some his mere presence was enough.

With *High Time,* the MC5 finally hit the nail on the head, but nobody was listening to the bang. As Fred Goodman wrote in *The Mansion on the Hill,* "No one cared anymore. Atlantic had lost interest in the MC5 and offered only minimal marketing support for the new album" (160). Only in retrospect has the album been appreciated. But then, that is the story of the MC5's career. If nothing else, their imprisoned former manager approved. "The third one sounds like the MC5, like they really sounded," says Sinclair. "Musically, I thought the third one showed how good they were and how hip their tunes were."

Dennis Thompson remains adamant that the album is a classic: "I was and still am a fan of *High Time.* Not to beat my own drum, mind you, but I still think it is one of the best records ever made by anyone. *High Time* is a natural progression from our first two records. On this record we managed to blend our high-energy live performing skills from *Kick Out the Jams* with the studio precision we gained on *Back in the USA.* I do not feel that we could have done much better than we did. Proud of that one I am."

Reviewing the album for *Rolling Stone* in September of that year, future Patti Smith Band guitarist Lenny Kaye wrote, "It seems almost too perfectly ironic that now, at a time in their career when most people have written them off as either dead or dying, the MC5 should power back into action with the first record that comes close to telling the tale of their legendary reputation and attendant charisma. This may appear particularly surprising, given the fact that the group's live performances have been none too cosmic of late, but then the old saw is that you can't keep a good band down, and it's never been more forcefully put than here."

Kaye closed by saying,

The capper, though, is saved for Dennis Thompson: his "Gotta Keep Movin'" not only defines the MC5 in the way that all of us would have liked to remember them throughout the past dismal year, but also manages to pull in every trick that literally made them the most exciting band in America for a brief and glorious time. It's all there—the precise breaks, the madly screaming dual guitars, the fanatic drive and energy. Make no mistake, they shovel it out as good as it ever gets, and that's pretty damn good indeed. For this, we can only praise the Lord and pass the ammunition.

Kaye's positive review was just one of many, but sadly the good press didn't translate into high sales, and Atlantic was getting restless.

In December, the MC5 were notably absent from a "Free John Sinclair" concert, organized by Leni Sinclair at the Crisler Arena on the University of Michigan campus, although they had previously performed at some "People's Ballroom" benefit shows for their former manager's defense at the Grande Ballroom. Dennis Thompson remembers that relations between the band and their former manager remained strained: "I am not sure if any members of the band spoke with John after his release from prison. I do remember not being invited to play with John and Yoko Lennon in Michigan at the huge benefit concert for his defense fund, though. That hurt. So, I certainly had no desire to contact John at that time."

Artists who did appear included Stevie Wonder, Bob Seger, Commander Cody and His Lost Planet Airmen, Detroit favorites the Up and, incredibly, John Lennon and Yoko Ono. Speakers included Abbie Hoffman, Black Panther leader (and Sinclair's hero) Bobby Seale, and yippie Jerry Rubin. When John Sinclair was permitted his phone call to Leni, she hooked it up to the loudspeaker system so he could address the crowd, unbeknownst to the prison staff. John Sinclair:

> I heard it on the radio. It was live on WABA. They can't really get in your bed and stop you listening to a radio. It wasn't against the rules. Of course, they had no idea what this thing was. It was incredible. John Lennon. Amazing. Stevie Wonder, Bobby Seale. God, I almost did a backflip when I heard fucking Seale. I got out three days later. If it hadn't been Friday night, I would have been out the next day. I don't think that was a coincidence. We'd been trying to put a lot of pressure on them for two or three years. Finally, John Lennon came in, and Jesus Christ, it was all over. Before that, he didn't know me. That was the amazing part to me. If he was a friend of mine, I could see it. But he just related to my predicament. A beautiful guy.

Leni Sinclair, who had been in charge of organizing everything and everyone, has patchy memories of the day:

I took some pictures of John and Yoko. The rest of the time, I was too busy taking care of business. I had arranged the hookup for [that] telephone conversation from prison, which was supposed to be just private between him and me, [but] it was broadcast to fifteen thousand people. I had two children I had to supervise. Then I had a literature table where we were trying to make some money. I was running around like crazy all night, but once in a while I managed to sneak downstairs and get a couple of [camera] shots off.

Unlike John, however, Leni doesn't think that the concert was solely responsible for her then-husband's release:

The concert was on the Friday night, and by the Monday, he was out. It wasn't the concert though. It was just a coincidence. The legislature had already voted to change the marijuana law. The concert speeded it up a little, and that's when they let him out. He was already slated to get out because the law had been changed, but John and Yoko didn't know that. They were like, "Damn, the power of the music." It certainly helped raise consciousness and raise awareness, and it might have sped it up. But without the concert, I don't know how much longer they could have kept him in for. What's interesting is that when he got out, the old law that he was sentenced under, for possession of two joints, expired on March 31, and the new law making it a one-year maximum for possession came in during May. So there was a month where there was no law for possession. We held a press conference where we were toking away in front of the TV cameras. When the new law took effect, the state had to release all the prisoners that were locked away under the old law. I think it was like 168 prisoners got out in one day. Me and John went to Jackson to welcome some of them, and they cried and hugged John, saying, "Thank you, thank you." To this day, John meets people that say, "I got out early because of you." That's gratifying.

Poet Allen Ginsberg opened the festivities at the concert, reading his lines, "Dear John Sinclair, we pray you'll leave your jail box." Speaking by telephone from prison, a choked-up Sinclair told the crowd, "I'm totally wiped out. I don't know what to say."

Stevie Wonder performed "Heaven Help Us All" and "Somebody's Watching You," deftly dedicating the latter to all the undercover agents in the audience. A far cry from the Disney performer he would later become, Wonder was at his gritty best in 1971, just a couple of years away from his classic *Innervisions* album.

Of course, most of the talk was centered on the fact that John Lennon and Yoko Ono were going to perform. Lennon was still one of the most famous musicians in the world, and his appearance took the event to a whole other level. People were taking notice of the injustices piled on John Sinclair, thanks in no small part to Lennon's involvement. The former Beatle took the stage at 3:00 a.m., and played for twenty-two minutes. Most of the songs were recent compositions, and Lennon closed the show with a song called "John Sinclair": "They gave him ten for two, what else can the bastards do?" As Lennon sang, "Let him be, set him free" and the show came to an end, the crowd marched out of the arena chanting, "Free John Sinclair." Within three days, they'd get their wish.

Writing at the end of December for the *Ann Arbor Sun* (and later reprinted in his own book, *Guitar Army*), Sinclair was clearly suffering from the shock of being free.

I'm just so *blasted* right now that I can't get very much together to say to you in this space, but there's no way I would let this issue go by without saying *something* to let you know how great it is to see all of *you* again out here on the streets—whew! And to know that it's you who got me out of that place—you and nobody else!

Before I go any further, I want to say thank you and power to ya, everybody who supported the Free John campaign for the past five years, everybody who's contributed in any way to this tremendous victory for all of us—because it is a people's victory, it's no kind of individual thing now and it never *has* been; ever since the bust came down five years ago, it's always been about the dinosaurs trying to stomp the rest of us out any way they can, and it's been about them trying to keep us separated from each other, isolated, powerless, and alone, so we can't do anything together to solve our collective problems, right? (317)

Printed next to a picture of Sinclair hugging his children for the first time in years, his article finishes with the lines "THANK YOU! SEE YOU ON THE STREETS! ALL POWER TO THE PEOPLE!" and he signs it "John Sinclair, Chairman, RPP." Those initials stood for the name of the organization that the former members of the White Panther party had recently formed. Sinclair had initially chosen the name the Woodstock People's Party, but after his brother David wrote him a letter in early 1971 claiming, "We're not feeling very Woodstocky out here," Pun Plamondon's choice, the Rainbow People's Party, stuck.

Essentially the WPP with a new name, the RPP consisted of John and Leni Sinclair, Gary Grimshaw, Pun Plamondon, Genie Plamondon, Frank Bach, Peggy Taube, David Fenton, and David Sinclair. Embracing elements of Marxism and Leninism, the RPP promoted the revolutionary struggle for a "communal, classless, anti-imperialist, anti-racist, and anti-sexist . . . culture of liberation." The rhetoric had been altered to slide with the times, but the socialist sentiments remained intact. Two and a half years in jail had, if anything, fired Sinclair up to continue the fight. Determined not to allow his time behind bars to be for nothing, he dusted himself off and marched boldly forward.

While still in jail, Sinclair wrote in the May 1, 1971, edition of the *Ann Arbor Sun*:

> We changed our name to the Rainbow People's Party because we feel that it's a lot more expressive of what we really are and what we want to be than "White Panther Party" could ever be. We realized that it's impossible to paste on names and organizational forms which other organizations and peoples have used successfully, simply because we understand now that our own situation as a new people in this place demands that we deal with it on our own terms. And we realized that we aren't really "white panthers" either—we're *freeks*, Rainbow People, rock 'n' roll maniacs who want to create a whole new way of life for ourselves and for all humanity, and the way we'll do it isn't by spouting a lot of slogans and trying to be "more revolutionary" than anybody else, but by *getting down* with our own people and working with you to build an alternative social order which will give shape to our holy vision of the Rainbow Nation.

So while the MC5 were desperately trying (and failing) to escape Sinclair's shadow, he was priming many of their original followers to continue the people's fight upon his release. When he did get out, he took over as chairman of the RPP and reasserted his identity as a "concert promoter, politico-cultural activist, and tireless propagandist." His brother David was managing the Up, and his friend Pete Andrews was managing a local band called SRC. John Sinclair joined them to form a production and management offshoot of the RPP called Rainbow Multimedia. Before long, Sinclair was managing a local hero, Mitch Ryder, and his band, simply named Detroit (that band also featured former Detroit Wheels Johnny Bee on drums and vocals and Steve Hunter on lead guitar). As John Sinclair remembers, "I managed Mitch Ryder for a while in 1972. He quit singing with the Detroit Wheels, and I managed the two different bands that the band members formed—one was called the Rockets, and one was called Detroit."

The Rockets included Johnny Bee and guitarist Jim McCarty, and were later signed to RCA Records. A popular figure in Detroit (the city), former Detroit Wheel Mitch Ryder was a good man to have along at the various rallies John Sinclair organized and/or attended. Ryder had become increasingly interested in politics as he got older, and so he was the perfect man for Sinclair to have around. Even if it didn't completely heal the wound caused by Sinclair's bitter split with the MC5, their association eased the pain a little.

Nineteen seventy-two should have been the year that saw the MC5 cement their blossoming reputation as one of the best rock 'n' roll bands on the planet, touring to promote their best album and one of the best records released the previous year. They were about to hit Europe and show the world exactly what they could do on stage. Things just weren't destined to run that smoothly, though, and as early as February, Michael Davis was forced to miss an important concert in London because Detroit airport security wouldn't let him board his scheduled plane. Despite flying out the very next day, his bandmates were not very pleased.

On February 13, the 5 appeared at the unlikely venue the Greyhound in Croydon to perform at a concert organized by promoters and the Fox record store. Charles Shaar Murray, writing for *Creem* magazine, was in attendance:

> The Fox in Croydon, Surrey, is a very long way indeed from the Grande Ballroom in *Dee*-troit, Michigan, and the MC5 were a very long way from home, but it didn't seem to matter. The stage was too small, there was no lighting worthy of the name, the gig was chronically underadvertised, and there was every reason to doubt that any significant proportion of the audience knew who the MC5 were. "Well, if they don't know who we are now, they sure as hell will when we're through," said singer Rob Tyner and took another slug at the band's bottle of Old Granddad. It takes quite a lot to shake up a band that's been together seven years. Even if the audience in Croydon had a fairly low level of MC5 consciousness, devotees of the underground press could recite the band's life and times verbatim, even if they'd never actually bothered to go out and listen to the records.

If the band was suffering from tension within the ranks in Croydon, Shaar Murray certainly didn't notice, calling their performance "a far cry from the freeze-dried sloganeering and clenched-fist Red Book politics with which most people link their names. Despite coming on, in Lester Bangs's words, like 'sixteen-year-old punks on a meth power trip,' the MC5's music, and its attendant ideology, are far more subtle than is first apparent . . . The MC5 don't leave you gaping in awe at their collective virtuosity, but they make you dance and they make you sweat. They play rock 'n' roll."

This might be true, but soon after this show, they'd be playing their rock 'n' roll without Michael Davis, who was fired. Dennis Thompson recalls the turbulent period:

> Mike's leaving the band all began, I believe, when he was replaced on bass for a couple tunes during the recording of *Back in the USA.* After that happened, one thing led to another and he just drifted from the center. His being replaced on bass during the recording of *Back in the USA* for [those] tunes never, never sat well with me, even to this day. Maybe it really hurt Mike down deep, I don't know. I am sure Michael can tell this story better than I, as his perspective will include more of what was going through his head back then. It really isn't my call to speak for him on this.

Michael Davis:

> I didn't see it coming. After we did *High Time,* between the time we finished the record and we did a few shows, then we were booked to tour England. The tour wasn't like touring is now. It wasn't like we had twenty-five dates on the continent, ten in the UK, fourteen in Scandinavia, out for three months or something. This was like we had three or four shows in England and two in Europe, and we were gone for three or four weeks. By that time, I had developed a serious drug dependency, and everyone except Rob was using. I decided that I wanted to do this all of the time. It wasn't just a party thing; it had become a way of life. I had kind of distanced myself from everybody else because of it. I lived in Detroit, and Fred lived in Detroit, but on the other side. Dennis may have lived at home. Rob and his wife had a kid so they wanted their own space, and I got a girlfriend that I could go live with. Fred was married to Sigrid then, and they lived in a place over on the west side of Detroit. So we kinda spread out and I wasn't seeing those guys very much. We'd rehearse now and again.
>
> We booked this tour to England, but when you start not hanging out with people and you don't have that sort of relationship, anything that comes along that demands your

attention is irritating. I started to not like anybody, and I didn't have much in common with anybody anymore. I thought I was doing pretty well. I was successful. I had a couple of grand in my pocket, and I could do any kind of dope I wanted to do, any time I wanted to do it. I was saving up for a Harley. Music was not really on my plate. They weren't liking me either, which was understandable. So when they booked the tour to England, I decided that I would go separately, I'd book my own flight, and I'd be there a couple of days after the other guys. Well, what happened was that when I went to the airport, as I was about to board the plane, there was a security check, and I had to take everything out of my pockets. Like an idiot, I had a syringe in there. A needle. I swear to God. I told the security guy that I had something in my pocket that I didn't want to put on the table. He took me out of line, and I showed him what I had.

Of course, immediately my bags got snatched off the belt and it was just paraphernalia. I missed the fucking flight to London, and it was a night flight too. Jesus, I also had a little folded up piece of cellophane with dope in it. I had it in a small pocket. As we were walking to go to the security office, I fished in the pocket (because I wasn't cuffed or anything like that), and I dropped it on the floor in the airport. When I got there they patted me down and didn't find anything. Now, this is how crazy I was: They let me go; they confiscated the needle; there were no charges. I'd missed the flight so I had to go the next day. I went out to the parking lot, gave it about five minutes, went back into the airport, and went down the aisle where we had walked to see if I could find [the cellophane packet] on the floor. And I did.

What happened was, because I missed that flight, I missed a gig at the LSE [London School of Economics]. There was a legend here in the U.S. that a London School of Economics gig was a big one. The Stones played there, the Yardbirds—everybody played the LSE. Sort of like playing the Whisky or something. So I missed the LSE. When I finally arrived in London, Dennis came to meet me in a cab and he said, "Everybody's pissed." I was like, "Yeah, I'm sure they are. Where's the dope? Have you found out where to cop? Let's go." Because I didn't dare bring anything with me. [I wasn't] that brazen to do it again and see if I could get away with it. They were pissed all right. We played a couple of shows, and then it was time to go to France . . . I have some photos of [my] room with me in a Mardi Gras costume and my Epiphone bass (that's what I was playing). Somebody came to the door and said that we were having a band meeting. It was in Wayne's room or Rob's room. I went there and they said, "We've all talked about it, and we've decided that we don't want you in the band anymore." My reaction was probably something like, "Cool.

OK, that's cool. After France, I'll just go home." They said, "You're not going to go to France." I wanted to go to France and finish up there but they told me that they'd already made arrangements, and that they had somebody to take my place. I said, "What's up?" and Fred told me, "I don't think you're into it anymore." He was right. I couldn't argue there, but they decided to take a vote on it. I went back to my room, and after a few minutes, Wayne and Fred came down and knocked on my door, and Wayne came in and told me that the vote was against me going. I said, "OK, get out of my room." That's about it.

I had to battle with them to pay for my flight home . . . I didn't want to stay there for another two weeks with nothing to do. The next day I was on the telephone with Ronan [O'Rahilly, a movie director], and he was mediating between myself and Fred and the rest of the guys. Finally he came in and said, "OK, we got you out." So I left.

By that time, it wasn't fun playing in the band anymore. The music we were playing was empty and soulless. The posturing and the talking on stage—it was embarrassing. When it was over, it was a relief. It was like I was out of that fucking dark cloud. From then on, I was on my own and I felt really good.

Wasting no time, and without looking for a new bass player, the four members of the 5 entered a London studio to record three songs ("Gold," "Train Music," and "Inside Out") for the soundtrack to Ronan O'Rahilly's movie, *Gold*. O'Rahilly had made his name as the founder of floating pirate radio station Radio Caroline, and in the MC5 he found like-minded people. According to Kramer, "He nearly saved the MC5." For the *Gold* soundtrack songs, Kramer himself played the bass parts, as well as piano on the title track.

The movie itself, dubbed "The Story of the New American Dream," was soon forgotten (it can't even be found on imdb.com, a rare feat indeed for a film). It eventually premiered in December of that year to little fanfare, partly because of the small budget and lack of a sizeable advertising campaign. *Shock Cinema*, revisiting the film recently, said:

It's always refreshing to stumble across an obscure, bizarre, and baffling relic from the groovy late-1960s, when coherence was at a minimum and radical ideas were happily embraced by open-minded viewers. This begins with an opening-credit montage that includes police brutality, dead Vietnamese children, JFK's assassination, Kent State, etc., so I was expecting a heavy message flick. But instead, it offered up a hippie-hodgepodge of political metaphors, barely-baked philosophy, sing-a-longs, bizarre camerawork, tinted stock, solarization, split screen, and gratuitous sex scenes that makes you wonder if the cameraman was on peyote. In other words, "Yow!"

Not a great success then, and not a classic now, the movie was certainly not the kind of project that would keep an unsteady ship like the MC5 afloat. Still, the relationship between the band and O'Rahilly had become solid, and the rebel broadcaster became their European manager. English bassist Steve "Annapurna" Moorhouse found himself in working with the band when they headed to France for a series of shows.

During this period, a string of prospective projects failed to get off the ground, and the countdown to the group's inevitable dissolution was well underway. During an interview with a French magazine, Tyner was quoted saying that the band was planning to record another live album in New York and, like their debut, it would feature all new songs. Kramer also mentioned the prospective project when he spoke with Nick Kent of *Friendz* magazine in March of 1972: "One time we were going to make a really weird album—maybe the next one ... which we're working on under the tentative title *MC5 Live on Saturn*."

When Kent asked if that record would feature "Black to Comm," Kramer replied, "Maybe. We've been playing it for six years and it's probably at the forefront of whatever we're into—it's an energy chant—it must have been through a thousand evolutions in character. We've all changed so much working over here—with Ronan and everything—that I don't know what direction our music will take. We'll just have to wait and see."

The album, tentatively titled *Live on Saturn*, would never happen. Although O'Rahilly was in discussion with Roulette Records about a possible deal with the band, this, too, ultimately failed to materialize. With their impending implosion getting closer at an alarmingly rapid rate, within months, the band would cease to exist (at least in any recognizable form).

On August 5, the MC5 played to sixty thousand people at the first annual London Rock 'n' Roll Revival at Wembley Stadium, on a bill that also included Little Richard, Jerry Lee Lewis, Chuck Berry, Bo Diddley, Screamin' Lord Sutch, Gary Glitter, the Move, the Platters, the Drifters, and the Coasters. Wayne Kramer remembers the eventful concert:

[It was] sixty thousand teddy boys, who are hard core fans of the 1950s, and the MC5 had decided that we were going to unveil the next move to the future at this gig. Fred came out as Sonic Smith—a cartoon character, a superhero. I painted all my skin gold and wore a black suit. Rob Tyner wore a gold lamé jacket and tight black pants, and he bouffed his Afro out to like three times the size of normal and filled it with glitter. When the teddy boys got a look at us, they didn't dig it. During the course of the set, a couple of them started throwing beer cans at us, and Rob Tyner made the mistake of throwing it back at a guy. It was the signal for the end because the stage rained beer cans . . . sometimes we made tactical mistakes.

Dennis Thompson:

The Wembley Stadium show was a complete fucking disaster. Total tactical group error. It was not the time to dress like spacemen at that gig. Way too many teddy boys in the crowd. We should've just worn our leather coats, black T-shirts and denims, and we would have killed that audience. But the teddy boys did not appreciate the MC5's latest stage costume incarnation. We ducked hundreds of beer bottles and kept right on playing, though . . . [*laughs*].

While on tour in Germany, Moorhouse left, and another English bass player, Derek Hughes, finished off the European tour. According to Dennis Thompson, "He was a true gentleman and a damn fine bass player. It was great to know him, and I thank him to this day for holding down the rhythm section as well as he did while he was with us." When the band returned to the U.S., Ray Craig filled in on bass, and when they went back to Europe in June, Hughes was again recruited. It barely mattered; in November, Thompson and Tyner quit the band.

The disintegration of the band gathered steam when they met at Tyner's house to discuss another forthcoming European tour. Thompson stated that he didn't want to go, preferring instead to enter rehab and get clean. Tyner voiced his support for the drummer, but when Fred Smith went to Tyner's house to try and straighten things out, the two of them ended up brawling.

The MC5 was over.

Dennis Thompson is adamant about the way things went down:

What I tell you here and now about me and Rob quitting the 5 is the truth, the whole truth, and nothing but the truth, so help me God. *I really did not quit the band.* I truly only asked to postpone a tour to Europe [in order] to clean up from a terrible heroin habit that was killing me and my family. I had made the decision with the help of my family to go to a methadone clinic every day, a sixty-mile round trip to a clinic in the city of Royal Oak. We had a band meeting at Rob's house, and that's when I said I could not do this tour, that I didn't think I could live through it. The Chinese heroin in London was ten times better than [what] I could get on the streets of Detroit . . . Rob said if I wasn't going [on tour], then neither was he. He supported my decision to clean up. Rob roomed with me on the road and knew full too well that I was a fuckin' accident waiting to happen . . . By the way, I did kick the Horse in his ass, and three months later I was clean and felt like a new man.

Kramer and Smith reconvened as the MC2.

Michael Davis recalls the entire mess:

Dennis called me at one point to tell me that he had quit the band, that there was no love in the band anymore. He told me that it just sucked. He said that there were big problems with Rob and the two guitar players. I knew Dennis was gone, but I wasn't interested. I didn't care what they were doing. I heard about the MC2 thing and the big fight at Rob's house between Rob and Fred. For the record, I'm really glad I wasn't around for that final year. Whatever 1971 was like for me, I guess 1972 was a lot worse for everybody else. I'm glad I was gone. I know those guys were using [with the exception of Tyner] . . . and things like that. It starts off being like a weekend thing, and then it's everyday, and then it's more than once a day. It's like a virus, and if you don't stop it, it just keeps going. I know Wayne was on [dope]; Fred was not so gone but he was drinking all the time. Dennis was into it, and Rob was the only one that wasn't.

With a few last commitments to uphold, Kramer and Smith played the final European shows with Hughes and a drummer called Ritchie Dharma. As Kramer said in *Grit, Noise and Revolution*: "We met our drummer in the dressing room the night of the gig. He didn't know who the MC5 were. We sucked. Fred and I were trying to sing, and we didn't even know the words to our own songs. It was terrible. We tried to play some songs that everybody would know, like old Chuck Berry stuff. Anything to get through the gig" (273).

Some of the rare footage that exists of Kramer and Smith, plus Hughes and Dharma, performing as the MC5 reveals some telling glances between the two guitarists. Kramer, drinking from a liquor bottle, seems determined to ride out the bullshit. Smith looks disgusted. By Kramer's own admission, this nonsensical version of their band "sucked":

My experience is not unique, that young people have a sense of invincibility and they work real hard, especially people in the arts like musicians, writers, photographers, dancers, filmmakers, and in a lot of work that you can do in the arts, you're laying the groundwork for a life's work—a career. In pop music, there are other forces that come into play that are much more powerful than young people think they are, or even are conscious of. Yeats wrote, "Things fall apart, the center never holds." That's what happens with bands. They fall apart. Just like anything in nature: it's born, it lives, and it dies. But nobody talks about that in the band business. All they talk about is, "You're gonna be a big star, you're gonna do well." So to find myself in this position where I'm trying to honor tour commitments [without my band] was disorienting. It's actually very damaging, because there's nothing that can prepare you for that kind of an experience. You can learn how to play your guitar and you can learn how to write songs, you can learn how to put a show together. But how do you learn how to fail? That was that experience—to see things falling apart. My experience was also not like a great many other people that were in the same position, in that I gravitated toward things that would kill my pain—my psychic pain, the pain of failure. The pain of youthful enthusiasm running out of gas. If you saw that footage, you probably saw me drinking whisky, and this is where all of the real damage gets done. Because it becomes a self-fulfilling and downward spiral. It's not going well so I take drugs. It's going bad so I drink. Because I'm drinking and taking drugs, I can't do anything positive to improve the situation. Like I said, it's not unique.

A guy asked me recently how is it that the Rolling Stones endured drug abuse and people dying and all kinds of changes, but the MC5 couldn't. Most rock bands can't. But the Rolling Stones had international success right out of the gate. They were on the first wave of the British invasion, and their first record was a hit. Their first single has a hit. Money has a great way of smoothing things out. Money has a great way of keeping the team going. The MC5 had no money. Most bands have no money. That's the illusion—that somehow success is gonna deliver me to a good life. And it's a lie. I call it one of the great lies of rock 'n' roll. That if I work real hard and have a plan, and I stick to my plan and my plan works out and I still don't have a good life, then I'm really fucked. What am I gonna do now? I had a plan. I used my plan. My plan worked, and I'm still fucked. Y'know, bands aren't designed to last. The natural cycle is that, anytime artists come together for a mutual purpose, whether it's a dance company, a theater group or a band, and they apply themselves, they will almost always achieve their stated goal. After that it has to change, it has to go some other way. The bands that didn't change and didn't go a different way, you can count on one hand. How many tens of thousands of bands have come and gone since the Rolling Stones came out. But there's still the Rolling Stones. The Who as well. That's about it. So the forces that were in play in the MC5 . . . we would have these group therapy sessions in a motel somewhere on the road. We'd all fishbowl out. After the first or second year, I said that I wouldn't participate in this anymore. Fred wanted to try to hold the band together, that was his business. But I said, "[Rob] ain't happy being in the band, I'm not happy with his performance in the band, him and I are having problems, let's just get a different singer." That was my attitude, in those days. Could it all have been repaired? That would have required power that none of us had—business power, psychological intervention power. None of us had the power to do that. Any time you add drugs and alcohol to the mix, it's almost a guaranteed recipe for disaster. I read an interview with David Crosby, and he said, "All those things we stood for in the 1960s—we were right on every one of them except for drugs." We fucked that one up. The rest of it—ending the war, peace is better than war, loving is better than hating, the civil rights movement, all the social justice issues—we were right about all that. I don't disagree with him.

The MC5's last ever show was, fittingly, at the reopened Grande Ballroom on New Year's Eve, 1972. That final show would feature all five members of the band, reunited by an eager promoter for one final fling at the venue where it all began, even though the old place had been standing empty for the past year. Michael Davis remembers an unpleasant evening: "It was nasty. After all the shit that had gone down and the band had failed and broken up . . . and then had gone on to become ridiculous caricatures in attempts to survive. It was really pitiful. Still, I was glad, because, in my mind, it brought some kind of closure to the whole deal."

Dennis Thompson: "Our swan song show at the Grande was sad, just real sad. No one showed up; the band had no juice; everything seemed fake and unreal. I think we all knew to a man that it was over. We just ran out of gas."

Michael Davis:

It sucked. We were bad. There was no spirit. We played the songs, but there wasn't a big crowd. I felt like we were ghosts up there . . . it was a really sad ending to what might have been. But there's no way to even know what might have been. It's ridiculous now that the MC5 are such a phenomenon. In some ways, I can't understand it, but in some ways I can. No one's ever done what we did, or even attempted. I've seen bands come along acting like the MC5, but they don't play like the MC5.

Wayne Kramer feels that, while not a great MC5 show, the evening could have been worse:

It wasn't any bigger disaster than many of the shows before that. Hell, no. You want to talk about disasters, there was the time in Belgium where our new manager Ronan O'Rahilly brought the president of Polygram Records in and had him ready to sign the MC5, and Rob Tyner . . . fell off the stage. That was a disaster. The show at the Grande was garden-variety. I've talked about it in magazines and newspapers, and so it's the one that everybody goes to. I've described it in pretty stark terms, from my emotional perspective. But no, it wasn't any bigger a disaster than a great many of the other MC5 shows. The MC5 was never consistent. We were mercurial, we would reach incredible highs, but was that show any worse than the night that I got so drunk that I missed the gig and they had to do the gig without me? That was a disaster. Or the night that Mike got so drunk that the guitar player from Brownsville Station offered to fill in for him. Or any number of nights when one of us screwed up or a few of us screwed up. We had disasters all the time. It wasn't any worse than any of the other ones. The story gets told a lot. I didn't need persuading to play because I needed the money. I remember being on stage, and all of the problems that the band ever had like the tempo problems, wrong notes—it was all in play. They kinda disconnect, when you're not really hitting on all cylinders, it ain't groovin' and you're just kinda goin' through the motions. All that was happening. But y'know, that wasn't any worse than any number of other nights. Who knew if it was really the final show? I know I left early, because I'd already been paid. I figured, what the fuck. This is embarrassing. I didn't know that we were gonna do that. Fred and I talked a lot on that European tour about what we would do when we got back. Who might be a good lead singer for the band? Were we gonna keep the band going or start a new band? Nothing was written in stone at that point.

Dennis Thompson doesn't remember the night fondly:

The final Grande show was a disappointment. I knew it would be, going into it. I think we all did—we knew there weren't going to be many people there. America had discarded us already—even our own town, because we weren't the flavor of the month anymore. The Grande was not in its heyday. They weren't even having shows there, so for us to put on a show there and have people come from scratch, it was like starting all over again. So we only had three hundred, maybe four hundred, people in the audience. Everybody was in a weird place, but we just did it because we thought we'd give it a try. Halfway through the set, Kramer realized that it was horse shit, that it wasn't working, and we'd already got paid so he walked up to Fred and he said, "Y'know, I think this is about enough." He played one more tune and hit the road. Fred agreed, we went our separate ways, and that was it.

"I was there at the Grande Ballroom for their horrid last show on New Year's Eve," recalls John Sinclair. "I felt sorry for them for having made such terrible choices in their lives and careers. I had spent twenty-nine months in prison and I was still better off than they were then. That was some sad shit."

Kramer offers his reasons why the band fell apart:

Well, you've got to remember the context of the day. [An Atlantic Records executive] looked at me one day and said, "You know what, Wayne? We have a concept here at Atlantic Records called sending good money after bad, and we're not going to do that with your band anymore." And he turned his back to me and wheeled around in a revolving chair and started talking to somebody in French as I stood there with my dick in my hand. So that told me that [the label] had decided that the MC5 doesn't need to exist anymore . . . We lost the support of the label at a time when everyone wanted to distance themselves from anything that was militantly political. Things were starting to calm down a little bit and they had new bands that just wanted to boogie. They had this new band from the South called the Allman Brothers, and all they wanted to do was boogie, man. So look at our situation again in the context of having lost the support of a label and having lost our manager and ultimately, lost the connection with each other. Rob Tyner said early on that separation was doom, and he was right. Because once we lost the spiritual connection, and once we lost the principles that were bigger than us as people, then we were no more than just another creepy rock band. And we were a creepy rock band with a big attitude and I, myself, had started to develop a pain-relieving campaign of serious drug and alcohol use, and that is the kiss of death for a band.

On hearing of the band's demise, the Grande's "Uncle" Russ Gibb says that he felt "sad and very old. They made the Grande, with 'Kick Out the Jams, Motherfucker.'" Leni Sinclair is proud of her involvement with the band:

I think what happened to that band is a great tragedy, but at least they were the best band in the world until they parted. That's how we looked at it. As far I was concerned, there was the Rolling Stones, the MC5, the Who, and then Bob Seger and Mitch Ryder. I wasn't that much into rock 'n' roll, in fact. If you look at what I took pictures of over the next twenty years, I drifted back into jazz and blues. I don't have pictures of Aerosmith or Led Zeppelin, or any of those big national rock bands. I didn't take pictures of because I was working on the light show. I was always working, and I just snapped a few pictures like of the MC5 at the recording sessions. I wish I had taken more pictures.

Stomper girl Debby Pietruska-Nathan is still at a loss as to why the band she followed to the bitter end didn't achieve a more recognized level of success:

I remember a transitional period where things were obviously not going right. I've always wondered why the bands from Detroit at the time, the MC5 particularly, didn't hit a more major level of success. There is a sadness attached to that, and I don't understand it because I *got* it. And I still do get it. Why somebody becomes famous and has a hit—the timing, the message, all the factors in whether or not that happens is so a mystery to me. Some of it is the politics of the time, it's what people are buying—it's a demographic equation. Maybe it was too specific, or too regional, possibly. It's something that I've thought about, but it's like one of those Buddhist questions—be in love with the question, because you ain't gonna get the answer. I don't know why they didn't get big. There's certainly superior musicianship than a lot of stuff you hear on the radio.

It occurs to me that not only [were] the record companies . . . operating in an increasingly conservative political climate, but also that American culture was becoming increasingly more celebretized, creating an exclusive culture that included pop culture. The whole ideology of the White Panther (later Rainbow People's Party) was antithetical to celebrity and exclusivity. It was based in socialism and communist ideas (communal love, sharing everything you have with others). The major record labels being based mostly in L.A. and, more specifically, Hollywood had already experienced the blacklisting of the McCarthy era, which was still resonating in the late 1960s and early 1970s.

"The 5 didn't end with an explosion, no cataclysmic event, no official press release announcement," says Gary Grimshaw.

If you weren't paying attention you would have missed it completely. All of my knowledge of the inner workings of the band came from Rob and Becky Tyner, my friends from long before the MC5 and long after, continuing up to this day. In our conversations in 1972, there was no grousing on their part about anyone. They just seemed disappointed in the way things turned out and would rather talk cheerfully about the future. If Rob had any bitter feelings (as I'm sure he did), he kept them to himself. I just figured he'd move on to new projects and perfect his role as father to his children, which is exactly what he did, so not to worry. I hadn't spoken to the other four members since 1968 and wouldn't again until the 1980s, so I had no idea what they were thinking in 1972.

Sadly, the five of them would never play on stage together again after the final Grande Ballroom show in 1972. And, as Leni Sinclair said, that's a great tragedy.

6
Hands Up If You're a Punk

T he MC5 may not have made a big dent on the billboard chart, but culturally they would make an impact that had far greater significance. Four bands are generally considered the major precursors to the music we now know as punk: Detroit's MC5 and the Stooges, and New York's Velvet Underground and the New York Dolls. Of course, this hugely simplifies matters. But there is little argument that these four bands had a massive influence on much of what was to come, for better and for worse. Though the four bands were very different from one another, they shared a raw edge that future punk bands would aim for. More recently, garage bands have deliberately tried to achieve the sound that MC5 reached by accident on *Back in the USA* (arguably, the White Stripes would not exist without the MC5's music). Everything they did, even all of the stuff that was reviled when they did it, would later be appreciated. Of course, by the time they got their plaudits, in many ways it was too late.

Michael Davis claims he knew little of the proto-punk bands that were happening in New York:

There's something about the atmosphere in Detroit. We knew about San Francisco, we knew about California, we knew about the whole psychedelic thing. There wasn't a lot going on in New York—New York was where you went to showcase your particular band. It was where you went to demonstrate to the media. It wasn't a place where rock bands were coming out of. To us, bands like the Velvet Underground were kinda carnivalish. They weren't real bands. There was this atmosphere in Detroit—and I think it's still there today—that Detroit is the center of the universe to its people. Detroit is the Mecca of real rock 'n' roll. Of course, this is poppycock, but that's what people really feel like—that Detroit is the center of it all. We thought that the Doors were mildly interesting, but we had a tremendous arrogance about us. That turned a lot of people off, but it also turned a lot of people on.

Wayne Kramer, who would eventually wind up releasing solo albums on punk label Epitaph Records, claims to have had little to do with the movement:

I wasn't particularly a Dolls fan. They were kinda raggedy to me. I like people that could really play, and I just didn't hear it. I didn't hear great songwriting, and I didn't hear great musicianship. I know that's a politically incorrect thing to say, and I know I piss off all my friends when I say this—Ron Asheton's still mad at me. But I don't hear it. I didn't come up in that era where it was OK to not play well. It's just not my approach to things. It doesn't mean that I'm any better than they are, or that they're wrong and I'm right. I'm not saying that. But my aesthetic, my sense of beauty in music, is not in punk. I'm not a punk. People tell me that I inspired the punks, but I'm not one.

In late 1974, former MC5 associate Danny Fields discovered a band in New York that had taken the 5's "leather street gang" image to the extreme. The Ramones were "brudders," and they were turning badass into both an art form and a uniform. Johnny Ramone: "We sent him [Fields] fliers all the time because we'd seen his name on MC5 and Stooges albums. We didn't know who he was or what he did, but we figured that if he liked *them,* then maybe he'd like us." "I borrowed money from my mother to buy them equipment," recalls Fields. "That was their condition of management: They needed a manager and money."

Like the MC5, the Ramones would achieve massive critical acclaim but would never be as commercially successful as they aspired to be. Like the MC5, they would suffer from infighting throughout their career. But unlike the MC5, the Ramones would soldier on for many years and make a succession of albums that varied in quality from average to excellent.

In 1975, Wayne Kramer was arrested, charged with conspiring to sell cocaine, and sentenced to four years in jail, though he would serve only two and a half. "While I was in jail, one of my pals bought me a subscription to *Billboard* magazine," he remembers. "I started reading about the Ramones—who all looked like Fred 'Sonic' Smith—and they were managed by Danny Fields. So all these articles kept saying that these kinds of bands were inspired by the MC5, and from where I sat, 'punk' did not have a good ring to it. So I was flushing the articles down the toilet, because in jail a punk is somebody that they knock down and make their girlfriend. You know, 'I'm gonna make you my punk'—and that kind of talk could get you killed, right?"

Over the next few years, bands and artists such as Patti Smith, Blondie, Talking Heads, Television, Richard Hell and the Voidoids, Wayne (later Jayne) County, the Dictators, and the Dead Boys would explode out of the same CBGB's New York scene as the Ramones had, and many would claim some affinity with the MC5. Members of many of these groups would cross paths with members of the MC5 in the future (including Patti Smith, Blondie's Clem Burke, and the Dictators' Handsome Dick Manitoba). Within the ranks of the Patti Smith Group was Lenny Kaye, the former *Rolling Stone* magazine journalist who, in 1972, had put out the *Nuggets* compilation, a double album of garage rock from the 1960s. It's difficult to believe that Kaye didn't incorporate a little Kramer and Sonic Smith into his playing, and the classic *Horses* album suggests Kaye had clearly been taking notes. Ironically, *Horses* opened with a version—a not entirely faithful version but a version nonetheless—of Van Morrison's "Gloria," the song that the MC5 had wanted to record as their first single before the Shadows Of Knight beat them to it.

Tom Verlaine's Television, and Blondie before them, featured a Fred Smith in their ranks, but this bass player had nothing to do with the 5's Sonic Smith. In the States, and in New York in particular, the arms of what was considered punk were spread a lot wider than they were in the UK, as both Blondie and Talking Heads would bear witness. The former, led by the incomparable Debbie Harry, shared their affection for girl groups like the Ronettes, the Shangri-Las, and any number of Motown artists with the MC5. The Talking Heads, too, were worlds apart from the simplistic fun of the Ramones, but Wayne Kramer and Rob Tyner would surely have admired their desire to push the boundaries as far as possible, while still remaining cool in the eyes of punk fans and critics alike.

Across the pond, something was brewing. Manager Malcolm McLaren may have been inspired to put the Sex Pistols together after a brief spell taking care of the New York Dolls, but original bassist Glenn Matlock says that their influences went further than that: "The MC5 were very influential in London. When we started the Pistols, apart from the English stuff, like the Faces, the MC5, Jonathan Richman, the New York Dolls and the Stooges were all we listened to. *Kick Out the Jams* was massive with us."

McLaren saw the MC5 live at the Rock 'n' roll Revival concert at Wembley Stadium, where he and Vivienne Westwood had gone to sell clothes to the teddy boys. As Jon Savage wrote in his excellent survey of English punk, *England's Dreaming*: "When a heavily made-up Little Richard made some comments about Black Power and then began disrobing in an extremely campy manner, the Teds booed viciously. The only new acts on the bill, Gary Glitter and the MC5, were hardly allowed the luxury of exhibiting any attitude at all" (50).

MC5 fans like Stomper Debby Pietruska-Nathan would find themselves attracted, if not completely drawn, to the burgeoning punk scene. "By then, I was in the theater. I was getting exposed to a whole new retro side of music to do with musical theater, although I wasn't terribly into that—I've only ever done one musical myself. But I liked what the punks were expressing. I liked the edginess of it. Certainly the Sex Pistols."

As Michael Davis recalls, "I actually read about the Sex Pistols while I was still in Lexington [prison] in *Rolling Stone*. I read about them being a phenomenon. I went, 'What the fuck is this?'"

Jon Savage would remark that "for all his posturing, McLaren was much closer to the post-hippie MC5 than he was to the dogged traditionalism of the Teds. At Wembley, the reality behind the revolutionary metaphor intruded with a jolt: far from being the proletarian vanguard, his customers were revealed to him in conversation as boring, repetitive and narrow-minded. The rock 'n' roll revival had been a useful polemic with which to crash through the detritus of hippie culture, but both Malcolm and Vivienne began to realize that it was itself even more ossified than the decadent King's Road culture they were trying to upset.

The Pistols would go on to become the faces of UK punk. Their name would forever be synonymous with controversy, and an X-rated interview with Bill Grundy would cause them to be hated nationwide. Within a couple of years, their second bass player, Sid Vicious, who had replaced the more clean-cut Glenn Matlock, would be dead from a heroin overdose. The legend of the Pistols would live on until their reunion in the mid-1990s, thanks to the success of one album, *Never Mind the Bollocks—Here's the Sex Pistols*. That was all the Pistols ever recorded—one studio album. Even the New York Dolls had managed to record two records, while both the MC5 and the Stooges recorded three, and the Velvet Underground recorded four.

If the Ramones adopted the MC5's gang image, in England, the Clash had taken note of the fact that music could be an effective means of conveying a message. Joe Strummer's band was the more political of the first generation of UK punks. As John Sinclair says, "I liked the Clash because they had something to say. I mean, look at the cover of their first album, with the Elvis thing. They were making a statement."

The Clash was the UK punk band that came closest to re-creating the MC5's powerful, political war cry. Aside from the fact that both bands enjoyed a hard chord and liked to push boundaries, they had little in common musically. Still, bandleader Joe Strummer would echo Kramer's career by later joining up with Epitaph Records, and the Clash's self-titled debut album, *London's Calling*, and *Give 'Em Enough Rope* are all considered classics.

It's generally accepted that the first-ever punk single was released by the Damned, and it was called "New Rose." The Damned was another UK first-wave punk band that would cite the MC5 as an influence. Says Wayne Kramer: "I thought the Damned were interesting. I really like them today. Captain Sensible's a ball. I adore him. I like the way that they still work."

Damned guitarist Brian James was equally as impressed by the MC5 and acknowledges the huge influence that they had on the formation of the Damned:

I'd heard the *Kick Out the Jams* album and I think I had a copy of *High Time*. I was playing at a sort of free festival that was organized by a friend of mine in Worthing [England], Ian Brunn, who organized Phun City with Mick Farren, where the MC5 played. They wiped me out. I really couldn't believe it. Dennis Thompson was, and still is, a great, great drummer. His snare playing was like a machine gun, like a *rat-a-tat-tat*. Live, it seemed like Wayne and Fred Smith with their guitars were mowing down the audience. All that sort of choreographed stuff that they do, it was just like, woah. It really was an attack band. They'd come on with all these strobes and stuff like that. The most rock 'n' roll band of the day, apart from my band Bastard, was the Pink Fairies. They were looning about—I think that was the time when Russ and Twink stripped off and were fucking about, pushing each other about. That was all kinda like English rock 'n' roll hippie madness, if you like. Out of the blue, this fucking [MC5] attack, and there's no other way to describe it, it was just unbelievable. The whole audience was like, "What the fuck is this?" They couldn't believe it. There were a lot of Hell's Angels there as security, because they'd always been associated with that sort of stuff—even they just stood there stunned.

So I heard the MC5 and they were right up my street. I was into rock 'n' roll bands like the Who, and people like Chuck Berry and Eddie Cochran. Plus the early R&B bands like the Stones, the Yardbirds and the Pretty Things. But the MC5 just put it all together. They stuck it all in this big pot, stirred it up and threw it at the wall. They stuck everything in. As a kid, I used to watch *Ready Steady Go!* on the TV: They'd have these black bands on like the Four Tops or the Temptations. They'd have these routines, and you kinda associated that with black artists—Tamla and the soul artists. But the MC5 were doing it. These were white guys beating the shit out of their guitars and ripping off Chuck Berry riffs at ten times the speed—as you can imagine, I was impressed big-time. Then I wanted to hunt out the other albums. The hardest one to find was *Back in the USA*. That was difficult to find in England for a long time. So when I met Rat [Scabies, Damned drummer], when London SS was auditioning, he'd heard one MC5 song, I think it was "Tonight," and he'd been impressed by that. The minute we starting rapporting, I thought, Wow, I've found my Keith Moon here. I wasn't even looking for a Keith Moon, but I've found a Dennis Thompson. He developed in the same way. I turned the other guys onto all their albums when we met Dave and then Captain. It was them and the Stooges that were the big influences for me and, therefore, the first Damned. Not so much the Dolls, although I found I had things in common with the Dolls, or with Johnny anyway. Johnny was very much a kindred spirit with his sound, as opposed to Wayne, who was a direct influence. Fred Smith too.

The other thing was, as a kid, one of the drummers that I was playing with, his parents were huge jazz fans. I'd be turned on to Coltrane, Monk and all these people, and amongst it, Sun Ra to a degree, but I never really liked Sun Ra. I thought it was weird for weird's sake. What was so cool was an electric rock 'n' roll band covering a jazz thing. It didn't matter who it was by, they just happened to pick the guy from another planet. Throw that in the soup too. No one was doing that. Then you found out later that they used to do a medley of James Brown songs. It's like, What the fuck? Where do they stop? It was a musician thing. Rob Tyner had a very distinctive voice, and he didn't look like the sort of white singers you used to see in England. He didn't look like Mick Jagger. He had this huge fucking Afro. It was like, You're not meant to look good, but you do. He didn't look sexy, but the way he sang, it didn't matter.

In Cleveland, writer-turned-front man David Thomas had formed a band called Rocket from the Tombs in 1974 with another writer, Peter Laughner. Thomas recalls discovering the MC5: "I was reviewing stuff. We'd go to shows, and he was reviewing things for other people, so that's how I ran into him. Peter was always really into the Velvets. I thought the Velvets did interesting music but I thought the rest of it was baloney. I tended to be more into the Zappa, Beefheart, MC5 sort of thing . . . the Stooges, but Peter was into the Stooges, too."

Another enduring icon who was influenced by the MC5, and who would have a lasting relationship with them is Lemmy, singer and bass player with English heavy rockers Motörhead. Formed in 1975 after Lemmy was fired from space rock band Hawkwind, Motörhead has always been unique in that the band attracted both punk and heavy metal fans. Lemmy: "I wanted it to be sort of like the MC5, since that was the big hero band of most of the underground, and throw in elements of Little Richard and Hawkwind."

It's little surprise that so many bands that came out of the UK and U.S. punk scenes worshipped at the altar of Kramer, Tyner, Davis, Smith, and Thompson. The MC5 had every fundamental component of a punk band. Controversial, often political lyrics? Check. Raw, garage-like production? Check. Internal fights and record company battles? Yup, that too. And we can add drug problems and later, tragically, band members' untimely deaths to that list too. Despite arguments from purists and the band members themselves, if the MC5 weren't punk, then nobody was.

7

New Lives, New Orders, New Races, New MC5

T he MC5 was no more. So, the five members had to find other ways to fill their time. First man out Michael Davis recalls that he had a ready-made career carved out for him, however:

I was a drug dealer, until they came and took me away in cuffs. I was even a drug dealer during the band, at the end. So I just kept on doing that. All I wanted to do was get high. Even during that time, I was a drug dealer but there were also some [musical] things I did with Fred. After the MC5 dissolved, Fred wanted to start his own band, and he approached me about being in it. He felt that I was a good singer. And I did too, but I didn't know anything about singing. I didn't know what it really took. I could do the "oohs" and "ahhs," and in the studio I could make harmonies—I did the whole falsetto harmony on "Poison" in one take—but I didn't know. I did it all by intuition. But I had no idea what it took to stand up and belt out destructive-type songs in front of an audience for three sets, and not be able to sing correctly. After *Back in the USA,* we hired a vocal coach to teach us how to breathe correctly so you don't destroy your vocal chords. We hired a drum instructor to teach Dennis . . . we hired an old black fellow to be my bass tutor. I took bass lessons. Here I am going to downtown Detroit, going to some old building and up some elevators to meet with a guy in a little room who's like forty years older than me and I've got records on major labels. This guy was teaching me major scales. I'm going, "What's this got to do with me?" We did all that to try to correct our problems. But anyway, I had no idea for a long time what it took to sing.

We put this band together that we called Ascension. Dennis was in it. I was not the bass player. We had this guy John Hefty from Detroit who I e-mail with every now and again. He lives in Denver. Anyway, he was the bass player. I was the singer, and with a Casio keyboard. I didn't know how to play keyboards either, but I had a little bit of something going on. We were playing "Getting Ready" by Smokey Robinson or the Impressions. We were doing Bob Dylan tunes and some Stones songs, some Motown, plus Fred had written some original songs. We had three sets of stuff, and [at this] Gala bowling alley. We did three nights, four sets a night. It was like being a bar band. We did the first night, and I was starting to really be hurting after that. We went back for the second night, and by the end of the first set, forget about it. I just couldn't sing. I'd ruined my voice. We knew we'd better not try that again. We still worked at putting together one set of ten or twelve songs. We had another couple of shows after that as Ascension. There's a tape floating around somewhere. It's awful though. It's awful because of my voice—it's terrible. It's flat and hoarse.

Dennis Thompson has his own memories of the short-lived Ascension project:

The tail end of the story is that about a month [after the final MC5 show at the Grande], Fred, myself, and Michael got together again. I was clean, Fred was clean, Michael was clean. We formed this band called Ascension. We rehearsed in my attic at about 110–115 degrees. A double-decker house with no air conditioning. That's how dedicated we were. We set the shit up in there and just got on. There was just boards—you had to be careful you didn't fall through the ceiling. We rehearsed up there and wrote five or six songs, and we put out a call to Wayne and Rob to ask if they wanted to come over and play. We didn't talk about putting the 5 back together, we just said come on over and play. Wayne declined and Rob declined. From my point of view, and Fred's and Michael's, we didn't wanna put the 5 back together, we just said, "Let's hang out together, and just jam," to see if there was a blend. We kept going for a little bit, got a bass player called John . . . an excellent bass player. Michael played rhythm guitar and sang. We played a few shows, but the whole scene had fallen apart. It was all about drugs. It was a really happening scene, and it just eroded. We went out and played, and the gigs were OK, with about three hundred people, but it wasn't enough to keep us going, so we broke up. That was the end of any affiliation among the MC5's members. The band had good tunes. "Summer Cannibals" was one tune that Fred used parts of for [Sonic's Rendezvous Band's] "City Slang." We gave it a good old effort, but it wasn't working.

Davis:

At some point, we decided to change the configuration. We got a guy named James Adam to play keyboards, he was the nephew of Jimmy Hoffa, the guy that they never found the components of his body. They put him through a grinder or something. So we changed the name to Sonic's Rendezvous Band. This was all Fred's trip. By now, Fred was really feeling his power and his potential as an artist. His guitar playing had really come along, and his songwriting really developed. We did at least one, maybe two, shows as Sonic's Rendezvous Band. [By then I had] already picked up two drug cases in the state of Michigan, then I got a third one, which was a federal charge. I got out of the two state cases, but with the federal charge, I was gone . . . when I did my plea bargain, I pleaded guilty to possession with intent. I got three years in a federal prison. That was 1975. I served just over one year. It was in Lexington, Kentucky, and it was an old navy hospital that was converted to a federal penitentiary. Medium security, so you could wear your own clothes. It was kind of a rehab place for drug-related federal criminals. There were mafia types, tax evasion types (although they were in a separate unit), bank robbery when supporting a heroin habit, and that's where Wayne wound up going. He wrote to me and told me that he had a federal case. I told him that if he had the same judge as me, tell him you did it because of your drug habit and that you want to clean up and get right, and they'll send you to Lexington, because it's cool here. It was co-ed—men and women. It was easy time. Sort of like being in high school in a way, on campus. But you couldn't leave.

I met a guy in there who was a pilot, a smuggler, and an actor. We hit it off right away—he had python-skin boots. We struck up a conversation, and we developed this plan to be artists and interior decorators of the jail. We invented a job. We proposed to the warden that we'd decorate the visiting room with animal sand paintings. They were done in acrylics, and they'd be really nice but we needed an office with a coffee machine, paints and brushes. The woodshop made our frames, and I stretched out my own canvas. We could go to work whenever we wanted to and knock off whenever we wanted to. We decorated the visiting room with beautiful paintings. I wonder if they're still there. I thought about going there and presenting myself to find out if my paintings are still up. It was a giant scheme to get out early.

I had gotten three years, but in the sentencing, I had gotten an A2 number, which meant that I was eligible for parole at any time, like the day after I got there . . . I went to the parole boards after eight or nine months. They denied me flat out . . . so I had my attorney put forward a motion to the judge that his orders for me to be eligible for parole were being ignored and denied. So he reduced my sentence to eighteen months, and I got out in thirteen because that was two-thirds of my time. I got clean in there, but that wasn't hard. The hardest part was the methadone clinic, because I had gotten on that. It took a while for me to get transferred all the way to Lexington. I had to go to Lyle, which is in Michigan, for holding for about two and a half weeks. There was a whole month where I didn't sleep very much because of methadone. Even though I detoxed in the clinic, when you go to zero, it tells a story. It was rough, getting off that. You can kick heroin in a few days, but methadone takes a long time because it's a pharmaceutical. It's a pure substance. The nature of it is more . . . it lingers.

Heroin is more like a bad cold for three-to-five days, then you're done. All of a sudden you wake up, and everything's cool, more or less. You've just got to keep it in your head that you don't do that anymore, unless you want to go through that again. The truth is, most people go ahead and do it again, saying, "It's only a few days, I'll get some meth." You have to really have a lot of time and space between the last day and when you really make the decision, Fuck that. It's like smoking. I just couldn't do it anymore. It wasn't a pleasure. I just walked away. I didn't have to put patches on my arm or see anybody. I didn't need to trick myself. One drag of a cigarette was enough to convince me. I didn't want it. It's the same thing with drinking. When I started treatment for Hep C, you can't drink. You negate the effect of the chemo. So for a year, I didn't drink anything . . . After I completed the treatment, it'd been a year, so what would I want to drink for? I might have a beer now and then, just once in a while.

[One time], a Japanese band stayed here for a few days on tour. They came to the house one night with a cooler with Pabst Blue Ribbon in it. I said, "Godammit, that's the first beer I ever drank." The first beer I ever got nailed on, sitting in a parked car with my buddies. We got a six-pack of cans of Pap's and got loaded. So I said, "Yeah, give me one." About halfway through, I started feeling the alcohol. It was sort of like I took a bad sleeping pill. I just thought, I don't dig this. But every once in a while, I'll taste a German beer or something. After a few sips, I start to feel it doing its thing. I start to feel sleepy. I lose my edge. I feel kinda lethargic and vulnerable. I can't even finish a whole beer. I have some wine with dinner, and that's cool because with food, you take a little wine and its part of the meal. It's not drinking to get fucked up. I haven't had any hard liquor or anything like that. It's like, "I don't fear this anymore." It can't take me over because, for one thing, I would never betray my wife Angela to go back to being how I used to be. Number two, now I realize that it's shit. It's fucking poison. You put something into you that takes everything away from you. It takes your strength away and makes you a puddle. I don't need that, not at my age. I don't need to be a sixty-three-year-old puddle. I need to be as strong as I can be. So I really have a resistance to it. In the holidays, I like to have a holiday drink but as soon as it doesn't feel right, I just put it down. I drink non-alcoholic beer. Becks NA is great. I like the taste of a beer—a good beer. It's the alcohol that I don't like. It took a long time to get there.

While Fred, Michael, and Dennis were putting together Ascension—the band that became Sonic's Rendezvous Band—Wayne Kramer had plans of his own:

Y'know, I'd been hanging out with some other musicians and I wanted to have some fun with music. I didn't want it to be so heavy. Everything in the MC5 had taken on this heaviness. We'd had to endure Fred's analyses in rehearsals, where Fred would have to break everything down for an hour or two hours, and I'd say, "That's all great, I appreciate it, but let's play." I wanted to play with other musicians. I wanted to play with people that had other influences, and I wanted to play with guys that played really well. Not that I'm being too hard on the players in the MC5—we all did the best we could—but I had a chance to work with a drummer that worked at Motown, who was just wonderful to play with. I wanted to play jazz, and I wanted to do other things. It was kinda liberating. I never really turned my back on the MC5 as if to say, I'll never do that, or, it never happened . . . I think it was a massive case of denial. I mean, I can't speak for anybody else, but in my case, I just denied what was actually happening in my life. It was too painful to bear. I lost my best friends, I lost my way to make money, I lost my status in my community, I lost my future since my whole future was tied up in those guys. I couldn't bear it, so I was looking for something to distract me. It was kind of a downward spiral.

Doing wrong was a way of getting attention, too. As a musician and as an untreated alcoholic and untreated drug addict, I'm driven by my ego. I need to have people around me telling me I'm cool. The group that I fell into were some bad people, and their measure of cool was different from the measure of cool in the rock 'n' roll world. Their measure of cool was harming people, of manipulating, of stealing, of lying. It was almost like a reverse world where bad became good. My ethics were flexible. It doesn't take long in that world to start building up damage, and building up trouble. If you do wrong enough, people will pay attention to you, but they'll be the police. At a certain point, judges will start paying attention to you. If you don't learn, at a certain point they have to do something to you. They had to do something to me, and ultimately they had to send me to prison. It's another un-unique aspect of my life. My life in that regard isn't any more unique than lots and lots of other people.

Kramer remembers his time behind bars following his arrest for drug offenses as slightly different from the "easy time" Davis recalled, despite being incarcerated in the same prison:

> You couldn't go home. If they didn't want you to eat, you weren't gonna eat. If they didn't want you to have a place to sleep, you didn't have a place to sleep. You lost your freedom. It was at the very end in the trajectory of public attitudes to corrections. It was at the very of the "rehabilitation" movement. Mike went home early. I stayed a lot longer than Mike did. I saw it go from the kind of place that Mike describes, with art, dayrooms, a piano, a TV—by the time I left, all the dayrooms were filled up with cubicles, and there were prisoners living in all the hallways. A drug war had exploded and the focus shifted from "rehabilitation" to "accountability." Now we're just talking about human warehouses. I went into a college dorm, but left a prison.

Difficult it may have been, but Kramer was able to continue playing music while in jail, as he told Nina Antonia, writing for *Record Collector,* in 1996:

> I read about [punk] at the time, but that music wasn't played on the radio in Lexington, Kentucky, and we certainly weren't playing it in our jailhouse bands. We played jazz and blues and funk. I had a regular band in jail, me and Red Rodney, the great jazz trumpeter. Red was an archetypal hipster dope-fiend jazz musician who got turned onto heroin by Charlie Parker. He took Miles Davis's place in the Charlie Parker quintet. Red was in his mid-fifties at that time, and unlike me, he was not a drug dealer—he was a musician who got caught up in a conspiracy. It was a great experience studying and working with him. In a lot of ways he turned into my musical father, my mentor and counselor. He died [in 1997] of cancer, but he did real well for the rest of his life.

After his release from prison, Michael Davis still had very difficult times ahead:

> I spent the U.S. Bicentennial as a guest of my government. Being in jail was a pain in the ass, but it was good for me because I got over my drug thing for a while, for about ten years. Then before I left Arizona, I started to use again. It was out of the blue, something came up, and before I knew it, I was a desperate fucker. Ten years later. Angela and I always have conversations about this, because somebody we know just OD'd in Detroit. This

person had put up a front that they were in recovery, that they were treating their Hep C, that they weren't using, that everything was cool. I told Angela, and she disagreed with me—I told her that if a person has the will to do it one time, the potential is always there for them to go back. It doesn't matter how long they've been away, the potential is still there. It's in the character. They may, at any time, change their mind. A person who never has done it, never will. It's technically still possible. If a person doesn't have it in their character to do it the first time, they won't. They have before, the potential's always there, in the mind. It's only my resolve that makes me who I am. Right here, I say, "No way, man." But what if I lost everything? What if there was a total disaster and I had nothing to look forward to, and I had twenty dollars in my hand? There's always that potential. But if I had never done that ever before, I would just go on.

While Kramer was incarcerated, a fairly hefty "Free Wayne Kramer" campaign began in the UK, the flames of which were fanned by writer Mick Farren. The "Free Wayne Kramer" pin badges were the fashion accessories of choice that year. Kramer admits today, however, that his guilt was never in question. "I was guilty as the day is long," he told Ian Fortnam of music365.com.

I went into such a downward spiral after the loss of my brothers, of my friends, of my job, and of my dreams and I discovered crime, and I thought crime was really fun. You know, I think I saw that movie *The Godfather* too many times, because all I wanted to do was dress in really flashy clothes, drive around in a big car, carry a pistol, eat dinner in nice restaurants, and talk about "taking care of business." And this was the strange, perverted fantasy I had, that I was some kind of hustler or something, and I got so deeply immersed in it finally that they did, in fact, lock me up for some of my less than honorable activities. It's what happens when you lose that spiritual connection to something greater than your self, because at that time there was nothing greater than me and my ego, and my troubles, and my worries, and my pain, and so I acted it all out. And I acted it all out in crime. And they have something for you when you do that; it's a game, it's a game of cops and robbers, and part of the game is that you get caught and you go to prison.

While Kramer was behind bars, Dennis Thompson was keeping himself busy. When Ascension came to an end, Thompson and former Stooge Ron Asheton formed themselves a New Order. Thompson:

Myself personally, around 1973, I had a Corvette 1967 that I bought . . . my dad helped me pay for it, and it was a muscle car. A 427 bhp race car. I sold that for $4000, and now it's worth $60,000, that car. I sold it for $4000, paid my dad off, took $1000 and went to California, because I was speaking to Ron Asheton on the phone. Ron said, "Come on out, I got a great thing going." I still wanted to play music, so I headed out to California with my $1000. I go out there, and he's with Jimmy Recca from the Stooges on bass and himself on guitar, and a manager named John, his friend, who was using money from a trust fund to support the band. He took the trust fund set aside for his education and paid the rent, bought the beer and the food. When I refer back to the New Order period, I have some great stories. I went out there and it wasn't what I thought it would be. I thought he had this project with a record label, I thought I was getting out there and plugging in. Something that was established. It turns out it wasn't established; he just had some gigs out there and was putting a band together. I had no place else to go and I liked Ron Asheton.

I used to hang out with the Stooges—I got tired of hanging out with the MC5 when they started to get really political, at the house in Ann Arbor. They started getting heavy into this political bullshit and I hated it, so I hung out at the Funhouse [the Stooges' house in Ann Arbor]. They were more fun. You go over there and it wasn't about politics, it was about life. Just jerking off, being young and having fun. I hung out with Ron and got to be friends with him. And Scott and Iggy too. Anyway, he didn't have much shaking, but he had a backer. We rehearsed every fucking day. Six hours a day in a rehearsal studio, and the Runaways would rehearse right next door to us . . . Jimmy Recca's bass playing is phenomenal, we're having a good time, we're rehearsing but we're poor. Really poor. That lasted for about two years—in 1975, I came back home. We found Dave Gilbert when he came to L.A. He was a good singer, but sort of a hippie. He was into folk music, but he had a phenomenal voice. Great, great pipes. We took him under our wing. He needed a place to stay so he stayed with us, and then he started singing with the band. Then we had another guitar player join us called Ray Gunn from Detroit. He had played in a band called Virgin Dawn and he was a good guitar player.

All of a sudden we had a working band. We were doing well, playing all the hot spots in L.A., like the Troubadour, the Whisky A-Go-Go—any place that was any place, we were playing 'em. We had a following good enough where the producer Neil Merryweather went in with us and we did four tunes. We had a deal with Arista on the table, and all we had to do to close the deal was play this show at the Starwood, where Arista's people would be. They sent their A&R people to the Starwood, where we used to kill 'em. We used to lay 'em flat. We were a good band—so fuckin' tight it was ridiculous . . . Anyway, Dave Gilbert was into THC/PCP—tetrahydrocannibinol. It's actually PCP, which is a large animal tranquillizer for zoos. That's what they sold on the street in L.A. Gilbert was fucking around with it. He showed up to that gig, he must have been nervous, high and with two whores—a black whore and a white whore—with black sunglasses like he was in the Blues Brothers. He came late, just made it. We put him on stage and here's our debut after two years of eating boot soup—we'd make a three-bean soup and it'd last us all week. We were flat fucking church-mouse poor. If we got beer on a Friday it was a big deal. Right next door to us where we lived on Sunset Strip, there was the Holiday Inn where all the bands would hang out when they came into town—the big bands like Led Zeppelin, the Who (I drank with both drummers). On the right side was a used sports car lot. I didn't have a dollar to my name.

Anyway, here's the finale. Dave shows up and he's so fucking high that he can't sing. He couldn't utter a word. He's vibrating. He came and stood next to the drums on my left and he's just shaking. I was like, "Get up there and fucking sing," because he sang eight out of the ten songs. He didn't even look at me, he was just vibrating. Nothing happened, so I threw a stick at Ron and gave him the finger-across-the-neck sign to cut it. We stopped the song and we had a tune that Jimmy Recca sang. I had a quick chat with Gilbert and tried to talk to him. I said, "What the fuck's the matter with you?" He couldn't talk. He was so fucked up he couldn't speak. After that song, we did another song that Dave sang, but he did the same fucking thing. Everyone realized we were in trouble. We were three or four songs into the set. Arista were sitting out there, and all we had to do to get a deal was do well that night. We told them we had an equipment failure.

We went backstage, and I took Gilbert's glasses off. I said, "What the fuck's the matter with you? You're fucked up on THC." Because we had been trying to get him off this stuff, take care of him, help him, and keep him away from these whores. The rest of us were sober. He couldn't answer, so I kicked his ass. When I was done, I hit him with a towel and then [another guy] who was bigger and stronger than me grabbed him and really started railing on him. We all had to pull him off . . . [then] who walks in while this was going on but Neil Merryweather and the guys from Arista. They walk in just as we're beating up our lead singer. That was the end of the New Order. There are a couple of bootlegs out there, and we have a complete CD that Ron Asheton put out called *The New Order*. They're really cool tunes. We never trademarked the name, so it was public domain when the Manchester band used it.

God bless him, Dave Gilbert died [in 2001]. Another time, he passed out with his guitar on his chest. So me and Jimmy snuck up on him, dropped two cherry bombs inside the hole in the guitar, and got a bucket of water propped up on a stick, so when the bombs went off he would move and the water would douse him. So we went and hid and the bombs went off—BOOM, BOOM—the guitar shattered and exploded (it was more than we expected), then the water dropped and he was sopping wet. He gets up and says, "*Goddammit.*" Gets up and pisses on the lamp, fries the lamp. That's the kind of shit we used to do in the New Order. We had a lot of fun.

Dennis Thompson remembers having a lot of fun during his time with the New Order:

Me and Jimmy Recca were the practical jokers. We bought a bag of catnip. Ron was a late-nighter, and he came in at about 8:00 p.m., and me and Jimmy told him that we'd scored and started smoking a joint. Ron smoked this thing for about five minutes saying, "This is good shit," before we told him that it was catnip.

One time, Arthur Kane from the New York Dolls came around. He was a real hard core alcoholic. Jimmy Recca and I went into the kitchen and made him a drink of every whisky bottle, every bit of leftover beer we had, Tabasco sauce, steak sauce, ketchup, mustard, salt, pepper—anything we could find. He drank it down and said it was "fucking great, man." Another time, Ron was pissing me and Jimmy off in rehearsal so we found an old boot in the alley and put it in the soup, and let Ron and John eat it. We said we weren't hungry that night.

For Rob Tyner—a dedicated family man—jail time was neither an option not a likely possibility after the demise of the MC5. He gigged around the Detroit area as the Rob Tyner Band, and after a trip to Europe, released a single with pub rock band Eddie and the Hot Rods in 1978 called "Till the Night Is Gone (Let's Rock)." Keen to pursue his political interests, Tyner also became involved with Scott Morgan's Guitar Army project, aimed at helping the nation's Vietnam Veterans.

With the New Order no more, Thompson had to find new means of employment:

I was aware of Fred's Rendezvous Band. In 1975 I came back to Detroit. I'm pissed off, but I'm not pissed off enough to quit music. I need to get a job. I've lost my car and all I own in my life is a set of drums. What I did is, the Motor City Bad Boys with the legendary Sirius Trixon were sort of a cool band. They were like a prop band and they used to play New York all the time. They looked good [and] Sirius Trixon had a good schtick . . . so I joined the Motor City Bad Boys and we mostly played in New York; we played in Max's Kansas City, and we attracted huge crowds and we did play well. We almost got a deal— Tommy Dean from Max's Kansas City almost got us a record contract but the record people said that if we fired the singer and got a new one, "we'll consider signing you" . . . We had a Cadillac onstage, a 1957 pink Cadillac. The front end of the Cadillac was built around the drum riser. We had one guy who was a greaser, Jim Jam, who would lean up against the car and smoke a cigarette for the whole set. It was really cool, but there was no record deal.

Motor City Bad Boy Sirius Trixon remembers the Tommy Dean contract debacle:

Tommy Dean, the owner of Max's Kansas City, tried hooking us (Sirius Trixon and the Motor City Bad Boys) up with a big name record producer/record label big shot. We had a meeting, and during the meeting, Mr. Big Shot pulled out a vial of cocaine, and me being the anti-booze/anti-drug person that I am, told him off and to take his drugs and record contract and stick it where the sun don't shine, and I immediately stormed out of the office. Mr. Big Shot was still very much interested in the band, but only if they would break all ties with me. There is no Sirius Trixon, there is no Motor City Bad Boys, simple as that. At the time, we had other offers coming from all directions.

Thompson:

At the same time, Fred had the Rendezvous Band. They were playing here in Ann Arbor a lot, they were playing at the Second Chance in Detroit. Wayne was playing in his band.

So all of us are out there playing in different units, but we're not communicating. I'd go and see Fred play, but he's now hanging out with Patti Smith . . . Fred became incommunicado with all of us. We used to call them the Smith brothers, because she looked like him. Me and Ron used to call them that. When we got back to Detroit with the New Order, we'd play the Second Chance, and so did Fred. The Second Chance was the one club in Detroit that made sense around that time, like the 100 Club in London. It was a cool club. So we're crossing paths. When the Bad Boys broke up, I went with a band called the

Secrets, with Bob Flat and Charlie Bell. It was a trio, and we styled after the Police and the Who. It was a great band, we sounded great, and every place we played, people loved us.

That was going well, and I got a call from Deniz Tek in Australia to do the New Race thing. Ron called me and asked if I wanted to do a tour with him, Deniz Tek, and Warwick Gilbert from Radio Birdman. It was only six weeks. So I left the Secrets but told them I'd be back in six weeks. I went and did that tour, and it was a successful tour. We had a good time. We played every venue of the B circuit. We rehearsed for a week solid, ten hours per day. I came back and played one show with the Secrets, and we were treated like third class citizens. The other band had the dressing room and we used the kitchen as a dressing room. I'd just come off this tour where I was treated with respect . . . the drummer of the MC5 is in the kitchen, changing his clothes. After that, I quit. It sucked. They [people in Detroit] had no respect for me, the MC5, or their history. These were disco days, the early 1980s. Detroit follows the scene. So I quit the Secrets, and that began my drop. That's when I stopped playing. This is 1982. By now, Ron and Michael had moved to form the Monsters band. This is after the New Race. Ron kept moving in his direction. Ron, Niagara, and Mike stayed together for a long time—six years or something like that. At that point, I'd been beaten up enough. I'd been trying and trying and trying, sacrificing, spending all my money, avoiding the day job, and making it work any way I could, and it wasn't working. The one tour, which was called "The New Race: The First and the Last," was great. But when you go out and play and it's great, and then you come back and get treated like shit—I couldn't take it anymore. I was heartbroken. So I quit. I played with my brother in a few nostalgia rock bands in bars, for money at the weekend, but that was it.

When Wayne Kramer came out of prison in 1978, he started gigging around the Detroit area, and it was at this point that his already unstable life was disrupted further by a living Doll. As he remembers, "I started a band in Detroit and I worked around the Detroit area. I went out and did a few trips. And I started a band with Johnny Thunders."

By that year, Johnny Thunders was already a legend within the punk and rock 'n' roll communities. As a member of the New York Dolls, Thunders had developed a style of loose guitar playing, based on the style of his hero, Keith Richards, that hundreds of future players would imitate to this day. The Dolls' self-titled debut album and their follow-up, *Too Much Too Soon*, are both inarguably classics that stand up alongside the three MC5 albums, the three Stooges albums, and the four Velvet Underground albums as the precursors to the punk movement. When original drummer Billy Murcia tragically died in England, the band's momentum was all but killed. Jerry Nolan took his place, completing the lineup with Thunders, front man David Johansen, guitarist Sylvain Sylvain, and bass player Arthur Kane, but the band never really regained their footing. Future Sex Pistols maestro Malcolm McLaren tried to help them out of the rut by dressing them up in red PVC and having them perform in front of a flag bearing the hammer and sickle. However, there was no coming back, and before long the band was no more. Thunders wasted little time in setting up his new band, the Heartbreakers, carrying Jerry Nolan over from the Dolls. Former Television bassist and punk style-guru Richard Hell was also recruited, as was Walter Lure. When Hell went on to form the Voidoids, Billy Rath was brought in on four-string duties to complete the lineup. The Heartbreakers' *LAMF*, recorded in 1977, was another classic album under Thunders's belt, and though his 1978 solo album *So Alone* was unreleased in the States for many years (something that would remain a bone of contention for some time with Thunders' adoring fans), it also features some wonderful moments (not least "You Can't Put Your Arms Around a Memory," with guitar and backing vocals provided by the Only Ones' front man and Thunders devotee Peter Perrett).

With Thunders battling to get his record released, and with Kramer determined to enjoy his freedom, the two somehow found the time to put a band together. "He'd been a fan of the MC5 and come to all our gigs," Kramer told Ian Fortnam. "When we would play on the East Coast, he'd show up and he'd be in the front row, and after I got out of the penitentiary he invited me down to a show he was doing in Detroit. I was real reluctant in the beginning because he was dope-fiending and I'd just gone through all of that. I'd just come out of the penitentiary and didn't want to go back. So I tried real hard, but—of course—to no avail, to stay out of bad behavior again."

The two had first played together when Kramer joined the Heartbreakers onstage at Detroit's Bookie's Club. Of that experience, a clearly elated Thunders said, "I had always wanted to meet Wayne Kramer: he's one of my teenage idols. He jammed with us on 'Do You Love Me,' and we got to be friends after that."

In many ways, the career of the New York Dolls echoed that of the MC5. Both were so far ahead of their time that they wouldn't gain the recognition they deserved until long after they had broken up. Drugs would seriously affect the ability of both bands to work up to their potential both onstage and in the studio. Both bands would have members pass away long before their time, with unresolved issues still sizzling away. And later on, both bands would be involved in a snobbishly maligned reunion. The teaming up of Thunders and Kramer seemed perfectly natural, though it was anything but.

Kramer:

> He was a nightmare to work with. Always, working with people who are using drug addicts is a nightmare. It ain't so much about Johnny as it is about me, because I knew in my conscious mind that this would never work. We will never be able to accomplish anything. We will not be able to make records and tour. As a drug addict myself, I know the script. It's ultimately predictable. But below my conscious mind is my character. I only know this now, in retrospect, with some clarity. There was something in it for me. I could get in a band with Johnny Thunders, and maybe the combination of both of our charismas would converge into the ability to make records and tour. I believed in my own omnipotence, that somehow I could fix it. That was what was wrong with me—I thought I had more power than I did. I was grandiose. Of course, it didn't work. It can't. It never will. On paper, it was a good idea, but it would be unnatural for it to work.
>
> It's just the way that heroin addiction works, you can't do anything until you cop. And somehow, in my naïveté, I thought that with my ego, I could fix it. I can fix this, I can handle it, you know, and of course, I can't fix anyone but Wayne. And I can hardly even fix Wayne by myself.

As mentioned earlier, Kramer was a fan of neither the New York Dolls nor punk in general. But he knows exactly what drove him to want to work with Thunders: "Ego, grandiosity. I'd just come out of the penitentiary and my feeling was that I didn't exist. I wasn't on the radar. Maybe this would help me get my name back in the papers. These things used to be important to me. I used to think that that was my life. I used to think that what I did was who I am. I don't believe that today."

The band was christened Gang War and the lineup was completed by bass player Ron Cooke (formerly of Mitch Ryder's Detroit and an embryonic Sonic's Rendezvous Band) and drummer John Morgan (brother of the Rationals' Scott Morgan), both respected working musicians in Detroit. A 1979 bootleg of the band's first demo features Philippe Marcade on drums, however, and Cooke was eventually replaced by Bobby Thomas, so it's clear that Kramer and Thunders were the spine of the lineup.

Talking to writer Ken Shimamoto in 2000, Gang War bassist Ron Cooke recalled:

> My relationship with the MC5 and Fred and those guys goes back a long time in Detroit, I mean from when we were like fifteen years old. When the MC5 weren't even the MC5, when they were hanging out in Allen Park, Michigan. I kinda went in and out of that scene with those guys for our entire musical lives, our entire lives, really. I mean we grew up basically down on the lower southwest side of Detroit, in the suburbs, playing gigs and being in battles of the bands and all kinds of nuts things like back in 1963 and shit. In Detroit, to a certain extent, it wasn't that it was cliquish, but there was a group of guys that kind of gravitated together.

By 1980, Cooke had fallen in with Kramer's new project:

> I was in the original Gang War [thing] with me, Wayne Kramer, and Johnny Thunders and a lot of crazy things that went down musically. [Gang War] was an endeavor to really try to produce some music and go out and do it. It was a short-lived thing, as far as my being in the group. I think we did that for like a year and a half. We called a bar up down in Ann Arbor and said, "We wanna play in your bar," and the guy goes, "Well, I'm not gonna pay you nothin'." I said, "You don't have to pay us anything." It was a guy I knew who owned this bar and Christ, they were lined up on the street trying to get in to see us, y'know. We did some pretty good jams in that group. Once again, some of the better stuff was live [rather] than the recorded stuff. Some of the recordings are kinda contrived, as far as I'm concerned. Some of the live stuff really was a little bit better.

Thunders relocated to Detroit with his wife Julie and their three children, Johnny Jr., Vito, and Dino, and Cooke recalls the temperamental guitarist enjoying his time in Ann Arbor. "We brought Johnny out here," he told www.i94bar.com.

> The best story about [him] in Ann Arbor is we had him out in the country in a farm situation and he says, "You gotta take me down to Ann Arbor, Ron, man. I gotta see some CE- MENT." Johnny Thunders in Ann Arbor was wild. We got him hooked up in this beautiful old

1958 Buick thing he had, this car. Oh, man, he was wild. I've got pictures of him with my daughter sitting in his lap in my living room. The guy hung out with us . . . the last time I saw Johnny was here in Ann Arbor at a gig, I think about a year and a half or two years before he died.

Perhaps understandably, when considering the social climate of the time, Mrs. Thunders found Detroit a less than savory place for herself and her kids, so she took off with them. Thunders stayed on, determined to make this project with his childhood hero work out, but during subsequent Gang War sets he would launch into tirade after tirade of misogynistic rhetoric. Johnny was hurting, and he knew of only one way to dull the pain.

Gang War drummer Marcade recalls Thunders asking him to join the band:

Johnny Thunders called me up and said, "Hey, man, I'm starting a group with Wayne Kramer! WHOA, this is gonna be great. Yeah, we're gonna be called Gang War. You wanna come and play the drums?" I said, "Yeah, great. I'll come right away. Where are you?" He said, "Ann Arbor." "So how the fuck am I gonna get to Ann Arbor?" "We have a manager guy and all that, and we got you a plane ticket. We'll come pick you up at the airport." So I got on the plane. But the only cheap place the manager could find for us to record was a little studio that was under some guy's house where they did jingles, not rock 'n' roll. So we show up and the owner of the studio sees this bunch of fuckers come out of the car. You know, Johnny in a ripped T-shirt, all fucked up, and the owner asked to see everybody's ID. Johnny said, "Fuck this crap, man, let's go somewhere else." The manager said, "Cool, cool it." So the manager starts negotiating with the owner of the studio. The manager was saying, "Are you crazy? This is Johnny Thunders, from the New York Dolls." The owner said, "No it's not, and don't try to lie to me, because my son, who is upstairs, is a very big fan of the New York Dolls, so if you're trying to pull some number on me, I'm gonna know right now." So he tells his son to come down, a big fat kid in his shorts, who comes down, looks around, and then says, "It is, that's Johnny Thunders!" So they got their mom, they got the Instamatic camera out, and they're all posing, and Johnny's all fucked up. [*laughs*] Then we went into the studio and Johnny was flat as hell. The owner of the studio, this guy smoking a pipe, dressed in his suit, was looking at Johnny singing, going, "But he can't sing!" I said, "Oh, it's great, it's fine." But the guy said, "He just can't sing." Then he kept asking me why Johnny kept making trips to the bathroom. I said, "He drinks a lot of water." Then, at the end of the session, the owner came up to me—I could see he was feeling bad about something—and he had a clean T-shirt in his hand. He said to me, "I feel really bad inside because my son's with a big star, but Johnny must be so poor, he's got that T-shirt, it's old and ripped, there's holes in it. Give him that so he can at least have a clean T-shirt to wear.

Mick Farren remembers the mess that was Gang War: "Gang War was a good band for about ten minutes. When I heard Wayne and Johnny were getting together, I thought, This is gonna be good until heroin takes over. And within hours, Johnny was back in the bag . . . and it all went to hell in a basket." As Kramer told the *New York Rocker* in 1980, "Johnny's got one foot in the gutter and the other poised to step on a banana peel."

Still, in their short time together, Gang War assembled a set of songs that would keep them gigging for approximately a year. Though heavily weighted toward Thunders songs, Kramer contributed the MC5's "Ramblin' Rose," plus "Hey Thanks" and "I Still Hate" (co-written with Mick Farren). Thunders compositions include "There's a Little Bit of Whore in Every Girl," "Alone in a Crowd" and "M.I.A.," plus the delicately titled "Just Because I'm White (Why Do You Treat Me Like a Nigger)." The set was the filled out with covers, including the Rolling Stones' "I'd Much Rather Be with the Boys" and Jimmy Cliff's "The Harder They Come."

The band's plan, reported the *New York Rocker*, was to put together an album's worth of material and then auction it off to the highest-bidding label. Sadly, Gang War were destined to remain the sole property of bootleggers until Skydog Records put out a live album, recorded in Toronto and Boston, in 1992. The album was re-released by Jungle Records in 2004. There were plans to record an album, however, and another New York Doll, Sylvain Sylvain, was suggested as producer, but he told the *New York Rocker* in 1980, "I'd like to know what kinda budget he has, first. I mean, I can work pretty cheap, but I don't know if I can work on his budget."

In the film *Born to Lose*, Kramer remembered,

We were playing a show somewhere in Michigan . . . and the show was tremendous, and we used to do this version of "My Sharona," which we changed to "Ayatollah." Johnny would get in this pretend political rant like he actually understood what was going on in world politics or something.

> We were using the club's office as a dressing room, and Johnny was in the drawers stealing the club's money. I said, "Let's get the fuck out of here right now." We packed up all our shit. He gave my girlfriend a stack of bills and she said, "What do I do with the money?" I said, "Get rid of it," so we stashed it behind the toilet. The police were called.

The *New York Rocker* reviewed one of the band's gigs at the Heat club in New York, in February 1980, saying that "while critics carped, the crowd gave Gang War one of those obligatory 'It's 3:00 AM, and we paid six dollars' ovations. The band returned for an encore of (get this) "My Sharona"/"Ayatollah" (Johnny ranting unintelligibly about Iran, hostages, and marines), followed by Chuck Berry's "Around and Around." Suddenly, Iggy Pop leaned out of the audience to sing and dance along, and the place went wild in a way that Gang War alone could never have inspired."

It makes sense that Iggy Pop would whip Gang War's crowd into a frenzy; as legendary as Kramer and Thunders are and were, neither of them could ever be perceived as natural front men. Great guitarists, yes, but not front men. Iggy Pop, on the other hand, is not only the perfect punk front man, he was already a hero to many Thunders and Kramer fans.

Gang War would tour through Canada and New England, and somewhere along the way, they talked Billy Rath into joining them. It was when they returned to New York, however, that things took another turn for the worse, as Thunders told *Zig-Zag* magazine. "We did two shows over two nights and Wayne Kramer didn't play . . . so it ended up with me and Peter Perrett . . . David and Sylvain came up and helped me . . ."

With the damage irreversible, Gang War never played together again. "The reason why we stopped playing together was Tommy Dean from Max's had booked Gang War," he told Nina Antonia in her book *Johnny Thunders . . . In Cold Blood*. "The way that Johnny and I worked the band was as partners. As Johnny's habit got more and more out of control, he phoned me and said, 'Look, Tommy Dean doesn't want it to be Gang War, he wants it to be Johnny Thunders, but if you come and play, I'll give you $100.' Of course, I said, 'I'm not going to come over there and play for $100. I'd stay at home and watch television for $100.' Every time we'd try to set something up, he'd fuck it up" (110).

Still, Ron Cooke told Ken Shimamoto that the band managed to have a few good times: "We had a lot of good gigs, we did the New York thing, Boston, Toronto—we

had a great turnout for like three or four nights at a big cabaret in Toronto. Rockin'
right along. Some people like it, some people don't, I guess. It was *knock down rock 'n'*
roll all the fuckin' way. Just drinkin', partyin', goin' one step in front of the fuckin'
law at all times. One step ahead of 'em, boy. We ran the moves. It was cool!"

Unfortunately, music wasn't the only thing on Thunders' mind. Despite Kramer's
best efforts, Thunders was determined to live up to the rock 'n' roll mythology.
Kramer remembers trying in vain to work with Thunders:

> I used to tell Johnny that that's an image. You can talk about it, you can perform it, but
> you don't have to live that way. You can live like a human being and have values and
> principles in your life. You don't have to perform as one. There'd be nights when we'd be
> on the road, and I knew he didn't cop any drugs that day because I was with him all day in
> the van. He'd knock shit over, untune his guitar, and yet he'd be completely sober that day.
> He was a brilliant showman. Very charismatic. He just had that disease, and it had a
> powerful hold on him. He didn't live long enough to get out it. That's the trap of the dis-
> ease—do you find the key to the door before they lock the door? You can't live for tomor-
> row. There is no tomorrow. There's only right now.

In retrospect, it seems obvious that the partnership of Kramer and Thunders
wasn't going to work; the Detroiter was emerging from his drug hell, while Thunders
was plunging headfirst into one of his own. At a time when Kramer needed stability
and an ego boost, he had actually hooked up with someone who provided the exact
opposite. Any hopes that Kramer had of straightening Thunders out were, by his own
admission, frighteningly naïve. However, there were two great tragedies that came
out of the whole Gang War experience:(a) they were unable to pull themselves together for long enough to record some decent output and (b) Kramer and Thunders
didn't part on particularly good terms. At a solo show in Ann Arbor soon after the
demise of Gang War, Thunders made fun of Kramer's conviction. The catty comments from both sides only went to prove that Gang War was never meant to be, and
the band quickly fizzled into a footnote on both musicians' careers. A quote from
Kramer on the Jungle release of the live Gang War album attempts to sum things up:
"Music is important to me and I value the honor, the opportunity, to be an important
musician. Johnny, on the other hand, didn't consider himself a musician. He considered himself an entertainer."

As he had always done when he had been knocked down, Kramer simply got back up and dusted himself off:

> Gang War wasn't the only thing I was doing. I've always produced bands, I've always written songs with other artists, and I've always been a session musician. So I carried on those activities, working with bands on the Lower East Side in Manhattan. Doing sessions in New York. I kept my own band together, working in the East Coast area, working those clubs up and down the East Coast. Then I joined Was (Not Was). That was a very exciting undertaking. I really enjoyed my time working with Don, Dave, and all these great musicians. The writing was first-rate; David Was is like a national treasure. I really believe he's one of the premier lyricists in America today, even the world. The people in the band were just superb musicians, and we'd rock the house. That was good fun. I'm still in that band. It's not really like a band, it's more of an informal association, a brain trust.
>
> I just played on the new album, so I'm still in Was (Not Was). I've toured all over America with them. I played on the very first record. Don and Dave's idea was to take different influences and try to kind of mesh up. Take the avant-garde jazz thing that they're big fans of and combine that with heavy beats. We're talking about 1979 to 1981, so beat music was really starting to evolve. Disco hadn't quite arrived yet, but there were dance clubs building up, mostly in the gay communities. twelve-inch singles were the rage, so we made a twelve-inch single of a heavy dance beat called "Wheel Me Out." It was a hit, and like I was saying about the Rolling Stones, when a band has a hit out of the box, it makes it a lot easier to carry on. None of these things were full-time jobs. The life of a musician is not a nine-to-five job, forty hours per week. It's an unorthodox lifestyle. That can be very good and it can also be very bad.

While it might not have been a full-time job, Was (Not Was) and the hit "Wheel Me Out" single provided Kramer with exactly the sort of boost he needed after the Gang War debacle. Formed in 1979 by the core duo of David Weiss (David Was) and Don Fagenson (Don Was) in Detroit, the eclectic self-titled debut album was released in 1979 to critical acclaim. Poetry, political diatribe, jazz, rock—the record featured it all. Little wonder then that Kramer was eager to join. Filling out the lineup on the first album were vocalists Harry Bowens and "Sweet Pea" Atkinson, as well as the Knack singer Doug Feiger, who popped up as a guest. On 1983's follow up, *Born to Laugh at Tornadoes,* Ozzy Osbourne can be heard rapping (strange but true), and

Detroit legend Mitch Ryder tries his hand at techno-rockabilly. Though the work was and remains infrequent for Kramer, Was (Not Was) certainly provides him with an outlet for some of the more abstract musical ideals he holds dear. And with that band, life is certainly never dull.

In 1976, Rob Tyner would take action that would anger his former MC5 bandmates, putting together a new band and naming it the MC5. Some promoters would sportingly bill them as the New MC5 to avoid confusion, but usually, they were simply billed as the MC5. Wayne Kramer wasn't happy: "I think he missed the band once it broke up. He started a new band called the MC5! . . . I wrote him . . . demanding that he stop using the name MC5. It was a very rough time."

The guitarist in the New MC5 (as we shall refer to them here for simplicity's sake) was Robert Gillespie. Gillespie met Tyner in '76 at the Red Carpet Club in Detroit. Following a lengthy jam, the pair decided that they should work together, so they set out to recruit a band. Drummer Ralph Serafino was next into the fold. Greg Arama (of the Amboy Dukes, now sadly deceased) was quickly replaced by Michael Marshall, and Bill Alexander completed the lineup (toward the end of the band's existence, bassist Marshall was replaced by Charlie Bell). Both Gillespie and Serafino maintain that the band were only ever called the MC5, though Gillespie has the feeling that Tyner really only called the band that to get back at Kramer and Smith for playing in Europe as the MC5 with three hired hands. Interestingly enough, at the same time, Kramer was playing around Detroit in a band called Kramer's Creamers. However, when that same band went out of Detroit, they'd play as the MC5.

Ludicrously, it's feasible that two versions of the MC5 could be playing in two different cities on the same night.

However, Gillespie is totally happy with the shows that this lineup of the band produced night after night, for eighteen months at least: "We were managed by Brass Ring. They did all these shows locally and in the tri state area, and we did all their shows with national acts in arenas. It was huge, and it was wonderful. We played with AC/DC, Alice Cooper, Blue Oyster Cult, the Cars, Cheap Trick, Pat Travers, and more. It was fun, man. I was playing with a rock star. It was awesome. Then we recorded some demos for Atlantic in New York City. This was around the summer of '78. They passed on it. I don't know why. At the time, the punk movement was happening and they might have thought that we were too heavy rock. I don't know. Atlantic put out the second and third original MC5 records, and I think the MC5 owed them money. There had been problems with drugs and stuff. Whatever the reason, they passed on us."

Serafino remembers Tyner being excited to be out with *any* MC5 again: "I had just got to know him them but he seemed really pumped about the band and excited about doing this thing. We became really good friends over the first couple of years. I didn't know him beforehand, so I don't know what he was like beforehand, but he took us under his wing. I was really young. I was nineteen when I joined that band."

Perhaps it was due to his tender years, but Serafino never considered the idea that he was filling Dennis Thompson's drum stool:

> We just did what we did. It was mostly new music. The only thing that had anything to do with him was that we were playing some of the old stuff. At that time, while we were playing those old songs, I thought about it. I wanted to keep it as close to the way he played it as possible because it was great the way it was and shouldn't be changed. I saw him at a couple of clubs and he used to call me Junior, and not in a nice way. I understood, you know. There was never a conflict between us. We weren't exactly friendly, but it wasn't mean either. I understood why he wasn't happy about all that. He didn't mean anything personal toward me.

Gillespie remembers one show when Ron Asheton of the Stooges turned up and began yelling at Rob Tyner during the set. Asheton was shouting, "What are you doing? This isn't the MC5!." Tyner responded with, "I ain't got no Corvette, I ain't got no Jaguar," in reference to the flashy automobiles purchased by his former colleagues.

Gillespie soon grew tired of the bickering:

> I remember early '78, Iggy was touring and David Bowie was playing piano with him. We were offered the show, but Rob wouldn't open for Iggy. That hurt me because I knew it would be sold out and great, but that was Rob's hard headedness.
>
> A lot of people had no idea that it was a new band, probably. They heard Rob singing and he was the voice of the MC5. It was tough, but my gut feeling was that I had to move on. I started playing with Johnny Angelos and the Torpedos, and I took Ralph with me. Rob was really angry with me and he wouldn't talk to me. He was really pissed and he held a grudge all the way to his grave. I was hurt that he was so hardheaded. It was over with. We had this thing that only went so far and it was over. There was this small clique here in

town that would say, "Huh, MC1." Of course, I always heard that and I didn't like it. That may have been half of it too. Mainly, I just wanted to get something rolling with a new band because I felt like we were defeated. We could open shows as MC5, big shows, but I wanted to make a record. Get my songs out there. It wasn't happening for us. That's when Rob went to London and made that record with Eddie and the Hot Rods.

The band consisting of Tyner, Gillespie, and Serafino should probably never have been christened the MC5, but the fact remains that they were. You can't change history. Gillespie and Serafino have saved ticket stubs and flyers from 1978, hard proof that in that year a band called the MC5 played shows with the Blue Oyster Cult, Alice Cooper, and others. Gillespie has a copy of *Creem* magazine from July 1978 that announces the MC5's reunion and their debut live appearance at the Red Carpet with the Rockets. More importantly, the songs that Tyner and Gillespie wrote together, songs that to this day remain in demo form, unreleased and unheard, are actually damned fine. (The New MC5 song "Taboo," written by Tyner and Gillespie, has been re-recorded by Gillespie's current band Powertrane, featuring Rationals man Scott Morgan on vocals, on their *Beyond the Sound* album. It's well worth picking up, and not just because of that song).

It was some time before Rob Tyner finally got around to recording his first solo record, but in 1990 he finally released *Blood Brothers*. Despite suffering from a less-than-perfect production job from then-guitarist Joey Gaydos, there are still some great moments on what would prove to be Tyner's only full-length studio solo outing. In "Grande Days," Tyner reminisces about happier days at the Grande Ballroom, while "Let's Rock" could easily be an MC5 song, despite the lack of adequate Fred Smith and Wayne Kramer replacements on guitar.

8
Monsters and Rendezvous

When Michael Davis found himself carted off to jail, Fred Smith continued to develop his new Sonic's Rendezvous Band. The first significant step was recruiting former Stooges sticksman Scott "Rock Action" Asheton. The MC5 and the Stooges had grown up together, signed their first record contract together, hung out together, and gigged together. It was only natural that now, as their respective bands had fizzled out disappointingly after making three classic records each, Asheton and Smith would join forces. Davis's place in the band was originally taken by Ron Cooke, before former the Up man Gary Rasmussen made it his own. Scott Morgan, of the Rationals, joined Smith on guitar and vocals, completing the lineup.

"Around 1976," said Rasmussen, "Fred just called me one day. He said, 'What are ya doin' this weekend?' I said, 'I don't know. What am I doin' this weekend?' He said, 'Well, we've got a gig in Maddix. If you wanna do it I'll send you some tapes.' So that was, for me, the beginning."

Scott Morgan: "Scott Asheton and I knew each other, and Gary Rasmussen also, through the same circle, and so when Fred and I needed a drummer for Sonic's Rendezvous Band, I suggested Scott, and we got Scott involved as the drummer in 1975. Then we needed a bass player after that, and Scott and I had been hanging around with Gary, so we told Fred that Gary's our man and he joined the band and it just stuck. So that was 1976, and that was the band that did most of the Sonic's Rendezvous Band stuff." Rasmussen remembers Smith as great to work with around this time:

Fred was great. It was inspiring to play with the guy, because he was never afraid to take it somewhere it hadn't been before. I still think Fred's one of the great guitar players. He liked working on the music. We would play often and always had new material going. If there wasn't a new song, we'd be tweaking on the old ones. So there'd be quite a few different versions of the same song. One will end differently, one starts differently, different speeds, things like that. Just working, and I think he enjoyed the work as much as any of the other stuff—maybe more than any of the other stuff.

Rasmussen feels that it's difficult to compare Smith's work with the MC5 and Sonic's Rendezvous Band:

Sonic's Rendezvous Band never really went to the studio and recorded very much material. Everything that exists is all live, where somebody happened to have a tape recorder, and most of them were done by fans. The band never recorded a show. We'd find out ten or twenty years later that somebody there recorded the show. In that way, it's hard to compare it to things, but I think it shows the development in Fred as a songwriter and singer. He sang a little bit with the MC5. When we started with the Rendezvous Band, Scott Morgan sang more of the songs, but as it went on, Fred became more comfortable being more of a front guy and singing the songs. I think Fred was brilliant. He had a knack. His songs are great songs.

Scott Morgan, speaking to www.i94bar.com, recalls:

We never had anybody, really, to put us in the studio. We never signed with anyone. We could've done more on our own, which is probably what we should have done. But we got to the point where we had some offers but we didn't think they were serious enough, so we decided to go in and just do our own record. We went and did "City Slang" and "Electrophonic Tonic" and put that out. In between the time that it was recorded and the time it came out, Iggy got those guys to go to Europe, and they went to Europe as his backup band.

The "City Slang" single [on Orchidé Records] would prove to be the only studio output from SRB, though it is an incredible piece of work. Without Tyner's soulful voice to soften it, Smith's guitar sounds heavier than ever, while as a guitar partner, Morgan proved to be a more than capable replacement for Wayne Kramer.

Still, with only one single in their back catalogue (despite a multitude of bootlegs and demos available to collectors), Sonic's Rendezvous Band barely got any recognition at all. "I think it'd be nice if people were into it and all that thing, but I think most of it was because we were not on a major label ever, and we didn't have records out," Rasmussen says. "We were an underground, cult thing. People that liked the band really liked the band, but we didn't have access to millions of people like we would've done on a major label. A lot of people were into our band as well because it was Fred's new band. But if it got bigger crowds at shows because of it, it wasn't hundreds more. Maybe twenty more."

Ultimately, it wasn't enough.

When Michael Davis was released from prison, he, like Fred, hooked up with an ex-Stooge. Ron, the other Asheton brother, to be precise. Davis picks up the story:

When I got out of the penitentiary in 1976, I immediately re-formed some decadent relationships. Not with heroin people, because I was done with that. I was seeing a parole officer, so I couldn't take heroin because they would have sent me back. But I went back to drinking in a big way, because I had just taken a year off. The first thing I did when I got out of jail was go in the liquor store outside the Greyhound bus station and get a pint of Jim Beam. I was wrecked by the time I got back to Detroit. That's what I'd been waiting for that whole year. I drank a lot, and I moved back to an area just outside of Ann Arbor with some friends. It was kind of a party house, out in the country. People would come over with their people, and we'd party with them.

Some time in the spring of 1977, Ron Asheton came over. He had this girl with him, this little dainty girl, with this Nancy Sinatra kind of hair. He had this other fellow with him called Cary Loren. They told me that they were starting this band, and they wanted me to play bass. They were like, "C'mon man, it'll be fun. It'll be a blast." I was kinda, "I don't know." I was thinking that I wanted to be in a band again, and Fred already had Sonic's Rendezvous going with some other people. I was just kinda biding my time, sitting and waiting for something to come along . . . and this was something. Ron and I had had a pretty good relationship in the old days. He was hurting from the Stooges' demise, and he was looking to pick up the pieces and get back on stage. He proposed this little sort of "supergroup" thing, and it sounded pretty neat. I said that I'd practice with them and see what it sounded like, and then I'd give it a shot. So we started Destroy All Monsters and practiced. There was like these horn players around, because the Monsters had evolved out of this art thing. People were around that had originally been in art school. One was Mike Kelly, who's a big time artist now, Jim Shaw, and Ben Miller, the sax player. The girl's name was Niagara—she was the singer. Cary Loren had developed this concept of the Japanese sci-fi thing, very Warhol. It wasn't what I was used to. It wasn't where I came from. It wasn't about high-energy rock 'n' roll. It was quirky and gimmicky. What I was about was leather jackets and amps on ten. Play full blast and shock people. Here comes this kinda cartoon thing, and for the lack of anything better I went, "Oh, I'll do it!" That's how it got started. Ron was kind of fitting into a superstar mode . . . posturing, cigarette holders, military insignias, and riding boots. Little Dutch Boy haircut.

It was cool, but it wasn't what I was envisaging I'd be doing. But then I didn't know what I would be doing. I thought I was through with rock 'n' roll. I thought I was gonna go into the arts in some way, and I was gonna go into drinking and partying. So this came along, and then that was the start of that. We went for six or seven years in that band, which is about the same time span as the MC5. I'm the kind of person who tends to not quit. Even if things look bizarre, I tend to not chuck it all and move onto something else. I keep on banging away until, y'know . . .'cuz I always think there's something good about it. If somebody strokes me the right way, and says, "Wow, great show," I think, "We're onto something! We just need to have more of my songs in there and we'll really be going."

The original lineup of the band featured Cary Loren, Niagara, drummer Mike Kelly, and guitarist Jim Shaw, although they were only performing at occasional parties at that time, as Ben Miller remembers:

It was very sparse. An odd mix of noise and songs. Occasionally Niagara would play some violin or say a few words and then leave the stage. Mike would dabble on the drums while Jim played guitar through an Echoplex. From time to time, Cary seemed to try and get the set off the ground.

Destroy All Monsters went through a transition between late 1976 into early 1977. Of the original band, only Cary and Niagara remained in Ann Arbor. At this time, Lar (Laurence Miller) had a band called EMPOOL, which was mostly psychedelic free improvisation (guitars, electronics, tapes, saxophone, occasionally drums) along with a number of other musicians, including myself and brother Roger (the original version of EMPOOL was just Lar and Andre Cynkin on guitars and electronics). EMPOOL played a couple of parties, but otherwise stayed "in the basement," much like Destroy All Monsters. As far as I know, these two bands were the only weird things happening in Ann Arbor at that time. Compared to where Destroy All Monsters were coming from, though, EMPOOL was more music-related. Some of our improvisations were structured around notated compositions. Cary and Niagara would drop in unannounced at our jam sessions and request we do their stuff; two- and three-chord songs with lyrics—the exact opposite of what we were doing. Perhaps by default from the fact that we were all outcasts of the music scene, the two groups eventually fused together into the second incarnation of Destroy All Monsters; a plodding garage punk sound with a lot of psychedelia hanging on the outer fringe. This was the fun version of the band where artistic intention was high. Band members were interchangeable and songs were not nailed down.

Front woman Niagara was a riot grrrl before the term even existed. She could turn from cutesy to aggressive in an instant, while writhing on the floor in her infamous "blood slips" (which, unsurprisingly, were women's slips, drenched in fake blood). Men feared her and adored her at the same time, and her influence on bands like Queen Adreena, Babes in Toyland, and Hole is immeasurable.

Before long, Asheton was in, Davis was in, and Loren was out. The band, with two underground legends on board, looked like they might at least have a chance of doing something significant. Miller remembers the band unconsciously adopting a more traditional style when Davis and Asheton came in: "I think it wasn't until our fourth gig that Michael had joined. Cary was still in the band, so it was an odd mix of psychedelic garage and heavy rock. With both Ron and Michael in the band, though, our rock sound was definitely becoming more traditional. Also, when Mike joined, the band's instrumentation finally became fixed, and so a certain spontaneity was lost. However, a much-needed consistency in our sound had finally been achieved. It wasn't really considered a compromise, it was just the way things rolled."

Davis remembers the band was far from rigid in its approach:

They'd come there in the evening, and everybody would have their own pint of Bacardi. Everybody had their own. And a six-pack. We'd put away half of that sitting in chairs before we'd ever go upstairs to rehearse. Everybody was out of it by the time we started to play. It was difficult to work with them and call it real work, but I was doing it too, so it was just loud and shitty and disorganized. As time went on with those guys, it got worse and worse.

David Keeps booked us about a month worth of jobs in England. We licensed our stuff to Cherry Red too; we were the third pressing for Cherry Red, I think, 003 or something. We were over there to play some gigs, and we played Dingwalls twice. The first show at Dingwalls . . . [they had technical problems and a muted reception] . . . there was dead air between the songs. You can't do that in front of an English audience. This is the crowd that brought you the Beatles and the Stones . . . the show was bad and the reception was bad—it was disheartening.

Like Sonic's Rendezvous Band, the recorded output of Destroy All Monsters was very small. They did manage to release two singles, the first of which, "Bored," remains something of a classic and a collector's item. Most of their product on the shelves and in the hands of collectors is live material of varying degrees of quality. Still, Davis is rightfully proud of some of the music that this band, possibly the most avant-garde of all the post-MC5 groups, produced. "My favorite one is still 'Nobody Knows,'" he says. "That came out really well. There's some live stuff that we did that's pretty decent. But 'Nobody Knows' is a good song; the Celibate Rifles covered that."

With punk music the buzzword of the late 1970s and early 1980s, Destroy All Monsters' art-rock was unfathomably dismissed as heavy metal by some, as Davis remembers: "We were kind of on the tail [of punk]. We started when that was really getting off. By the time we got to England, it was 1980. Ska was the rage, and we got really rejected because they thought we were heavy metal. We preceded the guys like Def Leppard that came along and made it cool again. When we were out, they called us heavy metal as a bad thing. Bad, bad. I left the band in June 1984. As far as I know, they never played another show after that."

Tragically, Ron Asheton was found dead in his apartment in Ann Arbor on January 6, 2009, having apparently passed away a couple of days earlier from a heart attack. The Stooges had reunited in 2003 and had become more popular than they ever were the first time around. Fortunately, Ron Asheton was able to experience the glory. Michael Davis will forever hold Asheton in the greatest respect.: "Ron was the Christopher Columbus of rock 'n' roll. He knew there was a new world out there and from day one when he was a teenager, he knew that was what he wanted to do. That was his calling, his mission in life."

Dennis Thompson also remembers his former New Order bandmate fondly: "I really liked him. We had lots of fun together. We both had things that we didn't like about each other, I'm sure. But we had a lot of laughs and we related to each other, ever since we were younger. There were times when I related more to Ron and the Stooges than I did to my own band (MC5). They knew how to have fun, and we started getting a little serious. We related as brothers. We got along pretty good, all the way along. It was a long road."

9
Dream of Life

I t was around 1976 that Fred Smith began a relationship with punk icon and poetess Patti Smith. The pair had met when Sonic's Rendezvous Band opened up for the Patti Smith Group on a few dates. Patti was overjoyed to have met someone who she felt both emotionally and artistically connected to, and she began expressing those sentiments to those close to her. The relationship blossomed and in 1978, shortly before the release of her third album, *Easter*, Patti took the huge and unorthodox step of moving to Detroit. In terms of her career and her life in general, this seems like an extremely strange thing to have done. New York was a whirlwind of cultural diversity. For a musician and poetess like Patti Smith, it was the perfect place to be based. Detroit, on the other hand, was a long way from CBGB's. Still suffering from the 1960s race riots, and with the auto industry in fast decline, the crime rate was soaring, and by 1978, Detroit was one of the most depressed cities in the U.S. When Patti Smith moved to Detroit, many people were moving away.

If her band harbored any hopes that the closeness of their group would get them through the fact that they were separated by a thousand miles, those hopes would soon come crashing down to earth. When legendary punk writer Legs McNeil paid a visit to Patti's building and knocked on her door, Fred apparently told him that Patti wasn't at home, in a less than friendly manner. McNeil left a message, but he never heard back from her.

On March 1, 1980, Fred and Patti were married, inviting only their parents to the very small ceremony. Conveniently, Patti didn't need to go through the rigmarole of changing her surname. That same year, Patti retired from performing live. In 1979, both the Patti Smith Group and Sonic's Rendezvous Band had effectively disbanded, and before long, the two of them were working on the album together that was to become *Dream of Life*. The two of them worked slowly, combining having as normal a life as possible with writing and recording songs for their new record. In 1982, Patti gave birth to a son, Jackson, who is now a musician and a well-respected guitarist (and married to Meg of the White Stripes).

"I grew up in St. Clair Shores, Michigan," Jackson Smith told me.

About eight miles north of Detroit. It's just a quiet suburb, pretends to be like a seaside town type thing, but doesn't really accomplish its purpose. A lot of old people, and once you're on the main road, it gets like any other suburb around here. A lot of gas stations, chemists and stuff. It's nice and for me, I'm a pretty quiet guy. I don't like to make too much of myself. I went to high school in New York City, and lived there for four years. The day I graduated I wanted to move back here. I can't function in those types of settings too well. I'm counting the months and the days until I moved back, and no one believed that I would. Two weeks after I graduated, I moved my stuff. That whole move was kind of a disaster, because we had a Cordova. I had a car my grandfather—my mom's father—had left me, a 1978 Cordova, but it didn't make it on the first trip. It ended up dying and we had to go back and get it in Morgantown, Pennsylvania, this really odd Amish town. The mechanics had this odd accent.

Smith doesn't recall having any knowledge of his parents' illustrious pasts when he was a child:

Growing up, all I knew was that my parents were musicians. I didn't know about the Patti Smith Group or the MC5, or any of that. My dad wanted [me to be] educated at a private school. He wanted me to be president or something like that. Kind of a lot of focus on schoolwork, and teaching me to be well mannered, well behaved. Even in 1987 or 1988 when they recorded *Dream of Life,* they somehow managed to keep me from knowing what was going on. I was only five years old, so it probably wasn't that hard. They somehow managed to keep me from realizing what was going on.

It's good because I went to high school with famous people's daughters and sons, and I'd look at the way they behaved like they were the famous ones. I've never been able to act like that or drink like that. I still hang out with the same old friends that I've had for years, a very small group. I don't think any of my friends think about me that way. People who just meet me maybe expect something else, but people that know me just think of me as, y'know, Jackson. People see my mom on polls for the "Most Influential Album," and seeing that, people expect that I'd be much better off than I am. People expect me to be pulling up in a sports car or something, but I drive a big dirty rust-bucket truck and I work fifty hours a week. There are people that expect the rock star kid. We would go to normal restaurants around town. Today I hung out in the same bar that my dad hung out in. We went to northern Michigan on vacation. My dad would get recognized around here. We'd go out to visit my mom's parents, and she'd get recognized, not so much my dad. But I just didn't think about it.

In 1988, a full eight years after the idea was originally conceived, the Smiths released *Dream of Life*. Demos had been scrapped, work had stopped and been restarted time and time again, but during the spring of 1988, the album was finally completed. Unfortunately, it flopped commercially, a fact that hit Fred Smith hard. Jackson Smith believes that *Dream of Life* "really represented him as a musician more than any other work he ever did." This may be true, and it may be why the fact that the public hadn't taken his and his wife's work into their hearts hurt Fred Smith so much.

One of the songs on the record is the very personal "Jackson Song." The song's namesake, however, isn't a huge fan:

I hated that song. I still hate that song. I heard that music, but I was still just like, "Oh, mommy and daddy are musicians and they're making music." But I still, to this day, cannot stand that song. I know it breaks my mom's heart, because this song was written with the best intentions. For me, it's a pussy-ass song. When I was a little kid, that song would get in my head, and I'd hear it and I could not get it out of my head and I hated it. The only thing that could make me get it out of my head was thinking about cheese, for some strange reason. That'd get the song out of my head somehow.

If his parents had set out to give Jackson and his sister Jesse Paris, born in 1987, a normal life by stepping away from the music business, it worked. Even later, when the young man discovered his father's past work, it felt like the music had been created during a different lifetime. Jackson Smith:

Growing up in the way I did, even when I found that stuff out, I think when I did I was at an age when I could kinda handle it better. It was like, "Really? No shit." But my mom was still my mom. To me, the MC5 is cool and it's adventurous, but it's something my dad did long before I was around . . . Honestly, I'm not really too fond of music being overly politi-cal. I like brainless music like AC/DC or something. I don't think that it's bad, it's just not really my cup of tea. My memories of my dad are my memories growing up—pitching or playing in my yard. When I think of my dad, that's what I think of. When I think of my mom, even now; she's far more known now than she ever was when I was growing up. When I go visit her in New York, she can't see all that well—she'll kind of walk downstairs, she still does the laundry, cooks dinner . . . she's still the same person. Me and my sister laugh sometimes, when she plays and we make fun of the fans that are hanging on her every word. She still hollers me out, and shouts, "Jessie, your room's a mess." I acknowledge it, but I can't think of my parents in a celebrity fashion. I don't look at them in that way. Some kids are different . . . my dad always wanted me to be like, how do I word this, he wanted to train me to be a tough guy and strong. When I was a kid, I remember he would have this John Wayne/Clint Eastwood thing about him. Then other times, he was, y'know . . . affectionate. He knew that acting one way with me would serve a purpose and acting another way with me would serve a purpose. He used to box when he was a kid, and I remember him playing around with me and trying to make me into a strong person, you could say.

While Jackson and Jessie were enjoying a regular childhood, Fred Smith was drinking heavily, and before long, Jackson would have to be stronger than he could have anticipated.

Working 9 to 5

Without a permanent job to provide him with income, Wayne Kramer had to look for other means to make money. Speaking with me in 2006, he said,

I continued to lead a band in New York and do session work in New York, and there was a point there where I got so sick of being poor between being in bands and between gigs that I noticed every actor I knew had what they called a day job. I always looked down my nose at people—musicians especially—who had day jobs. My attitude was, If he could really play, he wouldn't have to have a job. But that's a kinda shitty attitude, because a lot of people can really play, but the truth is, being a musician is very hard. Trying to support yourself as a player is almost impossible. The average income today for professional musicians in America is $36,000 a year. That's not a lot of money. And most musicians work part time because there's not enough work available. They have to do something else. There's about sixty thousand professional musicians in America working right now: Half of them work for religious organizations. The megachurches, y'know. They all have bands, and they all get paid on the books. Gospel singing, they all have bands. I finally said, "Why can't I have a day job?" So I just started looking for work. What could I do? I don't know; I'd never done anything. I was in my mid- to late thirties, and all I'd ever done was be a professional musician. I found that I was pretty good with my hands. I had a good spatial sense. I was lucky enough to meet a guy in New York that was a cabinetmaker, and he was also a music fan who knew my work from music. He needed some help, so he took me into his shop as his apprentice. I learned carpentry, and I continued to work as a carpenter for the next ten years and I really enjoyed it. It's honorable work, it's creative work, it's steady, and actually, it was liberating for my music work because now I didn't have to play for less than I wanted to play for, because I wasn't desperate for a $250 job at CBGB. I'd say, "No, the price is $1000. If you want me to play, that's the price." At $1000, I can afford to pay my band, I can pay my bills, and I can live for a week or so. At $250, I gotta ask people to do me favors and it's just not a good position to be in. It made it so that music was something I did because it was important for me to do, because it was work that I enjoyed doing, and I was pretty good. My life started to settle down a little bit. I started to get a sense that it might be possible that I could have a manageable life. I didn't have evidence of it yet, but it was a step in a certain direction. It was a step away from the anti-world and into the world of possibilities.

I built some nice stuff for people. We built nice furniture and nice inspirations for very wealthy clients. It had to be done right, and I learned a great deal. In fact, when I left New York I moved down to Key West, and I built two custom homes down there with another guy, and really enjoyed the work. I'm still a carpenter. I'm a carpenter today. I built my studio, and my office. I build stuff in my house all the time. I built a studio in Nashville called Alex the Great, and I did a deal with them. The guys were very cool and they're my deal friends. I said I'd build the stuff for them if they gave me free studio time, because I was coming to L.A. and I'd written ten to fifteen songs, and I wanted to have a calling card when I arrived in L.A. So we bartered. I wasn't just playing for fun, but I wasn't desperate. My mother always used to say, "Music's good, Wayne, but learn a trade so you can fall back on it." I always thought, "Yeah right mom, whatever." But one day I called her up and I said, "Mom, I've learned a trade." You wanna live in the real world, get a real job. It did a lot for me. One time I was in Key West with another carpenter, driving to a job in his truck, and a truck pulled up next to us with some other carpenters that we knew. Something had been on television the night before that had some footage of me playing in the MC5. This guy, a buddy of mine, yells over and says, "HEY KRAMER! I saw you on MTV last night. You used to be cool." That was good for me. I need to hear that.

Michael Davis, meanwhile, continued to search for a musical outlet:

I messed around for a few more years, and in 1987 I left Michigan and went to Arizona. I played in a few bands there, one of which did a lot of touring in Europe—a desert rock band called the Luminarios. That was a strange old band; it was kind of a singer/songwriter deal. This guy had had a band called the Sidewinders; they changed their name to the Sand Rubies, and they broke up but they had a big record deal. This guy was like a multimillionaire who inherited millions, and I played in his band for a while and did a lot of touring.

Dennis Thompson, too, found himself working a day job, a career chance that would last the best part of thirty years:

From 1975, off and on, through 2000, I had twelve jobs. But on a résumé, you'd call me a computer numerical control machine center programmer. I programmed and set up robot machine centers to machine parts for the F-16 Eagle fighter plane, the M1A1 tank, then I was in the prototype business. I worked on brand new stuff that was just coming out. Turbochargers for cars—I'd make setups and do the machining. Most of the jobs I had were of that nature, and I ran big machines called boring mills. In 1982, I met up with a guy who put together a family entertainment center, like Chuck E. Cheese. You go there and have pizza, and they have robots that play music. It was called Major Magic's All Star Pizza Revue. This guy had his shit together. There was a lot of money involved. They went head to head with Chucky Cheese, and what I did is I hired a full factory's worth of fifteen people and we built the life size, pneumatically operated rock 'n' roll and country music characters, like Disney's *Pirates of The Caribbean*. There were three stages. One was a country music stage with two big huge bears. The center stage was for a crocodile on piano, a girl fox on guitar, a big lion called Flash played drums, and a walrus played the trumpet. They were huge, they were bigger than life-size. The fox, her name was Barbara Stringband, she was like eight feet tall. They had twenty-five different movements each. I got all the music together for the show, like twenty songs. I wrote a couple of birthday songs for kids' parties. I programmed it all, and I built four of those across the country, taking a crew with me to set them up. I did that for about two and a half years. That was a ball. That I loved. It was music, it was machining, it was everything I liked. I had guys working for me that ran lathes and were welders, women that made clothes and guys that worked with fiberglass and guys that worked with latex. The reason I had to quit was that there were so many companies doing it, there was a glut. A saturation of the market.

Around the year 2000, my mom died and I quit the toolmaking business. I didn't like it. I was really good at it. Really good. My father was a toolmaker, my brother was a toolmaker. I was excellent at it, but I just didn't like it. I would always stand by the door staring outside, thinking, What am I doing? I'm stuck in prison. That's why I developed my drinking problem, and my cocaine problem, which lasted twenty years. I could hear a guitar solo here and there, or a drum part that sounded like [my] stuff. The dark period—no renaissance going on here. I made a living, bought a house—I tried to live the American lifestyle like here in Detroit. I went to the Detroit College of Business and took three courses in accounting. I took some courses in creative writing. I dabbled here and there trying to learn something else, but mostly what I did was work. My mom died in October 1999, and after that I went on a binge and I got a DUI, and I sobered up. Those years from 2000 up to 2003, I was floating. I would pick up work and I had a little bit of money saved up, and between myself and my wife Patrice we would make ends meet. I started playing again—just picked up sticks and working on tunes, but not playing with anyone. I had twenty-five years of working real jobs and not being happy except for the robots. That was fun.

On September 17, 1991, while sitting behind the wheel of his car, Rob Tyner suffered a fatal heart attack. He left behind his wife, Becky, with whom he had remained since 1966, and his three children, Robin, Amy, and Elizabeth. On February 22 of the following year, the four remaining members of the MC5 performed together onstage for the first time since the Grande Ballroom farewell, in order to raise money for the education of Tyner's children. What should have been a celebratory event, however, still managed to leave attendees with a sour taste in their mouths. For Davis, the news of Tyner's death had left him numb:

I think Scott Morgan called me. And my mom sent me an article from the Detroit paper which had a big thing about Tyner's death. Somebody popped for a ticket, and I went. Things between me and Rob were about as estranged as things could get . . . I can't point to any event or anything like that, but he and I weren't on the same page at all. He was way over there, and I always got the feeling that there was something in our past that had alienated him, but I didn't know what it was. I felt ambivalent when he passed. It's too bad. I couldn't say that I was overcome with grief. I was just, Well, we've all gotta go sometime. That's about what my attitude was. I had kinda lost a connection with Tyner early on with the MC5. I didn't feel anything against him, so it must have been something he felt against me, but I don't know what that was.

Kramer, too, had some unresolved issues with Rob, which, tragically, will never be resolved:

Y'know, in Detroit I ran into him in the supermarket one day and we had a quick exchange. The next time I heard from him was in the 1980s. I was living in New York and he called me up and asked me if I'd be willing to go on an MC5 tour with him again . . . some promoter thought that they were gonna sell out a sports arena or something. He did his best to be the old witty, enthusiastic Rob, but I really resented him for a lot of years . . . Today I understand that the center doesn't hold and it goes away, but for a long time I resented everybody. I don't today, but I did for a long time. I have some awareness today that I didn't have then.

I was living in Nashville, and one of my friends from Detroit called me and told me [that Tyner had died]. I was on crutches; that's why I didn't go to the funeral. I had wrenched my knee playing racquetball. I couldn't handle an airport and flying. I couldn't bend my knee. For the oddest reason, I didn't feel bad for Rob. I knew him pretty well, and he was a spiritual guy. He had a sense of the mystery of existence, that there are things that transcend all categories of human thought. At some point, the conversation has to ascend to a transcendental level. When I first met Rob, what attracted me to him was that he had studied Buddhism. He was the guy that helped me break away from that first-century religious thinking and open my mind up to the idea that there were other concepts of power greater than human power. Or, what happens after we die? How old is the universe? How long will things last? What does it all mean? I wanted to know. I think the thing that religion does for us is it takes the sting out of some stuff. It takes the sting out of death. I wanted to believe, and I did believe, that Rob wasn't afraid. I don't know. I want to believe that, but no one knows. But denial again figures in. I lived in a world of denial, and I probably still live in a world of denial to some degree. I'm aware of it a little bit now, so I try to cut through and say, "Well, what's really going on here?" But it took a while for that to sink in, that he wasn't on the earth anymore. I don't know if it's ever really sunk in completely. Even here today, I don't know if it's sunk in completely. He's still present in my dreams and my memories. It's like James Dean, y'know? James Dean will always be that beautiful young man. We'll never know James Dean at sixty-five with no hair and a big belly. Elvis we did. But when people die before their time, they get fixed in that place. I wasn't around Rob for all those years after the MC5, so he exists in my mind as we all did when we were in the band together. He still exists that way. I don't live in my yesterdays, but if I touch it, if I go there, that's what I get. Plus, it was a great tragedy for his family.

We're all gonna die. It always seems more painful when people die at forty-six instead of eighty-six or seventy-six. It's something that's unresolved. You can't ever make peace with it. When your parents die, over time you push it away from your conscious thinking, but it's always there. I lost my mother recently, and I thought at some point, If she's gonna die, when she goes then that'll be the end of a chapter of my life. But when she did die, the chapter didn't end. It just stays open. I don't know if I buy this idea of closure. Maybe there's something to it, I don't know. I have so many friends that have gone before their time. The list is heartbreaking. I lost one last week, before his time. It happens all the time and it doesn't get better. It all just diminishes you. Life goes on, and it goes on without you. Life will continue on without me. If I have to bring it all home, I have to say that life is for living. Life is for producing. Life is for joy. Life is for creativity. Yeah, you can't escape the pain of death and the loss, but life follows life. If you add up the loss of Rob, and then four years later Fred died, which came as no surprise, it sent me a message . . . I didn't kill them. I get the sense sometimes that people make it out like I killed them. I didn't kill anybody. But it told me that I'm only here temporarily. If I'm gonna do anything, all those dreams and ambitions I had when I was a little boy, if I was gonna realize them, if I was gonna make a contribution to the world, if I was gonna create some art that might help somebody else, then I'd better get to work. I started to look at things in terms of, How much time do I have? Do I have ten good years? I don't know. Do I have fifteen? Maybe, I don't know. But I do know that every hour that I waste, I don't get back. So it's time to man up—life up!

Dennis Thompson remembers receiving a very difficult phone call:

I was at home and I had a phone call from Ben Edmonds, the journalist from *Rolling Stone.* Ben gave me a call at about 1:00 p.m., and said that Rob had died from a heart attack. I heard his voice on the answering machine, and I went and picked up the phone. That was it. Rob was the healthiest guy out of all of us. He wasn't supposed to die. If anybody should've been dead, it was me and Michael. Or Wayne. But anyway, he had a heart attack. He had a heart problem since he was younger.

    I went to his funeral—it was a big, huge . . . funeral. Lots of people. A twenty-one-gun salute—Rob was working with Vietnam vets and doing some good work in the community. Later, the four of us got together as the MC4, played the State Theater, and left an open mike for Rob. We played four songs. It was weird. Fred was drinking a lot, I was doing coke, I don't know what Wayne and Michael were doing. I was drinking and doing coke so I was pretty high but capable of playing. My playing was fine. Fred was an alcoholic, but I didn't know that then. We had one rehearsal before we played that show. Fred walked into rehearsal with two bottles of chardonnay. Wayne, Mike, and myself were already jamming.

We were waiting for him and he's late. Then he came in, sat down, and didn't start rehearsing until he'd drunk both bottles. Two full bottles of Chardonnay. When we started, I said, "I've had more fucking fun sitting in a dentist's chair getting a goddamn root canal than this rehearsal." Wayne looked at me and gave me those knowing eyes like, "Yeah, I know what you mean." Fred was fucked up, but we didn't know how bad. It wasn't even three years later and he died.

Perhaps partly as a result of unresolved issues, the show for Tyner's children was a very difficult and awkward affair for everyone. Kramer:

I don't know how to describe how I felt about it. I can describe what happened and the events in a linear narrative, but y'know, I knew that I couldn't change anybody. And I knew better than to drink with Fred. I really didn't have too many preconceived ideas of what that show would be like. By that time, who knew? I didn't know. I knew that it was gonna be complicated. I think I hoped that it'd be fun. I do remember at one point in the performance, when we were playing the last tune, "Black to Comm," looking out at the audience and realizing that these were the children of the people [who were there] the last time we played this. When we played it the first time, no one had ever heard anything like that, and when we played it then, nobody had heard anything like that. There were so many resentments and unresolved issues. I felt like it was a time to make some amends and to raise some money for Rob's family—seemed to be the right thing to do. I'm sure you've discovered by now that having been in the MC5 has left none of us independently wealthy. There's no money. We knew that the Tyners weren't wealthy people either. So if we could come together at least . . . that wasn't such a bad thing to do. It was the beginning of a healing process, or it could have been. Some things started in that direction. Because all of a sudden, we had to come back together as grown-ups now; a lot of time had gone by. But still, it was a hard thing to do. Maybe for other bands it's not so hard, but the guys I've talked to, it's hard for anybody. Anybody that comes back into a band situation with guys they played with when they were young and you try to do it again, it's hard.

Michael Davis remembers the difficulty of trying to get everyone on the same page:

It almost didn't happen, because Fred was so immovable. I don't know what his problem was, but he would not take the stage. He kept saying, "Wait a little longer, wait a little longer." I get the psychology, making the crowd into this emotional thing so that when you do come out, they're just in a frenzy. But he took it past that. They were over it. The promoter was coming in and saying, "They're leaving. They think you're not gonna play. It's too late." It was unreasonable. When we went out there, we had only rehearsed a couple of times and we were trying to play together. Maybe it was interesting to people, it wasn't phenomenal . . . I was wearing an MC5 T-shirt like I was really cool. I was up there bopping, and I sang "Kick Out the Jams."

One poignant moment came in the form of an impassioned speech from Kramer, just before playing "Kick Out the Jams." Addressing the crowd, he said, "The worst thing that we did was that we lost each other. The MC5 represented a lot of things. We represented possibilities—a possibility of new music, possibility of a new lifestyle, possibility that we could change the world. But in the end, the worst thing that we did is that we lost each other. So tonight I'm here to reclaim those possibilities, and to reclaim my lost brothers. So Rob, if you're out there, and I know you are, and you're listening, this one is for you."

Tyner was the second of two former colleagues Kramer lost in 1991; on April 23, Johnny Thunders died in a New Orleans hotel room. He was thirty-nine years old.

In 1999, eight years after Tyner's death, a live album was released of a concert performed in 1977 by a band billed as the Rob Tyner Band (actually the New MC5) at the ironically named Kramer Theater in Detroit. Sadly, considering that there are only two Tyner CDs available, his band just can't generate the energy to do songs like "Kick Out the Jams" or "Back in the USA" justice, at least on the album. Of the four Tyner/Gillespie-penned songs, "Taboo" is the best. "Rock and Roll People" is a sad record of Tyner treading water, and one that is best forgotten, because Rob Tyner, as one of the greatest rock 'n' roll front men to ever walk the earth, deserved better. When I sat with Robert Gillespie at his home, he played me some recordings of this band that were a lot better. Quite why this recording was released is a mystery.

More tragedy would follow just two years later. On November 4, 1994, Fred "Sonic" Smith died of heart failure. To the three surviving members, the news came hard but as no surprise, as Davis remembers:

Dennis called me. He said that Fred was gone. He told me this whole story about how they had taken him to the hospital sometime before he actually died. He was treated at the hospital and he was released. We knew something was wrong in 1992, at Tyner's thing. The three of us, without Fred being present, said, "When I see you again, it'll be at Fred's funeral." We knew. He wasn't acting himself, he was chalky looking, grey. There was no life in his eyes. I don't know if he was drug dependent, I don't know if he was just alcoholic, I don't know if he had Hep C, I don't know if his liver was shutting down, but something was bad. Something was real impenetrable. He was there but he wasn't. It was like he didn't exist. He just looked bad, and we knew that he was sick. When I saw Fred at some music theater, we'd just put our hands in cement for some museum and signed guitars. I saw him sitting at the bar talking to somebody. All of a sudden, he just lit up and went, "Michael!" One second later, he was gone again. Just for that second, he was happening. Within a second, he faded back into whatever. He had an attitude. He was a big star now. I think he was married to Patti by then, which might have had something to do with it. I've met Patti. She told me that I was her second favorite member of the MC5. You can't win 'em all. Of course, I saw her at Fred's funeral and she's nice.

Kramer agrees that Smith's passing was all too predictable: "It was pretty obvious that Fred's alcoholism had reached a terminal stage. He was in very bad shape. You could see it in his skin, the amount that he drank . . . I mean, I'm a sober alcoholic, and in 1994 I was still drinking. For me to observe somebody drinking more than me, it was painfully clear to me and Michael, we talked about it and said, 'Jeez, he ain't gonna make it.'

I was the closest to Fred. Fred and I were little boys together, we grew up together, we went out and played together. All those youthful dreams and plans, the social and emotional evolution—teenagers, hormones, girls, being tough enough to fight in school, all that stuff. We were inseparable. I don't get to touch that too much. When I went to prison and came back, it was like me and Fred weren't close anymore. I was still close with Mike. I never saw Dennis or Rob. But I tried a couple of times to connect with Fred, but it was like he had made a line in the sand and said, 'This is my life before and this is my life now; and they don't cross over.' So I never really got to know him after I got back in 1978."

Jackson Smith:

Once my dad passed away, at the memorial service I met all those MC5 guys for the first time and I remember them just being stunned that I didn't know who they were. But I didn't, really, for another couple of years. [Thanks to] my mom, I started to figure things out. After my dad passed away, our financial situation was not the best by any means. My mom had to start going out to make money the only way she knew how. That was the way I became exposed to what she does. I suppose at the time that happened, it wasn't that big of a deal to me because there were all those years before that I didn't think about it. I can't really say that it was ever that big of a deal.

When he passed away, my initial reaction was like, for many years, I had to . . . he wasn't around, so I was the man of the house. I think it was the way he taught me to be, I was more concerned with being there for my mom and my sister. I don't think you ever really get over something like that. But for many years, I was crushed but I didn't take the time to grieve for myself. I was more being there for my mom and my sister to help them grieve. It wasn't for a really long time before I finally was able to let go.

Smith's more recent colleague in Sonic's Rendezvous Band, Gary Rasmussen, remembers taking the difficult phone call:

I was home, and Patti called me. When I answered the phone and heard it was Patti . . . Fred always called me so immediately there was something wrong. It was a shock.

A lot of people remember him for playing guitar. He was a living-on-the-edge and go-for-it kinda guy. Playing wise, I don't think he was limited by what he thought other people thought. He was doing what he thought was right.

Dennis Thompson:

Patti Smith called me up. She said that Fred asked on his deathbed if I would speak on his behalf at the St. Mariner's church. Right when she called, I had a bottle of Jack Daniels and I was listening to "Over and Over." I had a blank page on the table in front of me and I was gonna write something to Fred. Just myself, personally. Something from me to Fred. I couldn't think of anything to write, and then I got the call from Patti and we're both crying. I said, "Yes, of course." I hung up the phone and got out the third album. On there, there's a picture of Fred as Sonic Smith. There's a quote, and that got me started. So I wrote a eulogy called "Cellophane Flowers at the Fork in the Road." I had the idea that Fred was a man of the future, that he was a futuristic thinking person, which is what he was. Always ahead of the game. Never a follower, always a leader.

The Return of Citizen Wayne

A s the 1990s got into full swing, Wayne Kramer had a creative spurt, and so, with the help of Epitaph Records, he began a solo career. Epitaph was founded by Bad Religion main man Brett Gurewitz, and it quickly became the place to be for pop-punk and hardcore bands like NOFX, Pennywise and the Bouncing Souls. It was an unlikely home for Kramer, and one that would eventually prove uncomfortable. Still, he initially enjoyed being a solo artist and all that that entailed:

I never didn't enjoy the band dynamic. I liked collaborating and with the MC5, we were tight. I never felt frustrated in the MC5, musically or artistically. I felt that anything I wanted to try, these guys were gonna help me try doing it. I never felt competitive with Fred about who wrote more songs, who played what solos. That's really never been my experience. I've had that experience after the MC5; I've been in bands with guys who would bust your balls and tell you that you ain't playing shit right. Just pickup bands in Detroit. I'd start bands, hire guys, they'd come in and be ballbusters. If you're not playing it exactly like the record, you need to go and practice some more. Musicians are as flawed as anyone else, maybe more so.

At Epitaph, it was all a learning process. This was a new era, and I was given this opportunity. This ties right in with the point about Fred dying. I knew that I only had so many years left to work, and so if I was gonna accomplish anything, I had to go somewhere where my job skills were marketable. I'd already been in New York for ten years so Los Angeles was the only place to go. I knew when I got there that I was gonna get an opportunity because I was the new kid in town, but the window would only be open for a minute. I would have to really get serious. Brett [Gurewitz] was running a company; it was artist advocate and he gave me a shot. It was very exciting, because things were exploding for the label. Right after I signed with them, the Offspring record took off. So all of a sudden there was money to try things, to tour and do publicity, make videos, all the things that go along with the record business. We were all doing the best we could. That's about the only way I could look at it.

Brett tried to position me to the punk rock world in the only way that they knew how to sell music, which was punk rock music to skateboard kids, mostly in Southern California. If you define punk in the narrow range that it's defined, that it's 160 beats per minute, guitars, chords, and lyrics to piss off your parents, then that's a component of me. That's a part of my character. I like playing fast, I like blistering chords and I like provocative lyrics. But it's only one component. I have a broad interest in the musical world. So I made four albums for Epitaph and they did well. We sold some records and it was a good experience. But at a certain point, it became clear to me that the dynamic of the record business was changing and my position at Epitaph was changing. As I grew from record to record, I was moving further away from the Epitaph philosophy. I mean, that's my perception of it. I listen to a Pennywise record, and those guys are friends of mine, but the new record sounds like the last record. I listen to NOFX, the records sound the same. Even Bad Religion, who are the best of the lot, the records sound the same to me. It's a formula that works for them, and it's the way the record business works. It's mass marketing. It's just that I don't see it quite that way, and so all my records started to change, and by the time I did *Citizen Wayne* [in 1997], it's got pianos, avant-garde horns, and poetry. So I reached a point where I said that working for Brett's label—as much as I love Brett—I wanna be on my own label. It's about owning things in this world. Brett loved what I was doing, but I think I was too demanding of them. They had teenagers that were willing to get in a van, drive ten thousand miles and all sleep together in one hotel room or a hippie crash pad. I wasn't willing to do that. I did that in the MC5 and for years after. I wanted to promote my records but I couldn't do it on my knees. I'm not a teenager, y'know. They've told me since that all the mistakes we made together is how they learned to retool so that they could work with Joe Strummer or Tom Waits. Because I didn't really fit the mold of the punk rock artist or the fans. I was older, and eighteen-year-old kids look at me and see a middle-aged man. You could tell I was older than they were. It's all about group identification. To their credit, they've successfully reengineer the company, and Brett's doing great shit with Soloman Burke, Tricky, Tom [Waits], the work he did with Joe [Strummer], Joe Henry . . . they're doing good shit. Someone had to be the snowplow, and I guess that was me. But the good news is that I learned that there was a new way to do a label, and me and Margaret [Kramer's wife] founded a label that was artist advocate. But I think we came to the record business a day late and a dollar short, because it's all over now. It's all about downloading. What's a record? Even the term is archaic.

In 1991, Kramer released *Death Tongue* on the Curio/Progressive label. Credited to Kramer, it was a collaboration between the guitarist and his old friend, Mick Farren, a journalist and front man with the Social Deviants. While not entirely a success, the record does have some interesting moments. The pair resurrects the title song from their *Who Shot You, Dutch?* musical, produced by Don Was. The cover of Richard Harris' "MacArthur Park" is surreal and doesn't work at all. The two best moments on the record are "Spike Heels" and "Fun in the Final Days" which, though co-written by Farren, definitely sound like Kramer songs.

It was four years before Kramer's next album (and his first for Epitaph), but it was worth the wait because *The Hard Stuff* (later re-released as *The Hard Stuff+* with extra bonus tracks) still stands up as the best solo record of his career. Aggressive, autobiographical and soulful, *The Hard Stuff* was a real return to form for Kramer. It also featured a lot of cameo appearances from working musicians in L.A., the city where Kramer had recently moved to from Nashville. Epitaph head honcho and Bad Religion front man Brett Gurewitz, Pennywise bass player Randy Bradbury, and the Vandals drummer Josh Freese all jumped at the chance to record with Kramer, having grown up listening to MC5 albums.

As Kramer says, "Brett said that there were a lot of musicians around L.A. that would love to work with me. I started calling them up and I found out it was true. I didn't have a sense of the influence of the work I had done earlier. I mean, musicians have always told me that "Man, I love the MC5. You guys were the best." But to get it on that level, I was a little surprised. Pleasantly surprised. It still is cool. It's humbling actually. I appreciate it."

Highlights of the record include "Junkie Romance," in which Kramer talks about the dangers of heroin addiction and the fact that it isn't as glamorous as rock stars often make it out to be, while tipping his hat to his former partner in Gang War, Johnny Thunders.

It's a chilling song, brimming with experience. Having seen so many of his friends die, Kramer was in the perfect position so say, "This shit ain't cool," and he did so in the form of a song that manages to stay on the right side of self-righteous.

Elsewhere, "The Edge of the Switchblade" is a beautiful, poignant tribute to Rob Tyner.

It's wonderful to hear Kramer singing about his old friend and partner so many years after the breakup of the MC5 and, in many ways, their relationship. On the sleeve notes, former Black Flag front man and celebrated solo artist Henry Rollins says of the record, "I love it when an old record can still kick the ass of anything released years later. Fire up *High Time* or *Raw Power* by the Stooges and most of your record collection crawls away to hide for fear of getting exposed for the over-hyped, pale imitation of the real thing it is. Even better when one of the purveyors of the real thing still delivers. Such is the case with Wayne Kramer and Co. on this record."

While not as consistent as *The Hard Stuff,* the second Epitaph record, *Dangerous Madness* (later re-released as *More Dangerous Madness,* with extra tracks) had some shining moments and was by no means a disaster. The title track, featuring backing vocals from soul star Terence Trent D'arby, is as fast-paced and energetic as anything Kramer recorded post-MC5. The next song, "Going Back to Detroit," is a slightly sorrowful look at his hometown.

In 1996 two more Kramer-related albums hit the shelves—the Skydog-released Gang War live album, and *Dodge Main,* an album of covers by a scratch band featuring Kramer, Radio Birdman's Deniz Tek and Scott Morgan of the Rationals/Sonic's Rendezvous Band. Released on Bomp/Alive Records, the album features covers of classic garage rock songs like the SRB's "City Slang" and the MC5's own "Over and Over," and it works surprisingly well.

The following year, Kramer released yet another solo record, *Citizen Wayne* (again, later reissued as *Return of Citizen Wayne*). With Was (Not Was)'s David Was stepping into the producer's chair, this was never going to be a typical rock 'n' roll record, but it certainly didn't suffer for its ambition. As well as co-writing many of the songs, Was also added programming to some of them and, as a result, *Citizen Wayne* is very much a collaborative effort. The highlight is undoubtedly "No Easy Way Out," a country rock tune (possibly influenced by his time in Nashville) with one of Kramer's catchiest choruses.

In 1998 Kramer released a solo album, *LLMF* (Live Like a Motherfucker). The bulk of the material is pulled from Kramer's solo albums, though he does rip through "Kick Out the Jams" toward the end. Still, it's not an inspiring performance, and in the author's opinion, *LLMF* is a particularly low point for Kramer.

Two compilation albums of interest were also released in 1998; the self-explanatory *Hempilation, Vol.2: Free The Weed,* and a collection of Detroit rock called *Motor City's Burnin' Vol. 1.* Kramer contributed a song called "If You're a Viper" to the former, and to the latter, "Friday the 13th," which features Kramer and John Sinclair. That album also includes the MC5's "Looking at You," and "Electro-phonic Tonic" from Sonic's Rendezvous Band.

In 2000, Kramer became involved in a band set up with the Damned's Brian James, though Mad for the Racket were not the average group. Kramer: "I'd known Brian for a while, and every time I'd see him when I was in England, he'd say, 'We should do something.' One day he called up and said, 'I have a label that might pay for me to come out there, so let's get a bunch of guys together and make a record.' I said, 'If you're serious, why don't you come over and let's write a record first?' because just to get a bunch of guys together doesn't mean it's gonna be a good record. There's been a lot of bands like that, with people that have been in other bands, put them in a studio and nobody's really a songwriter, so they just do the best they can. It's all about the songs for me. But he came over and we wrote a record. We wrote some good songs. I said, 'OK, we've got the songs. Now let's call Stewart Copeland, Duff McKagan, etc.' It was fun. It was a good project and I like Brian a lot."

Brian James tells the tale from his side of the pond:

I'd met Wayne off and on over the years. I'd met him in New York a couple of times, and I lived in France for about five years and saw Wayne over there. We had this vague kind of, "One day we've got to do something together. It'd be a lot of fun . . ." and all this. When I moved back to England, I was talking to a friend of mine, Ian Brunn, the same guy who put on the Phun City thing and went on to manage the Stranglers, Big Country, and a bunch of stuff, so he's been involved in the music business, and we were just wondering what to do. I said that I had some songs written but didn't know who I wanted to work with. He said, "Make a list of musicians that you'd like to work with and maybe we can sort something out from that." So I phoned Lemmy [of Motörhead] and he was up for doing something. We'd always had this conversation that we should do something together before one of us dies. It got a bit morbid, really. I phoned Stewart Copeland, because he's an old friend. He played on some of my solo stuff. He was up for doing something because he'd only been doing movie music and stuff like that so he wanted to do some rock 'n' roll and have a good time. I phoned Wayne up . . . It was one of my old heroes saying that he wanted to do a whole album with me. I didn't even know if he was gonna go for the three song [proposal]. I was on the next plane over to LA. I had a few ideas, he had a few ideas, we worked 'em out together and then invited musicians in. The only reason that Lemmy wasn't on it was that Wayne thought he'd want to sing a few songs, and that we should keep it to the two of us. I could see his point. So we just called people we knew, basically. All apart from Duff. I'd never met Duff before, but I knew that he was the one responsible for Guns N' Roses recording "New Rose" on *The Spaghetti Incident* album. He lives between Seattle and L.A., and fortunately he was in L.A. at the time. We met up for something to eat, and he was like, "I want to do the whole album with you guys. Don't get another bass player in, I'll be really offended." He was on board big time. Wayne spoke to Clem [Burke, of Blondie], who was a friend of both of us. The album just fell together. It was easy.

The album, *The Racketeers*, features guest appearances from the Police's Stewart Copeland, Guns N' Roses' Duff McKagan (now of Velvet Revolver), Blondie's Clem Burke, the Sisters of Mercy's Adam Pearson and Primal Scream's Mani, among others, with Kramer and James the only mainstays. Kramer doesn't remember having any problems getting anyone to jump onboard:

It's all about work. We were very fortunate that these guys were available. Part of the idea of Mad for the Racket is that it's more of a collective, a free-floating collective based on our songwriting, than it is a band in the strict sense with a lineup. We can make another record with some different people, and every time we tour we can have different people. For example, on some dates, Mani from Primal Scream will play bass with us. That makes it more exciting for me. Maybe next year we'll have a Czechoslovakian synthesizer player in the band. Who knows? We might get a girl singer. We're like the Golden Palominos. Run more like a collective. The songwriting and guitar playing of me and Brian, but built around that core, we can constantly change the cast of characters. Because the most fun about being in a band is in the beginning—when you're writing the songs, making the records, doing the first dates. The business dictates that you keep doing it, but I don't wanna do that. I only wanna do the stuff that I wanna do. I wanna do stuff that I think is important. That stretches me out.

Of his relationship with James, Kramer said, "We're both students of the electric guitar, and we're both trying to express ourselves with the electric guitar, to find our own voice with the electric guitar."

Despite an excellent first album, Mad for the Racket have yet to record together again, which is a shame, because back when it was released, Kramer revealed that there were plans to take things further. "We'll probably start writing in the spring. If Brian and I can be left alone—'cuz I write all the time. I have a new solo album that I'm recording now and I have songs left over from that. If you wanna be a writer, you have to write all the time. It's just a matter of getting together, pulling out what we've been working on, seeing what we've got and getting a collection together. Brian comes over to L.A. because I have a studio. It's inexpensive to have him come now: We put him up in a little hotel in the neighborhood."

As Kramer would later reveal, however, things just didn't work out: "We had a lot of plans, but the logistical problem was huge. He lived in England, I lived in L.A., and there was no money. It takes money to run a railroad. Running people around gets expensive. We did a little bit of touring and it could have gone further, but it just wasn't in the cards. It was too hard."

Still, Brian James is extremely proud of his involvement in the project:

I thought it sounded good, and it still does. It stands the test of time. It's a rock 'n' roll album, so it'll sound good in another twenty years. It could have been recorded ten years earlier. It's one of them. We did a couple of gigs, and that was about the size of it, really. We got Mani in for the gigs, which was great fun. He's a great bass player. Wayne was great to work with. He likes to be in control, which was fine. We both wrote the songs, and then if I had a problem with anything, I'd just stand up. He has a way of doing anything, and if that's the way he wants to work, that's fine by me, unless you upset me, which never happened. Doing the gigs was a dream come true, for a guitar player to be playing with one of his favorite guitar players. It's like when I worked with Iggy. You don't know whether to try and play as much complementary guitar as you can, or just stand back and watch the guy in action. You get paid to be part of this thing that you would pay to see. Working with Wayne was great fun. I'd drop everything to do it again. Let's see what's around the corner.

Even with Mad for the Racket taking up so many of his days, Kramer still found time to co-write and record two songs for Henry Rollins's album, *Get Some Go Again*. "I co-wrote two songs on that. He's a joy to work with. He has this image of being this stern taskmaster, but underneath all those muscles, he's a hipster. He reads good stuff, he listens to good stuff. He's an ideas guy. It's the stuff he appreciates and it's what he aspires to."

The two tracks with Kramer, "Hotter and Hotter" and "L.A. Money Train," are as good as a collaboration between these two artists should be, with Kramer's furious, free-form guitar complementing Rollins's bullish vocals.

The only other release of note in 2000 was *Cocaine Blues,* a compilation of Kramer's work recorded between 1974 and 1978. The first four tracks are recorded live with the Pink Fairies, including a half-decent run-through of "Kick Out the Jams" and a bizarre cover of Bob Seger's "Heavy Music" that features an excerpt from James Brown's "There Was a Time." The remaining six tracks feel like bits and pieces that Kramer had lying around, including a cover of Jimmy Cliff's "The Harder They Come," and a few songs co-written with Mick Farren.

Much more interesting was the compilation that Kramer produced the following year, *Beyond Cyberpunk.* Kramer:

> It's a great collection of artists that I think were doing good work then and are doing better work now. The way the music industry is structured traditionally, bands like Pere Ubu or Richard Hell won't get exposed. It'll be a little cult record somewhere. This gives me a chance to bring in brand new music. I have the first new Richard Hell track in eighteen years. Dee Dee Ramone's on there, Stan Ridgeway, then a couple of new bands that I think carry on the spirit of adventure in music—Mother Superior. It was a great opportunity to do work that I think was important!

The compilation is simply fabulous, taking in new tracks from legendary underground artists like Ron Asheton, Richard Hell, Pere Ubu, David Was, Chris Spedding, Dee Dee Ramone, Mudhoney, as well as Kramer himself, who contributed the excellent "Crawling Outta the Jungle." As a fascinating exercise in proving that the once great were still very relevant, the album works wonderfully well.

Along with a heap of solo reissues (thanks to his own newly set up MuscleTone Records), 2002 saw a new Kramer solo album, *Adult World.* The record sees Kramer performing songs that are as middle-of-the-road as anything he had ever written. Even the appearance of Swedish garage rockers and MC5 aficionados the Hellacopters on "Talkin' Outta School" couldn't change the fact this album has more in common with Bob Seger than the MC5. That's not to say it's bad; the title track, "Brought a Knife to a Gunfight," and "Great Big Amp" are great songs that display just how good—and underrated—Kramer's songwriting is. It was missing an edge, though, a sense of excitement that is synonymous with Kramer's music.

Another guest on *Adult World* was the avant-garde jazz troupe X-Mars-X, led by Chicago bandleader Mark Williams. That same year, Kramer made an appearance on their self-titled album, a record that isn't for the fainthearted. Kramer may have gotten to live out his Sun Ra-fueled jazz fantasies with Williams, but the album is the most challenging and gloriously self-indulgent piece of work that Kramer ever put his name to.

In 2002, Kramer contributed an excellent version of "Bonzo Goes to Bitburg (My Brain is Hanging Upside Down)" to the Ramones tribute album *The Song Ramones the Same,* and two years later he had Johnny Thunders on his mind again, contributing "Children are People Too" to the very personal Thunders tribute album *I Only Wrote This Song For You.*

In 2004 Kramer linked up with the Axis of Justice, an organization that raised important issues through music, something that was instinctively right up Kramer's alley. Other key musicians involved included former Rage Against the Machine/Audioslave man Tom Morello and System of a Down's Serj Tankian. Rage Against the Machine had previously covered "Kick Out the Jams" on their *Renegades* album, and though their contemporary rap-metal didn't have anything in common with the MC5, they were certainly singing from the same lyric sheet—involving themselves in various political rallies and being labeled "unpatriotic" because of it.

Undoubtedly the busiest member of the MC5 during the 1990s and the early part of the new millennium, Kramer saw much of his solo work as a chance to exorcise some demons:

Well, you know, I had to accept the loss of the MC5. After prison and all that, I found myself in a real bad place where I was a very bitter man. I'd watch MTV and I'd just work myself into a rage about all these bands that I'd see. Maybe they had the look of the MC5 or they had distorted guitar tones or they spun around on stage like I used to spin around, and it used to just make me angry. And I'd sit there and I'd just stew and I'd say, "These fucking bands, this ain't shit, my fucking band could eat them alive." You see, I'd never accepted the loss of the MC5, I'd never accepted that that part of my life had ended, and so, when Rob Tyner died, it all came crashing in on me. That feeling of "You know what?

This will never come again, this is not gonna come back." It's the process of grief and loss, of anger, of denial, and finally of acceptance. And really I had to grieve over the loss of it all—I had to weep over it—but once I had, I didn't have to be bitter over it anymore. That actually liberated me and allowed me to go on and do the work I do today, and be able to honor the MC5, and tell the story of the MC5 in the work I do. I look at telling the story of the MC5 as part of my job. It's the last great untold story of the 1960s. So, ultimately, I have no regrets about the past, but neither do I close the door on it.

The Future's Here Right Now

idway through the 1990s, Future/Now Films director David Thomas and producer Laurel Legler began researching and putting together the idea for a documentary movie about the MC5 titled *A True Testimonial*. Seven years later, the film was ready for release. Advance screenings were shown in movie theatres and the film was ready to go, but various issues between the surviving members of the band and Future/Now has resulted in the film's release being delayed indefinitely.

When I spoke to Dennis Thompson in August 2009, he suggested that there was a day during March of 2004 when the movie could have been given the green light, following one last ditch attempt by Legler and Thomas—they asked Thompson to convince his surviving bandmates to give the movie the go-ahead, but to no avail. Naturally, the filmmakers had invested heavily, and the whole idea of the film not seeing the light of say was inconceivable and devastating. The stress was, according to Thompson, difficult for everyone to deal with: "I caught shingles two days after Dave Thomas and Laurel Legler came to beg me to mediate a deal to get their movie out. It was last call. The shingles went in my eye—I could have lost an eye. The thing with shingles is, they don't itch, they hurt. A lot of people wind up with ghost pain for the rest of their life. That's how stressful that was." At the time of writing, the movie still lies dormant.

It's a wonderful piece of film though, showing the band at their worst and their best, and one can only hope that if and when it finally does get released, it regains some of its early momentum.

In the meantime, fans can find comfort in the very economically produced *Kick Out the Jams,* a film put together by Leni Sinclair and Destroy All Monsters man Cary Loren out of some archive footage Sinclair found. Sinclair:

It was some 8mm footage. When I found that film, I told Cary Loren and he said we could make a little home movie out of it. Just something to make some money, and I was desperate to make money. I was really in bad shape in New Orleans—I was down and out. Anyway, it was just a small project for the fans and family. Cary took it upon himself to get an editor and continue with the process after I went back to New Orleans. He took about ten minutes worth of footage and stretched it out to almost forty minutes. It was really never meant to be a public authorized released. We were just playing around . . . this video was done, and somehow Cary Loren managed to get both sides together to sign off on the project and have it released. I am not very proud of it. If I had time and money I'd take it back in the studio and re-cut it. Make it more perfect. Just like the "Kick Out the Jams" album, we really didn't know what we were doing with the movie cameras. A lot of friends that say, and people at collectors conventions, they tell me that they have MC5 parties and crank it way up. It's like a home movie. Maybe the real movie will come out one of these days.

From an artistic point of view, and in light of the controversy surrounding *A True Testimonial*, it's unsurprising—but still a shame—that Sinclair is modest about her *Kick Out the Jams* film (which is now available on DVD). The sound is very rough, and some of the budget psychedelic effects look pretty basic when viewed today. But it's not without its charms; the home video feel and Sinclair's obvious affection for the band gives *Kick Out the Jams* an intimate air that large-scale productions lack. The recent DVD release features footage of John Sinclair performing a reading in 2003, which makes for compelling viewing.

In 1999, the indie label Total Energy released a collection of early MC5 recordings, discovered amid the dust in Wayne Kramer's tapes, called *'66 Breakout*. As a historical document, the album works remarkably well. Songs like "Looking at You" and "Black to Comm" benefit from the scratchy feel of this important collection. Reviewing the compilation for the now-defunct *Etch* magazine, Toni Jedlowski said, "Possessing the '60s daisy-chain flower-power message of combating the pride and prejudice of the time, the MC5 brought potency that was in contrast to the surreal, shallow hippie quest. Evading protest whines and earthy tree-hugging peace fests, their image was rich, sinful and coated with a chrome-plated glare, like a forsaken automobile, taken for granted, yet a component of life that remains as long as it is deemed necessary."

Many MC5 bootleg-quality CDs have appeared in recent years, but '66 *Breakout* is one of the best, interesting and historically significant.

Then, amid all of the uncertainty about *A True Testimonial,* something happened that shocked every MC5 fan in the world: the surviving members decided to reunite.

Wayne Kramer says that it was, rather bizarrely, the clothing giant Levis that prompted the decision:

A journalist called me and asked me what I thought about Levi marketing MC5 T-shirts. It floored me, because no one had called me. This is a serious problem. It's a big, big, big company. My wife is also my manager, and she's nobody's fool about business. She understood what this meant [Neither Kramer nor Davis had given permission for the T-shirt]. She opened up a channel with Levis, and said, "Let's find a way to work this out, because otherwise this is a big problem." My wife is pretty creative, and she found a creative solution, which was that we would agree to let them go ahead with their line if they would underwrite a reunion concert. They're very hip people and they thought it was a great idea. So I was presented with this possibility, and I thought, "Why not? Let's see what happens." I'd put a lot of stock into experimental activities—experimental art, experimental social sciences. And we did. The result was encouraging.

The venue booked for the reunion show was the 100 Club in London, the same place that the first-ever UK punk festival took place. When the idea started to gain ground, no one was more surprised than Michael Davis: "In my mind, I had buried it. I had buried the MC5. We were icons, but with two deceased members, there was no chance. We couldn't go back out and play. It's a history book. I had no hope of ever playing with them. The idea of playing with Wayne and Dennis again—we had gone to Detroit when Rob Tyner passed away to raise some money for his children's education. We had met up when Fred passed away, but not to play or anything. So between when Tyner passed away and London was ten years, and that was a fiasco of an event anyway."

Kramer:

I'd been out of the MC5 for a long time. I'd had a wonderful creative life and career going, a dozen solo albums, I worked as a producer. What did I need it for? It was a great legend, but let's leave it. It wasn't a compromise. I didn't have a good reason not to do it. It didn't mean that I was gonna stop being Wayne Kramer, it didn't mean that I was gonna stop doing music for film [another fire that Kramer has an iron in—eagle-eyed viewers of the recent Will Ferrell movie *Talladega Nights: The Ballad of Ricky Bobby* may have noticed that one Wayne Kramer contributed some of the incidental music]. Like I said, none of these things are nine-to-five, forty-hour a week careers.

Dennis and Mike were open-minded. We had the advantage of growing up a little bit in the meantime. I tried to bring in as much content as I could with Charles Moore and Buzzy Jones being from the era of the MC5 and still active players, and very forward-leaning players. Still on the cutting edge of music. Guys like Nicke [Royale, of the Hellacopters], Lemmy [Motörhead] and Ian Astbury [of the Cult], I've known them from around the community. So I thought, We could do this, and I think in the end that we did a credible job. I'm a builder as a carpenter, a builder as a producer, and a builder as a bandleader—it's all the same. When we said that we were going to do this concert, we then said, "Let's film it. Let's build a product on top of that, then we can build that into something else." It was a good show, but emotionally it was exciting because I play an MC5 song from time to time at my gigs because they're my songs too, but to play a whole set of MC5 songs and to have the whole audience sing along word for word . . . I guess that happens to other artists, but that'd never happened to me. It was an exciting prospect. Kids that could be my children or grandchildren were in the crowd.

For Davis, the event on March 13, 2003, wasn't what it might have been:

It wasn't how I envisaged it. It wasn't what I wanted it to be. I guess I wanted more input. I wanted more territory. Old habits are hard to break, and it was tough at the start. Angela had a lot to do with making it happen in the first place. We started off on a bad note because [certain people] wanted to sue Levi's, and I didn't want to. I wanted to use Levi's as something to start something. I didn't just want to get a check, put it in the bank and that's that. It just sounded great to me, to be back on a real stage . . . to play with my old guys again, high-energy music instead of this jangly thing. I thought, Man, that's it. That's who I am and that's what I want to do. I thought it was great that Levis was putting out MC5 stuff, and I thought that we could really get something out of that. It was really tough, because Wayne's got his solo career and stuff like that. You've got Dennis, who hasn't done anything for thirty years, and then you've got me, who's just done a little bit. So it was really tough to pull it together. Angela was attempting to be a peacemaker.

We agreed to come to England and play at the 100 Club, and get free stuff and get handshaken and sign autographs. Talk with the press. We were what's left of the MC5, and by God, we could still kick out the jams. Really, that's what it was about to me. I'm still alive, and I know what it took to make that stuff, so why shouldn't I have the opportunity to share?

For Dennis Thompson, the show couldn't have come soon enough:

All my life, I wanted the band back together again. In 1985, I got a call from a production company. They offered us $10,000 a piece to do a two-week tour of the States. I called everybody, everybody said "yes," apart from Fred, who said, "Let sleeping dogs lie" . . . so we didn't go.

Before [the 100 Club] show, I'd been going to the gym for three months and played every day. The gig was right down from the hotel, and before we went to play, I sat in my room alone and just broke down. Bawling like a kid. All those years of not knowing what it was that I missed. I missed my band and my music. Everywhere I went, "You were in the MC5—what are you doing working in a tool shop?" I went through twenty years of that crap. When we had the chance to play, I didn't give a shit if it was in a back alley. Everybody rehearsed for it, and it came off great. One thing led to another, and nobody planned anything except Wayne. The *True Testimonial* movie was happening and bringing us closer together a little bit, at least making us more visible to each other and the world. The great idea was to record the show; and then maybe do a small tour. When our management put out the idea that we were available for a tour, we got *a thousand* phone calls. We wound up with a U.S. tour, Europe, Australia, Japan . . . the rest is history.

We could go out every year from May to September and any festival anywhere would have us. Every time we go out, we get better. We just keep getting tighter and tighter, to the point where people are asking us if we're gonna write new material. That's gonna be the next challenge. I'm done—I've already written two songs. All my life I've wanted this band back. I don't care if there's just one other of us left. Me and Wayne or something. I wanna play with the only guys who I really believe are the best players in the universe. They really understand music.

The DVD of the 100 Club show, *Sonic Revolution: A Celebration of the MC5*, captured the show in all its nostalgic glory. As the new millennium rolled in, reuniting seemed to be the thing to do for any band that had any sort of legendary status at all, regardless of how many of their members had passed away. Everyone from the Doors (fronted by the Cult's Ian Astbury and calling themselves the Doors Of The 21st Century) to the New York Dolls (already minus Johnny Thunders and both of their drummers, bassist Arthur Kane tragically and suddenly died shortly after the initial reunion shows at London's Royal Festival Hall), the Pixies, Blondie, Twisted Sister, and a John Entwhistle-less the Who were back on the touring trail, and even the Stooges came back to give it another go.

With Iggy having had a successful solo career in the meantime, and with both of the Asheton brothers still alive and well, the Stooges were perhaps in the best position to reunite, and the standard of their live shows proved that their decision to reform was a good one. The MC5, despite making a point of not referring to their 100 Club show as a reunion, received more criticism than most. Not only were they missing key members, but they were working in partnership with Levis, a huge corporate entity, to make the show happen. Shortsighted and harsh fans viewed the whole event as "revolutionaries selling out." This is absolute nonsense. Previous chapters have revealed that this band and its members have always put their music first, and have been signed to two major record labels in the past. Using a clothing firm to help get their message across does nothing to contradict the ideals of the MC5. In fact, if Levis played a hand in helping get these three musicians on a stage together again, then God bless that denim.

Crucially, the band was excellent at the 100 Club, as the DVD proves. Maybe there were too many corporate invitees in attendance, too many industry insiders, but come show time, the band could do little more than play, and they played extremely well indeed. Critics cried that nobody could replace Rob Tyner, and they were right, but this is a moot point. In fact, the three remaining members realized that Tyner was irreplaceable and so they didn't even try, employing a variety of singers rather than one permanent new guy. The same goes for Fred Smith, who would also never be permanently replaced—for the 100 Club show, Nicke Royale of the Hellacopters played second guitar. As for the vocalists, David Vanian of the Damned sang on "Tonight" and "Looking at You," Motörhead's Lemmy sang "Sister Anne," and the Cult's Ian Astbury sang "Kick Out the Jams" (having already worked with the Doors of the 21st Century—this is a guy that likes to sing with legends behind him). As for the rest of the set, Royale took the lead on "Gotta Keep Movin" and "The

American Ruse," and Wayne Kramer sang "Skunk (Sonicly Speaking)," "Poison," "Rocket Reducer No.62," and, of course, "Ramblin' Rose." Michael Davis stepped up to the mic for "Shakin' Street" and "High School."

Reviewing the film of the show for Detroit's *Metro Times,* Chris Parker came out strongly on the side of the band:

> Reunions are too often a knotty proposition; nearly impossible when crucial members are dead. You can never recapture the past. Having said that, reunions work if the intent is to experience the moment, which in its own flawed way can be perfection (which is, after all, the nature of rock 'n' roll). As Yogi Berra once said, "If the world were perfect, it wouldn't be."
>
> So leave the MC5's past where it belongs—with the dearly departed Rob Tyner and Fred "Sonic" Smith—and rejoice with those remaining the immediacy of the band's bowel-agitating ruckus. For sixty minutes, the three MC5ers left standing and a guest list of infamous shouters [vocalists] covering Tyner—rip open London's 100 Club in this 2003 cinematic document, reprising old glories with a din that's none the worse for wear.

A promo video for "Kick Out the Jams" referred to in Parker's review as an early attempt by Leni Sinclair to help sell the MC5's music with film footage, which just goes to show how far ahead of their time the 5 and their associates were. Leni Sinclair:

> OK, we had this idea for the MC5—that we were gonna try to sell records by making a short film. It was one of the first rock videos, although at the time it wasn't video. I think only the Doors made a similar video before we did. In one tune, there were three costume changes and two venue changes. We just wanted to make it like a light show. Just show people what this band could do. Just advertising, at three and a half minutes long. That video took us two weeks to edit on the movieola. It's much easier nowadays to edit to sound. Thankfully, we did take some movie footage.

As expected, both the 100 Club concert and the subsequent DVD received mixed reviews. Anybody who attended the 100 Club concert or any of the subsequent shows will verify that the chemistry between Wayne Kramer, Michael Davis, and Dennis Thompson still exists, and there is no reason in the world why they shouldn't be on-stage together playing the songs that they used to play together. They stated it isn't the MC5, hence the name, DKT/MC5.

Still, the show did raise enough interest to make Kramer think that a full tour might be a possibility:

Some time had gone by and then the idea of doing a couple of shows in America came up. I said, "We know agents. I think we could do a show in Detroit, probably Chicago and maybe New York. Let's try and do three shows." We told the agent to see if he could get us offers. Touring is so expensive, so we wanted to see if we could get enough money to pay for the tour. In three days, it went from three shows to a world tour. When the promoters started hearing that we were willing to come and play, it was very exciting, and humbling at the same time. So now we have this little cottage industry. A little thing to celebrate the legacy. And it is a legacy. This is not anything new. The performance itself every night is new, and there are things that we'll play at night that are new. It may be new to the audience—they may have never been exposed to this before. But what the [new] band is, is a legacy. It's not the MC5. It's like the New York Dolls. They put out a record, but it doesn't sell. Cheap Trick puts out a record, it doesn't sell. Nobody cares about that. Records don't sell anyway. You can't sell anybody a record nowadays. But I play music for people, and in terms of the MC5's music, there are people that want to hear the MC5's music. I'm playing music for people that want to hear the music that I made. That me and the other guys made. That's what we do. It's really outside of MTV and the record business, and all the other trappings and considerations. We play in mostly clubs for a cult. We're a cult band. We were designed to be a cult band. Even though we wanted to be a big mainstream band, I don't know that that was ever in the cards for the MC5. We were never good little soldiers. We never went along with the program. They tried to plug us into the pop business in those days and it didn't work, and we're not part of the pop business today. We wanted to be one way, but it's actually the other way. We'll probably make a record. At least, we'll write ten or twelve songs, we'll record them and we'll figure out how to get them to people.

The band, dubbed DKT/MC5 (using the initials of the surviving three members) would tour with a revolving cast of musicians stepping into the huge shoes vacated by Rob Tyner and Fred Smith. To Kramer, the idea of recruiting a permanent band was too uncomfortable:

I don't think so. I think it's better fluid, unsettled and iffy. It's more work . . . they're in their own bands doing their own tours. So for me to find people that were available and that had enough of a connection to the music to be enthusiastic about it, it's hard. People's schedules, etc. But I think it makes for a better tour. The idea of having a permanent singer . . . I don't know, it seems like we'd end up playing state fairs and casinos. Which we may anyway. They pay very well, I understand! The artist in me wants to stay at least living and breathing. I don't want to be a cover band of the MC5. I want to do the songs authentically and accurately, and I like the fun that we have. Maybe I'll change my mind. I do change my mind from time to time. As long as we have new blood coming into the band, it's fun for me and I can get it up and remain enthusiastic.

It's a similar argument to the one that Kramer put forward when discussing Mad for the Racket; the more musicians he plays with, the more interested he remains. Davis, at least initially, was excited just to be playing with his old friends again:

There were six more dates added here, ten more there, a few more over there. It turned out we did a bus tour of the entire U.S., played thirty-three cities, with Mark Arm [Mudhoney], Evan Dando [the Lemonheads] and Marshall Crenshaw. How was it? It was exciting, it really was. I had a ball. To go to New York and have all these people clamoring on us. Marshall played guitar. He's a very successful writer for pop radio airplay. His music is very accessible, and he's successful like that. He did a cover of one of our songs, and it was badass. I meet this guy, he's from Southfield, Michigan, and he's this king of a mild-mannered guy. He wears a lot of brown and grey; he's a family guy. So we do the entire U.S. with some great shows and some not so great shows, then we're back to Los Angeles and we've got Australia, New Zealand, and Japan in two days. There's a big Detroit music thing in Australia. Deniz Tek from Radio Birdman was going to be our second guitar player in Australia and Japan. [Then we did Europe] We played about a hundred shows that year. We had Nicke, then Gilby [Clarke, Guns N' Roses]. Lisa [Kekaula, Bellrays] joined up with us, and Johnny Walker from the Soledad Brothers. Greg Dulli [Afghan Whigs] showed up with us on our last show.

Marshall Crenshaw, who, coincidentally, is from Berkley, Michigan, was offered the position of second guitar with DKT/MC5 for the American tour, following a phone call from Wayne Kramer early in 2004. Although he is loath to admit that he was stepping into anyone's shoes, Crenshaw was essentially filling in for Fred Smith. Crenshaw prefers to refer to himself as the "other guitar player." Still, Crenshaw's inclusion caused some controversy among long time followers of the band who insisted that the laid-back, unassuming guitarist was just too "nice" to stand in Sonic Smith's spot. Crenshaw, though, had no reservations about accepting Kramer's offer: "I was surprised to get the call, the proposition, but I didn't think about it for more than a split second, I just said yeah. I was familiar with their body of work. I saw the band back in my teens. I was ready to jump on it. I thought it was a good call for Wayne to make, but it did come out of left field."

Crenshaw, a solo artist, enjoyed the experience and the camaraderie of being in a band. A friend of Kramer's since 1981, the singer and guitarist didn't have any issues with Thompson or Davis, and he enjoyed playing the MC5's rich body of work night after night: "I liked playing 'Starship' a lot. I hurt myself playing it. The first week of the tour, I didn't have any earplugs, and I haven't really been the same since then."

Despite protests from the naysayers, Crenshaw is adamant that his time with the band was a success, particularly the guitar partnership he forged with Kramer. Rather endearingly, Crenshaw wishes the whole thing hadn't ended as soon as it did: "I really loved playing with another guitar player when that other guitar player is somebody who really has style and is really inspired. I thought that he and I really made some great noise together. I thought it was righteous."

Mudhoney front man Mark Arm had first heard the MC5 in the early 1980s:

I think Kim Thayil [Soundgarden] might have played "Kick Out the Jams" for me. They were a big influence [on Mudhoney]. They were up there. If you listen to [Mudhoney's debut EP] *Superfuzz Bigmuff,* the initial blast, I recall that we were listening to a lot of MC5, Stooges, Blue Cheer, Neil Young, and the Wipers. And we all came up through the American hardcore scene, so we were listening to the cream of the crop. There's a bunch of shitty hardcore out there, but we were listening to bands like the Void, Minor Threat, Black Flag, of course, Negative Approach. We were listening to stuff like PiL, too, but that didn't come into it musically, I don't think.

They contacted me, just to feel me out. Initially, it was gonna be just for the Australian leg of the tour and I was like, "Yeah, I could do that." It was like, this could be great or it could be awful. I was like, it's at least a trip to Australia! See some old friends there that I haven't seen for a while. Later, Mark Lanegan [couldn't do] the whole U.S. tour, and they asked me to do the whole thing. I was like, "Urrgghh!" It was this weird incremental thing. I was getting pulled in. They asked me to come down to L.A. for a couple of rehearsals. I went down there. I knew Wayne had been playing for years and roughly what he was doing—he had been, like, in training so to speak. But I didn't know about Michael and Dennis, and about what they'd been doing. Within five minutes, my fears of where they were at were laid to waste. They were smoking, the three of them. From that point on, the fear was about whether I could bring anything to it. Like, Am I gonna fuck this shit up? Am I gonna be the asshole that destroys this thing? After that first practice, they seemed pretty happy with where we were at. They were very encouraging, very cool. We practiced for a couple of days, then I came away from L.A. thinking that it was gonna work out. One of my fears was that I didn't want to be like Ian Astbury mimicking Jim Morrison. Rob Tyner had such an amazing voice, I don't think I could if I wanted to. I did the best that I could with the limited resource that I have.

Lisa Kekaula, singer with rock 'n' soul band the Bellrays and dance act Basement Jaxx, remembers sifting through her husband's record collection and finding the MC5:

My husband had the records, and we were going over stuff that he had heard, that really didn't match anything else that we listened to. Not that we were necessarily looking for something that was rock 'n' soul, but it was not something easily definable. I'd never heard of them. His dad had told him how many songs had curse words in them when he was a kid, and this was one of the ones he pulled up—"Who Are You?" and "Kick Out the Jams, Motherfucker."

It's not like we [the Bellrays] intended to make something that sounded like this, but since we listened to it and we're musicians, it becomes part of your background. As soon as you hear it, whether you want it to influence you or not, it's going to. I just happen to welcome that kind of influence. Let it in. We actually let in a lot of what they listened to in order to become what they were. What they were doing really made sense to our way of thinking about music. They call the MC5 the precursors of punk. What most people know as punk today, and most of the punk that's risen to the top, is usually devoid of that R&B element. That's really essential. The Ramones went for that doo-wop thing. For us, it just felt like a natural progression. When trying to say that that's part of the pantheon of punk, there are a lot of people that will argue that it isn't. I don't agree with that.

Kekaula's first show with the DKT/MC5 was in L.A:

I did "Human Being Lawnmower," so I knew that tune. I got to do some other stuff in 2004, when Evan [Dando] left. I was asked to come in and do the European dates, off the cuff. You've got to be ready. It was really fun.

I had the benefit of actually seeing it before. I saw it when they came to L.A. and they had Evan and Mark [Arm]. I knew what it looked like. I'm in a different position to what Mark would have been in, because he started it off. I knew it was whatever I was going to bring to the table, and they knew how I did the songs. They were the same tunes, but with me doing them. I'm not going to ever try to replace anybody, because I don't think people are replaceable. I just try to honor the songs as best as I can, which I think is the best way to honor Rob and Fred.

Kekaula claims to find the three veterans in the band to be great company:

They're really great guys. It's not like they're sitting there living in the past, telling stories about the old days, but they also don't mind if stuff comes up. I feel like we're lucky to be there through some of these tales. They're good fun to tour with, but mostly they're just good humans. They're respectful people. I think people picture the MC5 when they started—the rebels. The guys are clean, and they're proud of being clean. It's just weird to see the way the fans react when they say, "Let me buy you a beer," and they're just like, "Thanks, but we don't drink anymore." The fans don't really get that you can still be a revolutionary and not get fucked up. How far can this thing go? That's not up to me. I'm a guest artist.

Kekaula has her opinions about why the MC5 are rediscovered by generation after generation:

First of all, if the media catches on to a band, it's gonna hit, and that happened when loads of bands started saying they were influenced by them, so then people looked back and said, "Who is this band?" Enough bands said they were influenced. It seemed like a cool thing for people to latch onto. Within the whole Detroit thing, you had these bad boys. A lot of people claimed that they loved the MC5, when maybe really they only heard "Kick Out the Jams."

Mudhoney main man Mark Arm is a longtime MC5 fan:

There are a couple of bands like that. Some bands that were really huge when they came out—Three Dog Night, nobody's going back to Three Dog Night records. No one's going back to Wham records, but people keep rediscovering Black Flag all the time. There's bands like that, and it's always the bands in the underground. People rediscover Neil Young, but he's still going. There's honesty and power in the music. It holds up and it seems relevant now. It wasn't just some hippie-dippy flower-power shit. I enjoy listening to some of that, but it totally seems dated. Whereas this shit, despite the fact that they're talking about something that happened in 1969 with "American Ruse," unfortunately it's completely relevant, and "Over and Over" is completely relevant. I wish it was dated. I wish we could all say, "Wow, that's a weird time. They must have lived in a really weird time."

Some fans were annoyed when actress Jennifer Anniston was seen wearing an MC5 shirt on the TV show *Friends,* but Kekaula has her own opinions about that too:

I'd like to say to her, "Hey, thanks for wearing that shirt." Maybe a bunch of other people picked up that shirt. There are all these weird double standards. If she's getting up there saying that she knows all about the MC5, then we've got something to talk about. If you're going up there supporting a band and buying merch, woo-hoo. That goes for any band out there. I'm not a purist in that way, and the reason I'm not is that I know if she had that shirt on, some money went into Dennis's mouth, Wayne's mouth, and Michael's mouth. And the Smith family and Tyner family too. So many people have this vision of musicians and of what's cool and not cool, but people don't care about the basic shit. Who's making sure that I'm eating? Nobody cares whether I'm eating, but they'll be sure to tell me whether they think I'm selling out by seeing somebody with a T-shirt on.

On the August 28, 2004, DKT/MC5 played at the Reading Festival in England, performing under cover on the second stage. Also on the bill that day were, incredibly, the New York Dolls, plus a young Texan rock 'n' roll band called Young Heart Attack who had recorded a cover of "Over and Over" for their *Mouthful of Love* album, and fellow Detroiters the White Stripes, who were headlining the day. DKT/MC5 had played a show at London's Astoria the day before the festival, so by the time they were presented to a tent full of drunken kids they were warmed up and ready to go. Nicke Royale was still on second guitar, while the guest vocalists were the Bellrays' Lisa Kekaula and Mudhoney's Mark Arm. Something of a legend in his own right among followers of grunge music, Arm was superb, but for this author it was Kekaula who really stole the show. Part Tina Turner, part, yes, Rob Tyner, Kekaula nailed every song, and added a touch of glamour to proceedings.

Around the same time as the Reading Festival, the band were presented with an Icon award at the annual *Kerrang!* Awards. The fact that a rock magazine that had evolved into the UK's best-selling music weekly with a very young average readership would choose to honor the band was further proof of the 5's enduring popularity. Very few *Kerrang!* readers, or even members of the magazine's staff, would have remembered the band splitting up, so the award was particularly poignant. Motörhead's Lemmy was originally asked to present the award, but in his absence the task fell to Ginger, singer and guitarist with British rockers the Wildhearts. He was suitably honored:

> I've always thought that musicians getting awards is stupid unless they're also inventing a cure for cancer or are involved in actively saving lives. Making people dance doesn't deserve a Nobel Peace Prize, y'know? Anyway, when I illustrated this point to the famous and semi-famous at the *Kerrang!* awards, the guys from the band weren't in the room and so couldn't hear my diatribe, so it was great to hear Wayne Kramer say exactly the same thing on receiving the award. We hung out for the rest of the evening and the band all invited me and my then-girlfriend to stay with them in the States. They were/are the coolest, smartest, most politically righteous band I've ever met. I'd marry Wayne if I was gay and he was cuter. Or if he was gay and I was cuter.

A few short months later, the band was back in the UK, this time playing at London's prestigious Royal Festival Hall. What promised to be a great night anyway was made even more special by the fact that the support band was the Sun Ra Arkestra. Sun Ra died in 1993, but his Arkestra had continued to tour, and their appearance with the DKT/MC5 marked something of a full circle for both acts. For that show, DKT/MC5 employed the services of former Guns N' Roses man Gilby Clarke on second guitar, while the guest vocalists were Handsome Dick Manitoba of early New York punks the Dictators and David Thomas of Pere Ubu. The Royal Festival Hall might have excellent acoustics, but it's far too formal a venue for the (still) energetic music of the MC5, and with most people sitting for the duration of the show, the atmosphere was slightly muted. Toward the end, however, security men were ignored, and some of the crowd made a dash for the front, igniting some semblance of celebration. The highlight of the evening was the finale, when the Sun Ra Arkestra joined DKT/MC5 onstage to run through a mind-blowing "Starship." Amusingly, the straight-talking Manitoba didn't seem to know what to make of it all. He was more suited to the hard rock audience that the band played to at the Download Festival on the June 12, 2005. The festival takes place annually at Donington Park, a venue associated with Monsters of Rock events, denim, and mullets. In many ways, little has changed. Download takes place over three days, and features the best in hard rock and metal that the world has to offer. Contemporary metal bands like Korn, Deftones, and Slipknot are guaranteed a huge reception, as are classic metal heroes like Metallica and Slayer. How a reunited 1960s proto-punk band would fare was anybody's guess, but the set was an absolute success. Playing on the Snickers second stage, second on the bill to Motörhead, the band included Gilby Clarke on guitar (which would have earned them a few brownie points from the Guns N' Roses fans in attendance), and an appearance from Motörhead's Lemmy on "Sister Anne" (more brownie points). The star of the day, however, was Manitoba, whose straight-to-the-jugular approach sat well with a crowd who just wanted to rock out.

Of the show, Kramer told me, "We're continuing to perfect the art of performance, and not necessarily just the songs. The show is a way to communicate experience, ideas, and feelings . . . It's an honor to carry the message of the MC5 to a new generation."

By the end of the tour, the vocalists that DKT/MC5 employed had stacked up, but Kramer had his opinions about who worked best: "Lisa is probably my favorite. Sometimes I think she channels Rob Tyner, y'know? She gets it, she nails it so hard. Her sense of melody is the MC5 sense of melody—that rhythm 'n' blues, almost gospel background that comes out. She kills me. I adore her. Everybody that's been with the band has been a ball. I love Mark Arm, Dick, Gilby, we've got Adam Pearson [Sisters of Mercy] on this next tour, and he's a ball. A great guy to have around and a super musician."

Michael Davis was less enthralled by the revolving door of front men and women that came through the band after the first tour:

As time went on, the MC5 became less and less what I aspired for with an MC5 show and more of an all-star revue . . . I decided that I had had enough, and that I would just focus on producing new bands. Whatever comes up, I'd do, but I'm not gonna do this . . . It wasn't what I had hoped for. But then if you asked me who I'd give the axe, I would be fucked because they are all my friends and they are all so talented and add so much. Maybe that is the problem for me—I really bond with people, so I had hoped to just bond with a couple of them and make a great band together. Bonding with a lot of people and making all kinds of great sub-bands is a lot of work.

However, Davis is confident that the band can pull it together and still have a future, although a serious motorcycle accident in 2006 and various health issues have made him re-evaluate his life and career:

> Let me just say that I have learned a lot. The trauma that my family and I have been through over the past year with my near-death experience on the motorcycle, and with the treatment for Hep C, with a couple of surgeries here and there, I'm a much stronger guy than I was a year ago. Other people have had their own difficulties.
> We've all come together stronger, because we've weathered the storm. I think we're gonna be alright, and whatever we do, we're still the same people that created the MC5, a portion of it. I'm really hopeful still.

Sadly, at the time of writing, Michael's hopes seemed dashed. DKT/MC5 is, according to Dennis Thompson in August 2009, over: "It's sad but we had a good run. Wayne has a career in Hollywood that is starting to take flight, as a writer and a musical scorer for films and TV shows. There's a new show on HBO that Wayne has done the music for. That's where the work is for him. I know he took a musical composition class."

There are other issues that may have contributed to the downfall of DKT/MC5. More bad blood is the last thing that this group needs, but it seems to have infected them anyway. When a version of "Kick Out the Jams" appeared on *Guitar Hero*, a video game, arguments began to break out between band members about who should and shouldn't have been involved in the recording. Thompson, for one, was hurt by the fact that he was ignored. Still, the fact that another generation of rock-loving kids are experiencing the magic of the MC5 should help heal the wounds.

It's doubtful that the MC5 will ever surface as a band again, but Thompson subscribes to the never-say-never philosophy, stating simply: "I guess you never can tell what will happen in the future."

Conclusion

I t occurred to me very early on when planning this book that, as a thirty-one-year-old Englishman (still living in London) who had only ever interviewed two of the MC5 over the phone, I was severely lacking in experience, or more accurately, experiences with regard to this band. In order to alter this fact, I booked trips to both Detroit (for obvious reasons) and Los Angeles (where both Wayne Kramer and Michael Davis now reside). Also around this time, it was announced that the DKT/MC5 would play the All Tomorrow's Parties Festival at the Butlins holiday camp in the Somerset coastal town of Minehead in the United Kingdom, on a bill with old friends Iggy and the Stooges. My trips to Detroit, L.A. and, ahem, Minehead were from then on known as my "trio of MC5 jollies."

When it came time to fly my ass over there, I sent out an e-mail to all of my friends to see if anyone could let me borrow their couch for a week. When Phil Durr—a Detroit musician (of Big Chief/Five Horse Johnson fame) and old friend—immediately told me that I could crash at his place in Royal Oak, Michigan, I was extremely grateful because I was able to keep the costs down. Research trips like this are often considered unjustifiable because of the costs, but thanks to the wonderful people that I have in my life, I was able to make it happen.

I flew to Detroit on October 6, 2006, and had interviews pre-arranged with Russ Gibb, Gary Grimshaw, and Jackson Smith. Gibb and young Smith I met over breakfast, and an old acquaintance of Fred's, Freddie Brooks, showed up with Jackson. It made for an interesting morning. Gibb proved himself to be a pleasant and forthright man, and he had an air of success about him. As someone who had made himself very wealthy through investing in the cable industry, he has every right to carry that air. I met with Grimshaw at his house in Detroit, and he couldn't have been more helpful. Much of those interviews are featured within the pages of the book that you're just coming to the end of. But it was the afternoon I spent with Dennis

Thompson that will forever stick in my memory. I had interviewed him a couple of times on the phone prior to the trip, but meeting him in the flesh was something else. Dennis is a wonderful man, a true gentleman. I also got the impression that he doesn't suffer fools gladly, and that he isn't the sort of person I'd like to be on the wrong side of. I had nothing to worry about though; we hit it off from the beginning. His then-manager (and Michael Davis's wife) Angela had come up with the idea of Dennis giving me an "MC5 tour," and so the two of us decided to head off in my rental car to Ann Arbor. Dennis hadn't been back to the Hill Street White Panther House since the 1960s and, despite the help of a GPS unit, it took us an hour to find the house once we'd arrived in Ann Arbor. When we did eventually find it, in the middle of a bunch of sorority houses with all manner of Greek letters above their doors, we knocked and were let in by a student with long hair. Forty years had passed, and nothing had changed there. We had a look around, and it was a pleasure to see Dennis genuinely excited to be in the house. Memories were flooding back, and he had a glint in his eye when he pointed out his old room and told me some of the unprintable deeds that had taken place in there. The icing on the cake was a young student named Geoff, who came down the stairs when he heard mention of the MC5. "Dennis 'Machine Gun' Thompson—pleased to meet ya," said Dennis, and young Geoff was visibly shaking. He ran to get his copy of Legs McNeil's book *Please Kill Me*, and show us the picture of the MC5 and the Stooges signing their record contract with Elektra in the very room that we were standing in. "You guys are the reason I chose to live in this house," said Geoff.

Dennis had brought along some MC5 gear (a poster and a CD, among others), and Geoff was obviously the deserving recipient. He certainly wasn't expecting a visit from the drummer of the MC5 (plus an English journalist tagging along behind) when he got up that morning. Geoff was, however, the perfect host.

Two short weeks after I returned from Detroit, I was back on a transatlantic flight, this time to Los Angeles (interestingly, I was sat near Sharon Osbourne for the outward leg, but she looked tired so I didn't approach her). I arrived at LAX airport in time to pick up my car, check into my hostel, shower, and run off down the Sunset Strip to see what pleasures awaited me. I stayed at the Banana Bungalow/Orbit hostel on the corner of Melrose and Fairfax to keep the costs down. I was a bit nervous, due to the fact that I had never done the whole backpacking thing and therefore had never stayed in a hostel with a shared dorm consisting of five other men before.

I needn't have worried. One of my roommates, an Australian skinhead punk named Adam with tattoos and piercings from head to foot, turned out to be an absolute diamond of a man, and most nights we found ourselves at a noisy concert somewhere in Hollywood. On the Wednesday of that week, I met with Debby Pietruska-Nathan at her home. The idea of speaking to the former Stomper was suggested to me by Angela Davis (good call, dear), and I was delighted when I learned that she lived in L.A. At that point, I knew that I'd be meeting with Michael, but Wayne had yet to confirm, and it was looking like I may be flying all the way to L.A. for one meeting. With Debby on board, I had at least two. She was great too; filling me with anecdotes and adding some much needed color to the book. Debby is now part of a local theater group in Burbank, so be sure to check out what she's doing if you're ever in that area.

That Thursday, I met with Mike, Angela, and their kids at their home. They couldn't have been more welcoming, and Mike turned out to be even more of a gentleman in the flesh than he was on the phone. He's very different that Dennis, who loves to talk and is a lot of fun as a result. Mike is a far calmer human being, a man who always looks like he's pondering something vital, but is still very friendly and warm. He has a sharp sense of humor, forthright and open opinions, and is fortunate enough to have a beautiful family and home. My afternoon with the Davises was one to cherish.

Fortunately, Wayne Kramer, through his wife and manager Margaret, confirmed that he would meet with me at his office on Saturday of that same week. Again, it was a great experience to talk with him. Wayne is one of those people who stays very quiet, but when he does say something, it's worth listening to. It was essential that I spoke to Wayne in person for the integrity of the book, and he was no disappointment. We sat for about two hours, and he was happy to answer anything I asked him, including some particularly difficult and personal questions.

After speaking to Dennis Thompson, Michael Davis, and Wayne Kramer, I realized that I had been spoiled. When I begin to write my second book, whomever it shall be about, surely I'll never be treated so well and so openly again. I consider myself very lucky to have had the opportunity to meet these three men.

On December 7, 2006, the DKT/MC5, with a line-up completed by Mark Arm, Adam Pearson and Lisa Kekaula, were in London, playing at the Underworld in Camden as part of a UK tour. I met with Angela Davis and Dennis Thompson for a short while, and it was great to see them again. They put on a great show, but in truth, it paled next to what occurred the following Sunday at the All Tomorrow's Parties Festival. This event occurs annually, but this December they were having an extra one, dubbed the Nightmare Before Christmas. Thurston Moore of Sonic Youth was curating the event. Some excellent bands played at the festival too, including Sonic Youth themselves, stoner rockers the Melvins, classic punks Flipper (featuring Nirvana's Krist Noveselic on bass), Dinosaur Jr., Detroit hardcore legends Negative Approach and UK 1970s post-punks Gang of Four. But it was the closing two bands that Sunday evening that really raised eyebrows—Iggy and the Stooges were to be followed by DKT/MC5. It was the first time that these two groups had been on the same bill for decades, and it felt right. It felt like things had gone full circle. The Stooges were incredible that weekend, Iggy the consummate performer, never stopping to take a breath and encouraging this foolish author to jump the barrier in order to get on stage—I badly sprained my ankle in the process.

As a result of my stupidity, I had to watch the MC5 boys from the back, leaning against a chair. It was still an awesome sight, though, made all the more poignant by the fact that former manager John Sinclair introduced them onto the stage. At one point in my life, I never thought I'd see the Stooges or the MC5 live at all, never mind both of them on the same bill, at a vacation resort in Minehead, Somerset, England.

I had an interview with Mark Arm scheduled for that weekend, and I also managed to squeeze twenty minutes in with Lisa Kekaula too. Before I sat with the two singers, however, I had an interesting conversation with Dennis Thompson. It seemed that, after the tour had come to an end in Belfast, the group was staying on in the Northern Irish capital to spend some time in a studio, writing and demoing material for a possible new record. Dennis told me that they already had some songs written; they just needed to see how they would turn out. It was, of course, possible that the whole experiment would be a washout and the idea of recording a new record, under the name DKT/MC5, would be abandoned. But Dennis gave me a slight glimmer of hope too.

Maybe a new album would be good, maybe it wouldn't. The New York Dolls came back and recorded an incredible new album with just two original members, so it can be done. But one thing's for sure—no matter how the record turns out, it won't disgrace anything. It's too late for that. This band has earned the right to do whatever they want, musically. Personally, I hope that it's an edgy little beast, full of the hooks that made *High Time* so great. But I'll listen to it however, marveling at Wayne's fretwork, Dennis's machine gun rat-tat-tats and Mike's killer bass lines, because three-fifths of the MC5 is still better than the whole of most bands. One side of me wants the band to stick a middle finger in the faces of the naysayers. Then I think back to what Dennis said to me while driving around Ann Arbor: "Fuck 'em."

Sadly, we now know that a DKT/MC5 album is extremely unlikely. Not *impossible*, but unlikely. While Thompson is keeping himself busy with his instructional drumming DVDs and his latest project at the time of writing, "a new concept performance art rock 'n' roll show" in Detroit, one suspects that he and his bandmates are only truly happy when they're playing together.

Fingers crossed.

Selected Discography

As the MC5 only recorded three albums, this section could be very short indeed. Conversely, due to the fact that countless odds 'n' sods albums have been released since their demise, this section could stretch out over many pages. Therefore, I decided to select the albums that I consider to be the most important, not only from the MC5, but also from other projects featuring the five members of the band. Some of them may take some hunting down but, in most cases, it's worth it.

MC5

The three classic albums

Kick Out the Jams (Elektra, 1969)

Back In the USA (Atlantic, 1970)

High Time (Atlantic, 1971)

Selected compilations

The Big Bang: The Best of MC5 (Rhino, 2000)

Thunder Express (Jungle/Skydog, 1995)

Are You Ready To Testify: The Live Bootleg Anthology (3 disc box set) (Castle, 2005)

Purity Accuracy (6 disc box set) (Easy Action, 2004)

Babes in Arms (ROIR, 1997)

'66 Breakout (Total Energy, 1999)

DVDs

MC5: Kick Out the Jams: A Film by Leni Sinclair and Cary Loren (Wienerworld Ltd., 2005)

Sonic Revolution: A Celebration of the MC5 (Sony BMG, 2004)

At the time of this writing, the documentary movie *A True Testimonial* is still awaiting release.

Fred Smith

Secondary Bands
Sonic's Rendezvous Band
Sonic's Rendezvous Band (6 disc box set) (Easy Action, 2006)

Contributions
Patti Smith
Dream of Life (Arista, 1996)

Rob Tyner

Solo albums
Blood Brothers (R&A, 1990)
Rock and Roll People (Captain Trip, 1999)

Also of relevance, in 1977, Rob signed to Island Records and released a single with Eddie and the Hot Rods called "Till The Night is Gone."

Wayne Kramer

Solo albums
Death Tongue (Epitaph, 1993)
The Hard Stuff+ (Diesel Motor/Muscle Tone, 2007). Originally called *The Hard Stuff* (Epitaph, 1995), re-released with extra tracks.
More Dangerous Madness (Diesel Motor/Muscle Tone, 2007). Originally called *Dangerous Madness* (Epitaph, 1997), re-released with extra tracks.
Return of Citizen Wayne (Diesel Motor/Muscle Tone, 2007). Originally called *Citizen Wayne* (Epitaph, 1997), re-released with extra tracks.
Adult World (Diesel Motor/Muscle Tone, 2002)

Secondary Bands
Mad for the Racket
The Racketeers (Diesel Motor/Muscle Tone, 2001)

Gang War

The following live disc is bootleg quality, but it's the only available recorded output from this project. *Johnny Thunders & Wayne Kramer's Gang War!* (Jungle/Skydog, 2004)

Contributions

Was (Not Was)

Was (Not Was) (Island, 1981)

John Sinclair

Friday, the 13th (Alive, 1995)

John Sinclair & His Blues Scholars

Full Circle (Alive, 1997)

White Buffalo Prayer (SpyBoy, 2000)

Underground Issues (SpyBoy, 2000)

Tweaker

The Attraction to All Things Uncertain (Six Degrees, 2001)

Blue Meanies

The Post Wave (Thick, 2000)

Compilation Albums

Wayne contributed "Children Are People Too" to *I Only Wrote This Song for You: A Tribute to Johnny Thunders* (Diesel Motor, 2004). And he contributed "Crawling Outta the Jungle" to his own excellent *Wayne Kramer Presents Beyond Cyberpunk* (Valley, 2001).

He collaborated with System of a Down's Serj Tankian and Rage Against the Machine/Audioslave's Tom Morello on "Get Up, Stand Up" for *Axis of Justice: Concert Series*, vol. 1 (Serjical Strike/Columbia, 2004).

Michael Davis

Secondary Bands

Destroy All Monsters

Singles and Rarities LP (Revenge, 1989)

Bored (Cherry Red, 1991)

Live LP (Fan Club, 1989)

There's an excellent box set of DAM and Dark Carnival (a post-DAM project featuring Niagara and Ron Asheton) material called *Hot Box* (Lost Patrol/Niagaraland, 2007).

Contributions
Ron Asheton/The Empty Set
Thin, Slim & None/Flunkie (Birdcage, 1996)
Rich Hopkins and the Luminarios
3000 Germans Can't Be Wrong (San Jacinto, 1998)
El Paso (San Jacinto, 1996)
The Glorious Sounds of Rich Hopkins and the Luminarios (San Jacinto, 1997)
Devolver (San Jacinto, 1999)
My Lucky Stars (San Jacinto, 2001)
Tinitus (San Jacinto, 2001)
The Fifty Percenter (San Jacinto, 2000)

Rich Hopkins and his band also contributed the track "You've Gone" to *Full Circle: A Tribute to Gene Clarke* (Not Lame, 2000).

Tokyo Sex Destruction
Black Noise Is the New Sound (Dim Mak, 2006)
Dollhouse
The Rock and Roll Circus (Dim Mak, 2004)
OJM
Under the Thunder (Go Down, 2008)
Grinder
Out of Our Heads (Detroit, 2005). Michael appears on the track "Out of Our Heads."

Dennis Thompson

Secondary Bands
The New Order
The New Order (Isadora, 1977)
The New Race
The First and the Last (Statik/Total Energy, 2004)

Various Members Appeared On

GG Allin

Hated In The Nation (ROIR, 1998) featuring Kramer and Thompson on the track "Gimme Some Head."

The Sillies

America's Most Wanton (Scooch Pooch, 2002) featuring Kramer and Thompson on the track "Punk Rock Girl."

Bibliography

Ambrose, Joe. *Gimme Danger: The Story of Iggy Pop.* New York: Omnibus, 2002.

Antonia, Nina. *Johnny Thunders . . . In Cold Blood.* London: Jungle/Cherry Red Books, 2000.

Bangs, Lester. *Mainlines, Blood Feasts, and Bad Taste: A Lester Bangs Reader.* New York: Anchor, 2003.

Bessman, Jim. *Ramones: An American Band.* New York: St. Martin's Press, 1993.

Bockris, Victor. *Patti Smith: An Unauthorized Biography.* New York: Simon & Schuster, 1999.

Carson, David A. *Grit, Noise, and Revolution: The Birth of Detroit Rock 'n' Roll.* Ann Arbor: University of Michigan Press, 2005.

A Celebration of the 40th Anniversary of Rock and Roll at the Grande Ballroom (Commemorative Program). Detroit: Drop of a Hat Studios, 2006.

Colegrave, Stephen, and Chris Sullivan. *Punk: A Life Apart.* London: Cassell, 2001.

Farren, Mick. *Give the Anarchist a Cigarette.* London: Jonathan Cape, 2001.

Gavrilovich, Peter, and Bill McGraw. *The Detroit Almanac.* Detroit: Detroit Free Press, 2000.

Goodman, Fred. *The Mansion on the Hill: Dylan, Young, Geffen, Springsteen, and the Head-on Collision of Rock and Commerce.* New York: Times Books, 1997.

Heylin, Clinton. *From the Velvets to the Voidoids.* New York, Penguin, 1993.

Jania, Karen L., ed. *John Sinclair and the Culture of the Sixties.* Ann Arbor: Bentley Historical Library, 2004.

Kilmister, Lemmy, with Janiss Garza. *White Line Fever: The Autobiography.* New York: Pocket Books, 2003.

McLeese, Don. *Kick Out the Jams (33 1/3).* New York: Continuum, 2005.

McNeil, Legs, and Gillian McCain, eds. *Please Kill Me: The Uncensored Oral History of Punk.* New York: Penguin, 1997.

Plamondon, Pun. *Lost from the Ottawa: The Story of the Journey Back.* Blooming-
 ton, IN: Trafford, 2006.

Savage, Jon. *England's Dreaming: Anarchy, Sex Pistols, Punk Rock, and Beyond.*
 London: Faber and Faber, 2005.

Simmons, Michael, and Cletus Nelson. *The Future Is Now!: An Illustrated History of
 the MC5.* London: Creation Books, 2004.

Sinclair, John. *Guitar Army: Street Writings/Prison Writings.* New York: Douglas
 Book Corp., 1972.

Websites

www.mc5.org

makemyday.free.fr (a gateway to all things MC5)

www.i94bar.com (an online 'zine, full of rock 'n' roll debauchery)

www.svengirly.com (the management, publishing, and merchandising company run by Michael Davis's wife and manager, Angela)

www.muscletonerecords.com (Wayne Kramer's label)

www.machinegunthompson.com (Dennis Thompson's site)

www.johnsinclair.us (John Sinclair's site)

www.lenisinclair.com (MC5 photographer Leni Sinclair is still selling her iconic pictures)

www.punplamondon.com (the former White Panther Minister of Defense is still busy)

www.russgibbatrandom.com (keep up to date with Uncle Russ)

www.thegrandeballroom.com (keeping the venue alive)

www.garygrimshaw.com (the MC5 artist's site)

www.67riots.rutgers.edu (a full account of the Detroit race riots of 1967)

www.blackpanther.org/legacynew.htm (a history of the Black Panthers)

www.niagaradetroit.com (Destroy All Monsters front woman)

www.thebookbeat.com (Cary Loren of Destroy All Monsters' bookstore)

www.grokmusic.com (music site, managed in part by Russ Gibb)

www.furious.com (*Perfect Sound Forever*, a music magazine)

www.myspace.com/brettcallwood (support your author)

Index